D1580304

6

May Rathbone

HOW ENGLAND SAVED EUROPE

BLÜCHER, 1816

From a lithograph after the painting by F. C. GRÖGER

HOW ENGLAND SAVED EUROPE:

THE STORY OF THE GREAT WAR (1793-1815)

BY

W. H. FITCHETT, B.A., LL.D.

AUTHOR OF "DEEDS THAT WON THE EMPIRE"
"FIGHTS FOR THE FLAG," ETC.

WITH PORTRAITS, FACSIMILES, AND PLANS

IN FOUR VOLUMES

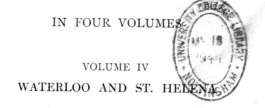

VOLUME IV

WATERLOO AND ST. HELENA

LONDON

SMITH, ELDER, & CO., 15 WATERLOO PLACE

1900

"England has saved herself by her exertions, and will, as I trust, save Europe by her example."—PITT'S LAST PUBLIC WORDS.

"A people which takes no pride in the noble achievements of remote ancestors will never achieve anything worthy to be remembered with pride by remote descendants."—MACAULAY.

e

CONTENTS

PERIOD VI.—THE HUNDRED DAYS AND WATERLOO

CONTENTS

LIST OF PORTRAITS

Facsimile

LIST OF PLANS

PERIOD VI

THE HUNDRED DAYS AND WATERLOO

A

PERIOD VI.—WATERLOO AND ST. HELENA

(From Wellington's entrance into France, October 7, 1813, to the arrival of Napoleon at St. Helena, October 16, 1815.)

CHRONOLOGICAL TABLE

1813. Oct. 16–18. Battle of Leipsic.

,, 31. Surrender of Pampeluna.

Nov. 9. Allies offer Napoleon peace at Frankfort; cross the Rhine, December 31.

,, 10. Passage of the Nivelle.

Dec. 3. Rising of Holland against France; Wellington crosses the Nive.

,, 9–11. Fighting before Bayonne.

,, 11. Treaty of Valancey; Napoleon surrenders the Spanish crown.

,, 12. Battle of St. Pierre.

1814. Feb. 1. Napoleon repulsed by Blücher at Brienne.

,, 21–24. Passage of the Adour.

,, 27. Battle of Orthes.

Mar. 12. Entrance of allies into Bordeaux.

,, 20. Napoleon marches on St. Dizier leaving Paris open to the allies.

,, 24. Ferdinand enters Spain.

,, 31. Allies enter Paris.

April 10. Battle of Toulouse.

,, 11. Abdication of Napoleon.

,, 14. French sortie from Bayonne.

1814. April 19. Soult and Wellington sign convention for cessation of hostilities.

   May 14. Napoleon lands at Elba.

    ,, 29. Death of Josephine ; restoration of Bourbons.

    ,, 30. Treaty of Paris.

   Nov. 1. Congress of Vienna assembles.

   Dec. 24. Peace of Ghent between England and United
States.

1815. Mar. 1. Napoleon lands from Elba.

    ,, 13. The Allied Powers issue a declaration against
Napoleon.

    ,, 20. Napoleon arrives at Paris ; Louis XVIII. flees to
Ghent.

   June 13. Napoleon leaves Paris for his last campaign.

    ,, 15. French columns cross the Sambre.

    ,, 16. Battles of Ligny and Quatre Bras.

    ,, 17. Wellington falls back to Waterloo, Blücher to
Wavre.

    ,, 18. Battle of Waterloo.

    ,, 21. Napoleon returns to Paris.

    ,, 22. Second abdication of Napoleon; provisional gov-
ernment formed.

   July 2. Convention to settle terms of capitulation for Paris.

    ,, 7. Allies enter Paris.

    ,, 15. Napoleon surrenders to Captain Maitland of the
Bellerophon.

    ,, 24. *Bellerophon* with Napoleon on board anchors at
Torbay.

   Aug. 2. The allied sovereigns declare Napoleon to be
their common prisoner.

   Oct. 16. Napoleon lands at St. Helena ; dies there May 6,
1821.

HOW ENGLAND SAVED EUROPE:

THE STORY OF THE GREAT WAR

(1793–1815)

CHAPTER I

ON FRENCH SOIL

WHEN San Sebastian fell the tumult of battle on the Spanish frontier for a time seemed to die away. Soult, shaken by the terrible battles in the Pyrenees, was in no mood to take the offensive. He wrote to Paris, indeed, declaring that unless he had 50,000 men who had never met the British, he could not answer for the South of France! His army had been drained of veterans to strengthen Napoleon on the Elbe and the Rhine, and his conscripts had emerged with sorely-shaken nerves from their rough wrestle with Wellington's war-hardened veterans in the Pyrenees. Soult, however, was busy with pick and spade along a front of more than twenty miles, turning the steep hills which form the

French frontier into a great natural fortress, which, he hoped, would prove impregnable. Wellington, on the other hand, was recruiting his army, which had out-raced its supplies and marched itself almost barefoot, and was exhausted with the breathless haste, the bloody battles and sieges of the wonderful campaign just ended. Wellington, a cool soldier, understood his own art too well to undertake the actual invasion of France till he had gathered up adequate resources for that stupendous task. Pampeluna had not yet fallen. Napoleon, who had just won the great battle of Dresden, might compel the allied sovereigns to treat for peace, and that would enable him to hurl an overwhelming force on the audacious English who had dared to invade France.

Waiting thus till Pampeluna fell, till the situation on the Continent became clear, and till his own forces were reorganised, Wellington kept guard on the slopes and peaks of the Pyrenees. But there was much suffering in his mountain-camps. The weather was harsh and tempestuous; the supply of food was scanty; and, from their bleak and wind-scourged bivouacs, Wellington's troops looked down on the rich plains of France with longing eyes. It is a curious fact that, exactly as was the case at Torres Vedras, there was a continual stream of desertions from Wellington's lines to those of Soult. In less than four months more than 1200 such desertions took place. The British private of that period was a magnificent fighter, but inaction galled him. The sense of patriotism was weak. To shiver through cold days and stormy nights, hungry and ill-clad, on the crests of the Pyrenees, after the hurrying excitements of Vittoria and San Sebastian, taxed his patience too severely, and the warm plains of France beckoned him too alluringly. Hence this curious drift of desertions from a victorious army to the very forces they had defeated.

Both the British Cabinet and the Allied sovereigns were eager that Wellington should cross the Bidassoa and display the British flag on French soil. The moral effect of the invasion of France by the victorious English would be immense. It would proclaim to the world the completeness of the French overthrow in Spain. It would dissipate, as with the prick of Ithuriel's spear, the spell of Napoleon's "invincibility." To see France invaded on the south while Napoleon himself was fighting desperately for existence on the east, would give new courage to banded Europe. And, as a political stroke rather than an effort of sound strategy, Wellington, with Pampeluna still unsubdued in his rear, determined to pass the Bidassoa.

The passage of this river was a soldierly deed, planned with magnificent skill and executed with magnificent courage. Graham, on the left, with the 1st and 5th divisions and some Portuguese, was to ford the Bidassoa near its mouth. The current

was swift; the tides rose and fell sixteen feet. No
one imagined that troops could cross such a stream
in the face of a strongly entrenched enemy. But
some Spanish fishermen had discovered three perilous
and uncertain fords, and Wellington was resolved on
the attempt. Its very difficulty, in a sense, made
it practicable; for the French counted the passage
impossible and kept careless watch. On the right,
the Light Division, with the Spaniards under Longa
and Giron, were to attempt an equally desperate
task. They were to storm a difficult line of crags,
rising like stairs till they reached the Great Rhune,
the whole line of mountain steeps being strongly
entrenched, and held by 5000 good troops.

On the night of October 6 the British were in
movement. There was blackness of rain and tempest
in the sky above as the columns moved down the
rough slopes of the Pyrenees, and there was blackness of vast defiles, opaque with night and depth,
beneath them. The gleaming lightning might show
to vigilant French sentinels the sparkle of metal
from the muskets of the soldiers, or from the huge
brass plates on their hats; and the troops as they
marched were ordered to reverse their arms and
turn the brass plates on their caps to the rear, so
as to escape that risk. The British columns had
reached their positions while the stars were still
shining. As the day slowly dawned, obscure with
rain and bitter with cold, the 5th division broke

from its cover, and, in two columns, moved swiftly across the sands left by the ebbing tide, and waded deep into the current of the Bidassoa. The swiftly-sliding waters reached almost to the men's armpits. The startled French from the farther shore poured hasty volleys upon them; but Graham's troops, as they came quickly up and in succession pressed into the river, were cheering loudly, the regimental bands playing the National Anthem. Without a check the columns crossed the fords and reached French soil. The 1st division followed. Maucune, who played so gallant a part at Salamanca, held the French bank with 5000 troops, but nothing could stop the British. Position after position was carried; eight guns were captured, and the French right was driven roughly back in a retreat which threatened to become a flight.

When Graham's columns had reached the French bank a rocket soared aloft from the steeple of Fuente-rabia, and in an instant Wellington's whole attack was uncovered. Seven columns, along a front of five miles, were in movement. The Bidassoa was crossed by ford or bridge at as many different points, and the attack of Wellington's right on the great mountain defences, the climax of which was the peak of La Rhune, was pushed with audacious valour.

The range of mountains attacked forms an acute angle with the course of the Bidassoa. As depicted on the map, it resembles a gigantic centipede, its tail touching the Bidassoa; the Great Rhune, at a distance of nearly ten miles, forms its erected head, and the lateral spurs, running down into the valleys, its claws. This hilly centipede stretches almost from the Bidassoa to the Nivelle, on whose stream the high peak of La Rhune looks down. The crest of the great range and all its flanking hills looking towards the Bidassoa were strongly entrenched. The long crest, it may be added, bore a series of names. The "tail" of the centipede is formed by the Mandale mountain; next comes the Bayonette ridge, from which, as a huge shoulder, the Commisari juts out. Then comes a steep and lofty spine called the Saddle, while, farthest of all and high above all, rises the Great Rhune.

Three columns were launched in parallel attack on this range of entrenched hill-summits. Giron, with his Andalusians, assaulted the Saddle; another column climbed the steep road—twisting with a hundred sudden turns, and blocked every few yards with abattis and retrenchments—which crossed the ridge under the frowning height of the Commisari. The hardest task was reserved for the men of the Light Division, who had to carry the Bayonette. From that frowning height a shoulder runs down more than half the flank of the mountain to a tiny plateau. There it splits into three diverging ridges which sink into the deep valley below. Each of these ridges was strongly entrenched. A star redoubt stood at their

junction; half way up the mountain shoulder was
another entrenchment; on the crest of the Bayonette
itself frowned a huge redoubt. But up that great
mountain stair, seamed with trenches and guarded
by batteries, the men of the Light Division raced
with hardly a check. The French were thrust back
over their entrenchments, bayoneted in their redoubts, or flung as mere scattered human spray down
the flanks of the ridges before the rush of the British.
One curious check, it is true, took place. The Rifles
were leading, and as their panting files struggled out
of the tangled brushwood on to the little natural
platform where the three ascending ridges met, and
which was guarded by a star-shaped fort, they closed
rapidly in upon that work to carry it.

The French, however, took the Rifles, from their
dark uniforms, to be Portuguese, and, plucking up
courage against such opponents, they charged in a
solid mass out of the redoubt, and drove the Rifles
back with loss over the edge of the descent. Just
then the 52nd came in sight. They were following
the Rifles up the steep ascent, and the mere sight of
their red uniform in an instant checked the exultant
French. They had no mind to meet British troops
in a frank charge. They hesitated; they began to
fall back, the backward movement became a rush.
The 52nd, running forward, stormed into the work
with their enemies, the Rifles racing round its
flank; and through the redoubt and up to the

very crest of the Bayonette the flight and pursuit swept.

Giron was checked in his attack on the Saddle ridge. Two French regiments, their front covered by a heavy line of abattis, barred the advance of the Spaniards with their fire, and nothing would induce the Spaniards to make the resolute push needed to break the French line. While the Spaniards hung sullenly back, refusing to follow their officers, a youthful member of Alten's staff came up at speed to learn the cause of the check. He was but a lad, a frank-faced British lad, and his boyish valour promptly solved the difficulty. Waving his hat, he shouted to the Spaniards to follow him; and, putting spurs to his horse, at one leap cleared the abattis, and broke in on the astonished French. The challenge of that boyish voice, the sight of the youthful figure leaping on the French bayonets, kindled the Spaniards to sudden fire, and with a clamour of shouts for "el chico blanco"—"the fair lad"— they followed him over the abattis, and the French were tumbled into disordered retreat.

Night by this time had fallen, and under its darkness the French abandoned that part of the Great Rhune which was still unattacked. Wellington had thus crossed a dangerous tidal river, and carried a range of mountains which Soult, with the labours of a month, had scarred with entrenchments; and he had done it all with little more than five hours' fighting, and the loss of less than 1600 men. The French, as a matter of fact, fought ill. The shadow of their defeats in the Pyrenees still lay chill and black upon their spirits.

On October 31 Pampeluna fell, vanquished by mere hunger. Its garrison held out with great stubbornness, and, when the gates were finally opened to the besiegers, not merely the horses and the mules, but the very dogs, the cats, the rats, the reeds that grew upon the glacis, had passed into the stomachs of the hunger-wasted garrison. Wellington was now free to push his operations on French soil. But first he had to teach his own troops, and particularly the Spaniards, that he meant to wage war in France in a civilised fashion.

He knew that unless he sternly repressed outrages on the French peasantry there would break out against him the flame of a guerilla warfare such as had wasted the strength and crippled the strategy of the French in Spain. And even if savage warfare did not bring in its train such a penalty, it was intolerable to the character of Wellington and to the temper of the English people. Wellington accordingly issued a proclamation calling upon his troops to observe the utmost order and humanity in their dealings with the French; and he supplemented his proclamation with the sternest punishments. "I do not care," he wrote, "whether I command a large or a small army; but, large or

small, I will be obeyed, and I will not suffer pillage."
"I have lost," he wrote at a later date, " 20,000 men
in this campaign, and it was not that General
Morillo or anybody else might plunder the French
peasantry; and I distinctly declare that I will not
suffer it where I command."

Wellington issued a proclamation inviting the
French peasantry to seize and bring to his headquarters all plunderers, promising to pay for the
damage they had committed, and to punish the
offenders. The inhabitants of one French village
shot an English soldier dead who was plundering,
wounded his comrade and brought him to headquarters, where he was promptly hanged. "If I
had 20,000 Spaniards, paid and fed," Wellington
wrote some weeks later to Lord Bathurst, "I
should have Bayonne. If I had 40,000, I do not
know where I should stop. Now I have both the
20,000 and the 40,000 . . . but if they plunder they
will ruin all." And finally Wellington sent back
25,000 good Spanish troops into Spain, because he
could not trust them in France, and he was willing
to postpone victory rather than to win it at a
shameful cost.

Wellington's policy stands out in vivid and noble
contrast with the savage methods adopted by all
other combatants in the great strife then raging.
Napoleon's methods in Spain are still the shame of
history. At the very moment when, on the southern

frontier, Wellington was sending back his Spaniards, and robbing himself of an army rather than suffer outrages to be committed, the Allied sovereigns on the eastern frontier were letting loose their Cossacks to spread havoc through the French provinces. Wellington's more humane policy was amply justified by results. How did it come to pass that Wellington in the south could effect more with a mixed force of 60,000 troops than the Allied sovereigns with 500,000 could accomplish on the opposite side of France? It was not merely that Wellington was opposed by Soult instead of by Napoleon. The justice and humanity he showed towards the French peasantry prevented the fire of a guerilla warfare being kindled against him. He had no foes except the troops arrayed under Soult. Perfect tranquillity reigned about his bivouacs, and followed him to the very edge of the battlefield. Nay, there ran before him the fame of his humanity, of the order and discipline of his troops, and this won him friends everywhere. He was able to secure more abundant supplies in France than Soult himself. "The English general's policy, and the good discipline he maintains, does us more harm," wrote a French officer at that period, "than ten battles; every peasant wishes to be under his protection." Soult himself complained of the French peasantry that "they appear more disposed to favour the invaders than to second the army. It is scarcely possible to obtain a carriage for transport," he wrote, " and I shall not be surprised to find in a short time these inhabitants taking arms against us."

The tempestuous weather now once more laid its arresting spell on military operations. It was winter-time—the winter of the Pyrenees ; and the snows and storms in the mountain passes were not more trying than the incessant dissolving rains in the plains below. The country was one great clay bed, laced with streams, and liquefying over wide stretches into vast marshes. The roads were mere ribbons of mud ; the streams were bridgeless ; the landscape was one rain-scourged quagmire. Soult, with a fortified camp and a great fortress as his base, and with paved roads linking his divisions together, had an advantage over his great opponent. The incessant rains were his safeguard. A hard frost, or forty-eight hours' sun, would have ruined him. But Wellington's divisions were parted from each other by moist stretches of mud almost as hopelessly as by spaces of fathomless sea itself. On the cross-roads, which formed the only lines of communication betwixt Wellington's camps, the guns sank to their axles, the infantry to mid-leg, the cavalry to their saddle-girths. There was nothing for it but to stand on guard and wait.

CHAPTER II

ACROSS THE NIVELLE

DURING this interval of waiting, the outposts of
the rival armies fell into the oddest relations
of friendship. They had a rough code of signals by
which they could communicate with each other ; and
if either side wanted, for a time, a particular post,
it would be yielded with good-humoured frankness.
The officers in charge of the French working parties
on the Little Rhune, busy throwing up entrenchments, chatted pleasantly with the officers in charge
of the British outposts, and exchanged bantering
pleasantries as to what would happen when the
business of storming these entrenchments was taken
in hand. The sentries on either side exchanged
news, or bartered tobacco for spirits, &c.

One curious example of the terms established betwixt the men at the outposts is given by Napier.
" The 43rd fell into line one morning, within twenty
yards of a French out-sentry. The Frenchman during
the whole operation composedly walked to and fro
on his beat, with his knapsack lying on the ground
to ease his shoulders. When the 43rd was ordered

to advance, a British sergeant went forward, helped the Frenchman to replace his pack, and told him to go away. Then the 43rd opened fire." Next morning the French, in exactly the same way, warned a sentry of the 43rd to retire. The soldiers were on terms of war with each other, in brief, but not of wanton murder.

In his "Adventures of a Soldier" Costello gives what we may call the view from the ranks, the sentiment of the privates; and his testimony is very striking. "Ours, indeed," he says, "was a noble enemy. They never permitted us to flag, but kept us ever on the *qui vive*. We anticipated little terror from capture, and though we ever found them to be our roughest antagonists, yet we always experienced a most generous opposition. Indeed there was, on the whole, such a chivalrous spirit between us, that our men had a kind of respect for even a wound inflicted by a Frenchman." Speaking again of the pause in the fighting which took place on the Bidassoa, Costello says, "Such a good feeling reigned among the French and our men, that they frequently went into each other's picket-houses—terms of intimacy which they extended to neither the Spanish nor Portuguese troops, for whom they expressed an unmeasured contempt."

Wellington, however, had sterner cares. He would sometimes complain, with a touch of bitter humour, that he had deadlier foes behind him than in front.

From amid his bivouac fires he had to watch the plots of Spanish and Portuguese statesmen, and his correspondence at this period reflects vividly the ceaseless anxieties these caused him. At the very time he was busy out-generalling Soult, Wellington warned the British Cabinet that there was a real peril of coming to open war with Spain, and he discussed how, in that event, he might be able to embark the British army at Passages, "in spite of all the French and Spanish armies united." "But," he added, "I should be much more certain of getting clear off, as we ought, if we had possession of San Sebastian;" and he urged Ministers to demand that a British garrison should be admitted into that fortress.

History is rich in satire, but what more striking example of the irony of history can be imagined than this — that at the very moment when England was spending the blood of her soldiers and the gold of her citizens to deliver Spain from Napoleon, she had also to consider the possibility of the nation she had delivered attacking her! The soil of Spain had been sown thick with British graves, but from that gallant seed sprang no harvest of gratitude. "It was," says Napier, "with an enemy at his back more to be dreaded than the foe in his front that Wellington invaded the South of France."

Wellington's difficulties, on the whole, and at this

distance of time, are hardly realisable. The Spanish authorities waged what was scarcely less than open war on his hospitals and communications. His great hospitals were at Santander, and the Spanish officials suddenly placed them all—doctors and patients— under rigid quarantine. Betwixt June and December 1813, 30,000 British soldiers had been wounded in the service of Spain. The return offered by Spanish gratitude was to make these wounded men close prisoners, with the view of driving Wellington to fix his hospitals in England!

And if Wellington suffered much from the jealousy and ignorance of Spanish authorities, he suffered almost as much from the stupidity of the British Cabinet. Reinforcements which would have enabled him to crush Soult were intercepted, and despatched on an irrelevant expedition to Holland under Graham. Wellington's troops were left to shiver, half clad, many of them barefooted, on the bleak slopes of the Pyrenees. His muleteers were twenty-six months in arrears, his troops seven months. Napier describes him at the end of 1813 —when all the victories of the Peninsula were behind him—as " having not a shilling to pay for anything in the country, and his credit gone." It is a fact that he had to borrow privately the money necessary to send a courier to Clinton on the east coast of Spain. He was so overwhelmed with debt that he describes himself as scarcely able to quit his quarters for the multitude of creditors lying in wait for him. The astonishing British Cabinet wished to despatch Wellington and his veterans to Holland, and Wellington had to remind them that a British army on the Garonne, with perhaps a rising on behalf of the Bourbons around it, would do ten times more to overthrow Napoleon, and to procure peace, than the same army occupied in besieging worthless fortresses in Flanders.

Never before or since was an unhappy general so sorely badgered or so ill supported. And, as Napier reminds us, "It was when crossing the Bidassoa, breaking through the mountain fortifications of Soult, passing the Nive, fighting the battles in front of Bayonne, and when still greater and more intricate combinations were to be arranged, that all these vials of folly and enmity were poured upon his head." "Who, then, shall refuse to admire," asks Napier, "the undaunted firmness, the unwearied temper and vigilance, the piercing judgment with which he steered his gallant vessel, with a flowing sail, unhurt through that howling storm of passion, this tumultuous sea of folly?"

It is unnecessary to waste space in describing the operations of this period on the east coast. They, in a sense, reflect no credit on the English army, but this was because the British Cabinet sent to the scene of action many commanders, but no general. The presence of the British on the east coast, how-

ever, served the useful end of keeping Suchet in
check, and the last British commander on that field,
Clinton, could at least claim that he had " held his
position in front of Suchet with much inferior forces
for eight months, and suffered no disaster."

Soult had constructed immense double lines of
entrenchments, stretching between the Nive and the
sea, and covering a front of sixteen miles.   He had
79,000 troops under his command, and conscripts
were rapidly flowing in.   The junction of Suchet
from Catalonia would nearly have doubled the
strength of the French on the Nivelle ; but that
general preferred—or found it necessary—to play a
lone hand.   And Napoleon failed to enforce common
plans on his two generals, though he approved of
Soult's plan of uniting both armies in Arragon, and
so forcing Wellington to fight a second battle of
Vittoria, with perhaps a result which would cancel
the earlier victory.

On November 10 Wellington moved to cross the
Nivelle.   His plan was to storm the Little Rhune,
which stood betwixt the river and the Great Rhune,
ford the river, break through the French centre, and,
if possible, cut off the right wing from Bayonne.
On the night of the 9th the British columns were
in movement to reach the positions assigned to
them.   They advanced in perfect silence, the words
of command being passed from officer to officer in
whispers.   Through the darkness could be heard

far off the chiming of the village clocks. An army 90,000 strong was in movement, but so perfect were Wellington's arrangements, that not a battalion strayed from its path, and not a sound reached the ears of the vigilant French sentinels. The bugles called and the drums beat in the British camps as usual before sunrise, so as to give the French the impression that the regiments were still there, while, as a matter of fact, they were lying on the ground within reach of the French positions.

Presently the first ray of the sun touched, as with a finger of light, the lofty peak of the Atchubia; a signal-gun from a British battery high up the hill flashed redly. In a moment the scarlet columns were visible, moving quickly down the flanks of the Great Rhune. L'Estrange, of the 31st, has left an amusing account of the scene at the ford crossed by his regiment. "When we came up to the river," he says, "it looked formidable enough, a strong stream running, and we did not know the depth of the ford. Mine was the leading company. My general, Byng, desired me to wade the river before the army came down, to prove its depth." L'Estrange obeyed the order; and a solitary figure, the water rising to his middle, he splashed across the river to the side held by the French. For aught he knew a thousand French muskets covered him as he waded ; and yet he never flinched, though expecting every moment to see the red flash of musketry, and feel the shock of the bullets.

In that day's brilliant fighting the most perilous part fell to the Light Division. Alten's men had to storm the Little Rhune, a "hog's-back ridge," rising at points to a height of 200 feet, and covered in front by an almost impassable marsh. The "bristles" on this hog's-back were huge perpendicular crags, and the French had turned them ingeniously into defences, connecting these splintered rocks with walls of loose stones, so that they formed a sort of rocky stair, each step in this gigantic stairway being a tiny fort. The whole was crowned by a star-fort on its peak.

The 43rd led the attack on the Little Rhune, William Napier being in command. He sent two companies into the marsh to keep down the fire of the French, and led four companies straight against the front of La Rhune. A direct rush was impossible; the men had to cross the marsh till they reached the base of the rocks, then swing sharply to the left along the ribbon of firm ground at the foot of the rocks, till they reached the shoulder of the ridge, where alone ascent was practicable. Napier strove to keep his men in hand, so that no rush should take place; but the ranks were eager, the men's steps instinctively quickened, the line curved forward. Suddenly there was the sound of galloping hoofs behind them. It was a youthful aide-de-camp waving his hat, and coming up at speed to join in the attack. That rush of hoofs

and the shout of the boyish voice kindled the 43rd
to a heat in which all restraints were dissolved.
The men, with bent heads and flashing eyes, broke
into a run, and nothing was left for Napier but to
try to keep the lead of his charging lines. Even in
this he failed, one Irish private, the worst character and most reckless fighter in the regiment, out-
charging even his colonel.

In the rapture of that wild rush, however, the
veterans of the 43rd kept their heads. They
reached the ribbon of firm ground at the base
of the cliffs, swung sharply round, raced to the
shoulder of the ridge, and leaped into the lower-
most redoubt, bayoneting its defenders. Then, for
a moment, they fell gasping and breathless. They
had charged at speed over half a mile of badly
broken ground. Presently they rose, fell swiftly into
rank, and stormed up this giant staircase, crowded
with foes, and every step in it flashing redly with
musketry fire. Castle after castle was carried. The
narrow paths were threaded, the loose stone walls
climbed. The struggle was often one of bayonet
against bayonet, of man against man; but nothing
could arrest the furious assault of the 43rd, till at
last the highest castle, called the Donjon, was
reached. There was a moment's pause while the
panting files of the 43rd drew together. Then came
a rush, the Donjon was scaled; and thus, to give
Napier's summary, " in twenty minutes 800 soldiers

were hustled out of this labyrinth." But the 43rd lost eleven officers and sixty-seven men in those few fierce and stormy minutes.

One picturesque incident marked this wild hill fight. The Donjon looked into the rear of a great star-fort beneath it, which was being attacked by the Rifles and the 17th Portuguese; and part of the 43rd, at the very moment when their comrades were storming the Donjon, knelt on the hill crest and opened a deadly fire on the star-fort beneath. Its garrison, attacked by the Rifles in front and smitten by a fire from above, broke and fled. From the lofty summit they had won, the men of the Light Division could look down on the whole landscape of the battle to the sea beyond, a splendid spectacle of war. "On the left," says Napier, "the ships of war, slowly sailing to and fro, were exchanging shots with the fort of Socoa; and Hope, menacing all the French lines in the low ground, sent the sound of a hundred pieces of artillery bellowing up the rocks, to be answered by nearly as many from the tops of the mountains. On the right, the summit of the great Atchubia was just lighted by the rising sun, and 50,000 men, rushing down its enormous slopes with ringing shouts, seemed to chase the receding shadows into the deep valley. The plains of France, so long over-looked from the towering crags of the Pyrenees, were to be the prize of battle, and the half-famished soldiers in their fury broke through the iron

THE HON. SIR JOHN HOPE

<small>AFTERWARDS FOURTH EARL OF HOPETOUN</small>

From a mezzotint after the painting by JOHN HOPPNER, R.A.

barrier erected by Soult as if it were but a screen
of reeds."

One redoubt remained on the extreme left of the
French, armed with large ship-carronades, which,
loaded with grape, wrought much slaughter amongst
the British. Leith of the 31st, Nichol and Dunn
of the 66th, gathered a few men together and carried
the redoubt brilliantly. "Indeed," says Henry, "the
three officers took it themselves; for they cleared the
ditch with a running leap, and dropped down amongst
the garrison before a man could enter to assist them.
As they leaped in, the French artillery officer, a red-
headed giant, and most of his men jumped out, but
not with impunity; for Leith, a Hercules in figure
and strength, knocked the red-headed officer down
with a brickbat."

Hope, meanwhile, had kept the French right occupied; Cole had carried the redoubts in front of
Sarre; Hill had driven back the French left. The
attack of the British centre was pushed till the
French line was pierced and the communication betwixt Soult's wings broken. The French right wing,
indeed, might have been cut off and destroyed; but
the short winter day was drawing to a close, the
ground was difficult, the field of operations very wide,
and Wellington found it impossible to reap the full
harvest of his victory.

In the night Soult withdrew his imperilled right
wing. He had been driven, in a little more than

three hours' actual fighting, from a position he had spent three months in fortifying. It is said that he had planned his lines on the model of those of Wellington at Torres Vedras, and hoped to have held them against Wellington as Wellington himself had held those famous lines against Massena. Soult reckoned, in particular, that it would cost the allies 25,000 men to force his centre. Yet his centre was pierced and his whole position carried with a loss of little more than 2500 men, the French loss being nearly double that of the English. The truth is, that the French were out-generalled as well as out-fought. Soult's best troops were amused with false attacks while an overwhelming force was thrown upon his centre. On the French side, too, while there were many individual examples of splendid courage, there was a marked absence of fighting energy. Soult's conscripts bore themselves as though they expected to be defeated.

CHAPTER III

SOULT'S GREAT RALLY

THE incessant rains, the swollen rivers, the impassable roads, once more arrested Wellington's operations, and Soult meanwhile fell back to the Nive, with Bayonne, at the junction of that river with the Adour, as his base. In front of Bayonne was a strongly entrenched camp, while Soult's outposts held in strength the entangled and difficult country in Wellington's front.

Early in December the weather for a few days mended, and Wellington determined to cross the Nive. This was effected on December 9; but Wellington's very success created a new difficulty, and gave to Soult a great opportunity, of which he availed himself with signal audacity and skill. The British held both banks of the Nive, but that river, wide and deep and at flood-level, owing to the incessant rains, divided the British army into two almost unrelated fragments, with communications betwixt them of the slenderest and most precarious character. Soult held an interior position, with good roads and a perfectly secure base in Bayonne. His business was defence; but he was too good a master of the art of war not to know that an energetic offensive movement is sometimes the most perfect method of defence. It was clear that he could throw a much superior force on either segment of Wellington's army at pleasure; and there followed five days of furious battle, in which Soult took the offensive and flung himself with magnificent valour and in superior numbers on each fragment of Wellington's divided forces in turn. But it was only to fail, though to defeat his attacks cost the British a terrible price in blood.

On the 10th, Soult, moving rapidly out of Bayonne, fell unexpectedly on the British left under Sir John Hope, while Clausel, with a powerful column, at the same moment attacked the Light Division holding the village of Arcangues. Hope had 30,000 men and twenty-four guns; Soult assailed him with 60,000 men and forty guns. Hope was taken by surprise; but the attack was delivered too late in the day to make a great success possible. The British regiments fought with dogged, long-enduring courage. Robinson's brigade of the 5th division distinguished itself by its obstinate valour; and when night fell, Soult's stroke had practically failed. After sunset a brigade of the Guards reached the field of action; later, the 1st division came up, and Hope's position was secure.

Hope was a man of gigantic stature; he rode the

biggest horse he could purchase, and his figure, through the smoke of an engagement, loomed in Titanic proportions. "We shall lose him," Wellington wrote, "if he continues to expose himself to fire as he has done in the last three days. He places himself among the sharpshooters without, as they do, sheltering himself from the enemy's fire."

Clausel meanwhile had leaped on the Light Division at Arcangues, some two miles from the point where Hope was fighting. The men of the Light Division were not soldiers to be easily caught off their guard, and the French resorted to an ingenious trick to deceive them.

On the morning of the 10th the pickets of the 43rd noticed that the men of a French regiment in their front were pushing each other about as if in sport, and their eddying gambols brought them every moment nearer the British position. The plumed hat of a French general officer, too, was discovered peering round a hut in the French line. The British company officers were keenly on their guard. Presently the apparently sportive French fell swiftly into line, a fringe of skirmishers ran out, and in a moment a vehement attack on the British was in progress. The French displayed such a strength, and came on with such a speed, that the 52nd and 43rd had to fall back at a run upon their brigade, which held the church and mansion-house of Arcangues. Only there could a successful defence be attempted. The roads were so narrow and so bad that the British could keep no formation; it was a mere race of broken soldiers, the French column advancing at speed betwixt the two regiments, and trying to get through the pass in advance of them. The British, however, came through first. As they reached the open plain, the apparently disordered soldiers fell into military order as if by magic, and a steadfast red line was drawn across the opening into the plain. In a few moments the French came up, breathless and eager, and found their advance barred by rolling volleys from the steady British front.

A cluster of British soldiers, however, was caught in the pass. It consisted of about 100 Riflemen and men of the 43rd, with one officer, an ensign of the 43rd, a youth only eighteen years old, named Campbell. They were a mere handful cut off by a column, and they were haughtily summoned to surrender. In reply, the boyish ensign of the 43rd, with a challenging shout, ran in on the solid lines of the French; the group of privates about him followed; the massive French column was torn through, and, though one-half of the British were slain or captured, Campbell himself, with the remainder, broke through and escaped.

The fiercest fighting of the day eddied round a great building belonging to the Mayor of Biarritz, and known as the "Mayor's House." It was sur-rounded by hedges, through which the French cut

gaps and came by fragments into the struggle. In
the mad fight military order on both sides was lost.
French and English clashed together in single combats, or in fragments of regiments, with the most
curious changes of fortune. The common feature
of all these separate combats was the fury of the
combatants. A strong French regiment, covered by
the drifting battle-smoke, passed clean through a
gap in the British line, and the 9th regiment, under
Cameron, while exchanging volleys at pistol-shot distance with a body of French in its front, suddenly
discovered this new hostile force taking up its position
in the rear. Cameron, a gallant soldier, left a line
of skirmishers to maintain the fight in front, faced
about the remainder of his regiment, and led them
in an angry bayonet charge on the body in his rear.
Nearly 100 men and officers of the 9th fell in that
rush, but the French regiment attacked was practically destroyed. When night fell, the British had
lost more than 1500 in killed, wounded, and prisoners;
but Soult's admirably-planned attack had failed, with
a loss to the French of over 2000 men.

To the mortification of failure the night which
followed brought to Soult an almost sharper mortification. Three German regiments passed over to the
British. They were amongst Soult's best troops, but
they were fighting in an alien cause. Their sovereign
was battling with Napoleon on the Rhine, and it
was absurd that his troops should be contending

for the French eagles against the English on the
Nive.

On the morning of the 11th Soult concentrated his
strength in front of the Light Division, and Hope
moved part of his corps to the right to strengthen
the threatened point. Soult, who had begun his
attack on the Light Division, hereupon swung round
his columns, marched swiftly to his right, and fell on
Hope's position, which he believed to be seriously
weakened by the reinforcements sent to Alten's
help; but once more his attack failed. Wellington
had drawn large reinforcements from his right to
strengthen his assailed left; and on the night of
the 12th Soult marched his troops at the quick-
step through Bayonne, and fell with fury upon the
weakened British right under Hill. Then followed
the battle of St. Pierre, described by Wellington
himself as "the bloodiest fight in the Peninsula."

Hill, with 14,000 men, occupied a front of two
miles. Pringle's brigade held a craggy ridge on his
left. The centre—a crescent-shaped hill—was held
by Sir William Stewart; Byng, with a brigade of
four regiments, held the right. The flaw in the
British position lay in the fact that its right wing
was parted from its centre by a marshy valley and a
chain of ponds. Hill's force consisted of 14,000 men,
and Soult fell upon him with 35,000. Abbe, an
energetic and daring soldier, led Soult's attack on
the British centre, while the British right and left

wings were both simultaneously assailed. In the
centre Ashworth's Portuguese, though bravely fighting, gave way, and two of Barnes' regiments moved
up to fill the gap they had left. But Abbe was not
to be denied. His leading battalions were shattered
one after another, but the French attack was fed
unceasingly, and Barnes' regiments in turn, after
losing half their strength, fell back, and the French
held the crest. Barnes then brought on the 92nd,
and that gallant regiment, moving steadily into the
fight, drove back the French, reeling from the shock
of their attack. Again and again, however, the
French renewed their onfall, till at last the 92nd, in
turn, yielded the ground, though still stubbornly
fighting.

On both the British right and left the battle raged
furiously, but with ill-fortune for the British, and
with some shameful incidents. The 71st was taken
ignobly out of the fight by its colonel on the left of
the centre, while on the extreme right the colonel of
the 3rd had also yielded the combat. No one could
exactly explain, least of all the guilty officers themselves, how this happened. Both bore the reputation
of good soldiers, but in the strain of that terrible
fight, a fight against what seemed overwhelming odds,
they suffered some temporary paralysis of nerve or
brain, and both paid the penalty of it afterwards in
an ignominious dismissal from the army.

Byng personally led the 31st forward in a furious

charge. He took the King's colour out of the
hands of the officer who carried it, and, bearing it
aloft, led the line forward. It was a gallant deed;
but incidentally the officer out of whose hands Byng
caught the colour felt the act to be a slur on his
own courage, and joined in the fury of the charge
with tears of anger and shame at the supposed slight
running down his cheeks.

At that moment the battle seemed lost. Hill had
watched the fight from some high ground near the
centre, and riding down at speed, he met the retreating 71st. He was a man of placid manners and
gentle speech; but, as he saw his regiments falling
back out of the fight, he was heard to mutter to
himself, "D—— it, this won't do." Wellington at
that moment had come up, and he whispered, half
jestingly, to his nearest aide-de-camp, "Hill is beginning to swear; we had better get out of the
way!"

The 71st was a Highland regiment of the highest
fighting quality, and its hot Gaelic temper was sorely
galled by that inexplicable order to fall back. Hill
halted the regiment, and sent it back with a single
gesture into the fight. The gallant Buffs, too, gladly
obeyed the order to "right-about-face," and moved
cheerfully to their position again. Then Hill threw
his whole reserves into the combat. The 92nd came
once more into the fray, and its Colonel, Cameron,
who understood his Highlanders, dressed his regi-

ment as if on parade, uncased its colours, bade his pipers blow their shrillest, and then, with waving flags and skirling pipes, moved down along the high-road on the French. A heavy French column was advancing to meet them; its temper was high, and it seemed as if, for a moment, Highlanders and Frenchmen, in the sternest fighting mood, would clash together. But that fierce Highland line, with its screaming pipes and wind-blown plumes, some-how curiously affected the nerve of the French officer in command of the column. He drew his reins; he made a hesitating gesture with his sword. The word of command ran down the French column; it halted, went right about, and fell back.

That sudden breakdown of warlike purpose on the part of the French commander cost Soult the battle. Pringle, desperately fighting on the left, had repelled the forces assailing him. The fight in the centre was restored; and the 4th and 6th divisions, press-ing on eagerly towards where the thunder of battle was rolling up the hills, had almost reached the scene of action. Wellington, too, had come up, and Soult, with all his great qualities as a commander, lacked the overwhelming fighting energy of a leader like Massena, who would not yield till his last cartridge and his last soldier had been expended. He abandoned the con-test. Hill's one surviving aide-de-camp, Currie, saw the 6th division coming down the hill slope in the rear to their help. He pointed to them, and said,

"There they come; but, thank God, we've beat the enemy without their help!"

Wellington, as he rode over the fighting ground, declared he had never seen a field so thickly strewn with dead. Upon a space of not more than one mile square, 5000 men had fallen in a struggle of less than three hours. On the British side the loss amounted to 1500 killed and wounded. The 92nd alone, who broke the French four times with bayonet charges, lost 13 officers and 171 rank and file. But the loss was heaviest in the higher ranks, for the officers had exposed themselves freely to maintain the fighting of the rank and file. Three British generals had fallen, almost every member of Hill's staff was killed or wounded; and when, late in the afternoon, an aide-de-camp carried an order to Byng's brigade to advance, there was no superior officer surviving to whom he could deliver it, and he led the brigade himself. Wellington summed up Hill's exploit in French; decorous English could scarcely supply the adjective he used. Hill, he said, met the enemy, "et l'a battu diablement!"

Soult, in a sense, is the hero of this great fight of five days. He had shown both generalship and courage in a very high degree, and the speed and decision with which he changed his attack from right to left, and from left to right, proved that he possessed the qualities of a great commander. And yet he had failed. He did not win a single foot of ground from his great opponent. He had repeatedly attacked with an army, and been repulsed by a division; and he was beaten not so much by better generalship on the part of the British commanders, as by the unconquerable valour of the English rank and file. If the slaughter of the five days be taken in the aggregate, and for both armies, it must have reached not less than 12,000 killed and wounded. And this huge slaughter left both armies occupying exactly the same ground as when the struggle began.

After St. Pierre the colonels of three regiments, the Buffs, the 71st, and the "Die-hards," or 57th regiment, were, in a general order, dismissed to England. Public opinion in the army heartily endorsed the judgment on the two first. The 71st had been commanded by Cadogan, who died so heroically at Vittoria, and in the few months which had elapsed since then it had become, under its new commander, sadly disorganised. So much mischief can a foolish colonel achieve in so short a time! But the colonel of the "Die-hards," to quote L'Estrange, was "as hard as nails, as full of fight as any Irishman or Scotchman, and adored by his own regiment." He was familiarly known as "Old McDonald." Perhaps his age was his disqualification. He died shortly after his dismissal; report said that the shame of being classed with the other culprits broke his heart.

With this contest ended the actual fighting for

1813.   Napoleon's position on the Continent was now
almost desperate, but his temper hardened as his
circumstances grew more hopeless.   A memorable
address to his Council of State at Paris, on November
9, was perhaps the most absolutely genuine out-
pouring of his innermost feelings amongst all his
public utterances.   "Wellington," he said, "is in the
south; the Russians threaten the northern frontier;
Austria the south - eastern. . . .   Every ally has
abandoned me.   The Bavarians have betrayed me.
Peace!   No peace till Munich is in flames.   I demand
of you 300,000 men. . . .   But it is men whom I
demand of you, full-grown men in the prime of life,
not these miserable conscript striplings, who choke
my hospitals with sick and my highways with their
carcases.   Give up Holland ?   Rather resign it to the
sea !   The word 'Peace' is ever in my ear, when all
around should re-echo the cry 'War !'"

But the empty veins of France, drained by so
many long campaigns, could no longer yield Napoleon
the blood he demanded.   France was exhausted of
men.   Its fields were tilled by women.   The very
boys had been drawn into the barracks.

Napoleon a little earlier had tried a characteristi-
cally subtle stroke of policy in regard to Spanish
affairs.   He still kept Ferdinand a prisoner at
Valençay.   He now secretly executed a treaty with
him, agreeing to restore him to the throne of Spain,
and to withdraw his troops from that country, on

condition that the British army should be required
to evacuate Spain also. On November 12, 1813, he
had written to Ferdinand saying "the present policy
of my empire" required that affairs in Spain should
be brought to a settlement. England, he wrote, "is
fomenting anarchy, Jacobinism, and the overthrowal
of the monarchy and the nobility, with the object of
establishing a republic in the country." The England
thus accused, it will be remembered, was the England
of Castlereagh and of Lord Liverpool! In order to
rescue Spain, therefore, from these English Jacobins,
Napoleon was willing to give it back into the hands
of Ferdinand, on condition he compelled Wellington
to withdraw beyond the Douro.

A treaty on these terms was despatched by
Ferdinand to the Spanish Regency, with a letter
requiring them to ratify it at once. Ferdinand, with
characteristic falseness, added secretly an explanation
that the treaty would be broken afterwards when it
suited Spanish convenience. The treaty of Valençay
gave back her king to Spain, and would have withdrawn every French soldier from Spanish territory;
and these were, for the Spaniards themselves, great
bribes. On the other hand, if Spain separated herself
from the European coalition against Napoleon, and
required the English army to withdraw from the
Peninsula, this would be an enormous gain for
Napoleon. The Spanish Regency, however, for once
showed both sense and courage. The offer of

Napoleon to withdraw his troops from Spain was unnecessary; his troops had already been driven from that country. The Regency expressed a decorous joy at the prospect of the return of their king, but declared that no public act of his, while he remained a prisoner in France, could be recognised by the Spanish Government.

On May 1, 1808, the Spanish crown had been surrendered to Napoleon, or rather had been stolen by him. He had held it for a little more than five stormy years, at a cost of blood and treasure not easily computed. That fatal theft, in fact, had proved his ruin. Now, like worthless counters, whose value is exhausted, he offered Spain her king and her crown again, only to find the offer refused! Wellington's shrewdness foresaw this move on the part of Napoleon. He dreaded its effects, and said, long afterwards, that if Napoleon had shown less pride and more common sense, it would have succeeded. The scheme failed, as we have seen, and Ferdinand was sent back at last without the guarantee of any written treaty, and in order to secure the release of Suchet's forces in Catalonia.

On March 24, 1814, Ferdinand crossed the Fluvia with the French and Spanish armies drawn up in order of battle on either bank, and became once more king of Spain; and Suchet, gathering up his scattered garrisons, fell back through the Pyrenees. Napier sums up the character of Ferdinand VII.

in sentences which have something of the gall and strength of Tacitus. "He had been a rebellious son in the palace, a plotting traitor at Aranjuez, a dastard at Bayonne, an effeminate, superstitious, fawning slave at Valençay; and now, after six years' captivity, he returned to his own country an ungrateful and cruel tyrant; he would have been the most odious and contemptible of princes if his favourite brother, Don Carlos, had not existed." Ferdinand's earliest performances in Spain justified those terrible sentences. Within six weeks of his return he dissolved the Cortes as a band of mere criminals, sent its leading figures into banishment or captivity, abolished the liberty of the press, revived the Inquisition, and restored in all its ancient strength the ignorant Bourbon despotism which had so long cursed Spain.

CHAPTER IV

THE BRIDGE ACROSS THE ADOUR

THE year 1814 is, in a sense, the supreme year of the general war with Napoleon. On January 1 the allied forces crossed the Rhine. On March 30 Paris fell. Eleven days afterwards Napoleon abdicated. On April 20 he left Fontainebleau for Elba. The soldier-king, who had dreamed of universal empire, and had shaken, one after another, all the thrones of the Continent to the very point of ruin, himself shrank to a toy monarch, with a tiny island for a realm, whose area could be reckoned in acres. During those three historic months the Napoleonic Empire fell, like the great image, with brow of gold and feet of clay, of Daniel's vision! Of the dramatic events which took place on the Rhine and before Paris, some brief account may be given; but place must be accorded first to the part played by Wellington and his troops in this the climax of the great European drama.

Early in February a sudden frost fell on the moist plains round Bayonne, and turned the leagues of liquid mud into stone. And the frost, which made the earth rigid, set loose all the streams of war. In

44

Wellington's forecasting brain the strategy of the coming campaign was already crystallised into perfect form. He would drive Soult beyond the Adour, cross that river himself, and carry the war into the fertile and open country beyond, seizing Bordeaux, where, as he knew from his spies, a rising in favour of the Bourbons would instantly take place. Wellington had 70,000 troops, including 10,000 cavalry, ready for action. Soult, leaving out of count his garrisons, could only put 40,000 men in line of battle. But Wellington's very success would tend to equalise the two armies. When he had thrust Soult back from Bayonne, he must leave a force of not less than 30,000 to invest that place, reckoned by Napoleon himself as one of the great bulwarks of France.

Wellington's plan was to cross the Adour betwixt Bayonne and the sea, a design which shows the scale and daring of his soldiership. It was there where Soult least expected him, but where all the natural conditions seemed to make success impossible. For the six miles of the Adour below the town it is a navigable river—swift, treacherous, dangerous. The spring-tide rises in it fourteen feet; the ebb-tide runs seven miles an hour. Its bed is fordless. Where the sliding current of the river meets the huge rollers riding in from the storm-swept Bay of Biscay is a dangerous bar, on which, in bad weather, a wild surf rages incessantly. A small squadron of French gun-boats guarded those six miles of river; the farther bank was strongly held by French infantry divisions. Yet across this broad and dangerous stream, barred with sand, beaten with surges, covered by the fire of French batteries, Wellington proposed to leap.

But first he must drive Soult from the nearer bank of the Adour, and Hill moved to turn the flank of the French. Harispe, who commanded Soult's left, fell back to Garras, but reinforcements coming up, on February 15 he made a stand on the heights of La Montague. Darkness was gathering. Wellington had only the 2nd division, under Stewart, with Morillo's Spaniards in hand. But the British general was in no mood to loiter. The Spaniards were sent past the French flank, and the 39th and 28th, under Pringle, were launched at Harispe's front. "You must take the hill before dark," said Wellington bluntly.

In front of the two British regiments was a steep ravine, black from mere depth; beyond was the high ridge on which stood the massive battalions of the French. The men of the 39th and 28th were tired with a long day's march; the shadows of evening were gathering blackly on the hill summit, the arms of the brigade had been piled. But the men caught up that stern phrase from Wellington's lips as a sort of kindling watchword. The colonel of the 39th repeated the sentence in ringing accents—"You must

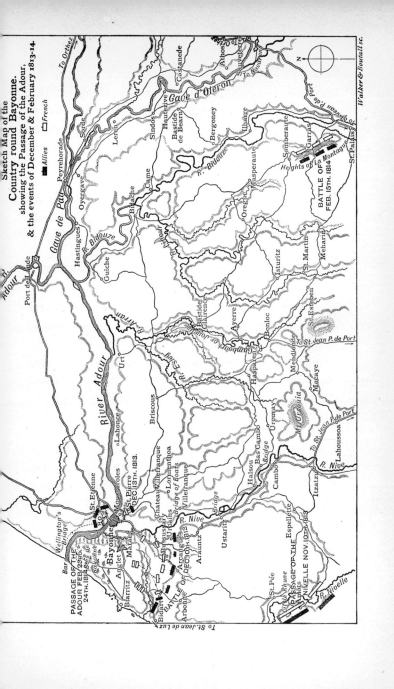

Sketch Map of the
Country round Bayonne.
showing the Passage of the Adour,
& the events of December & February 1813-14.

■ Allies □ French

N

Walker & Boutall sc.

Gave d'Oleron
Gave de Pau
R. Adour
Port de Lande
Peyrehorade
To Orthez
Sorde
Hastingues
Overgave
Lerin
Bellocque
Sindos
Hauterive
Bastide de Bearn
Bergoney
Isaarre
R. Bidouze
Somberaure
Garris
Gabat
St. Palais
Heights of La Montagne
BATTLE OF
FEB. 15TH. 1814
Masperaut
Orega
Clarenne
Isturitz
St. Martin
Meharin
St. Esteben
Bastide Clarence
Ayerre
Bonloc
Meindide
To St. Jean P. de Port
Hasparren
Mataye
Mt. Ursuia
To St. Jean P. de Port
R. Nive
Ustaritz
Larceveau
Bidache
R. Bidouze
R. Bidouze
Guiche
Urt
Arran
R. Esat
Rhune to Cambo
Briscous
Lahonce
River Adour
St. Etienne
Mousseroles
St. Pierre
DEC. 13TH. 1813.
Chateau Villefranque
L'Ormenthoa
Villefranque
Bridge of Boats DEC. 1813.
Bayonne
Marac
Anglet
Boucau
Bar
Wellington's Bridge
PASSAGE OF THE
ADOUR FEB. 23RD. &
24TH. 1814.
Biarritz
Bidart
BATTLE OF
Arbonne
ARCANGUES
DEC. 10TH. 1813.
Brindos Marais
Arcangues
Arauntz
R. Nive
Bridge
Halsou
Bas Cambo
Bridge
Ugarana
Cambo
Izatzt
To St. Jean P. de Port
R. Nive
Lahoussoa
St. Pée
Mt. Rhune
To St. Jean de Luz
PASSAGE OF THE
ESPELETTE
Espelette
Ainhos
BATTLE OF THE
NIVELLE NOV. 10TH. 1813
R. Nivelle

take the hill before dark." Then followed the orders: "Fix bayonets," "Shoulder arms," "Double quick;" and the next instant, in close column, the 39th plunged into the ravine, followed by the 28th.

The men did not fire a shot. They carried their heavy kits, and, as they climbed the steep hill beyond, breath and strength seemed, for a moment, to fail them. Pringle, who led the column, fell wounded, but the steady files never paused. They reached the crest, and, wheeling to the right, proceeded, with close and deadly volleys, to sweep the ridge. Harispe led forward his battalions in what seemed over-powering strength to drive the scanty British force down the slope, and at several points the hostile lines clashed sharply together. The officers on either side were in personal combat; the colonel of the 39th himself was thrust through by a French bayonet. But the 28th was by this time up, and with incessant volleys and forward rushes with the bayonet, these gallant regiments pushed Harispe's massive battalions off the hill. Wellington, with his staff, watched the fierce struggle through the darkening shadows of night and the eddying clouds of battle-smoke till the line of the English fire had swept over the crest. Pringle's men *had* "taken the hill before dark"!

The French, as it happened, had already lit their bivouac fires; and when the fight was over, the British soldiers flung themselves down round these to enjoy the rest they had won so gallantly. Henry, in his "Adventures of a Military Life," describes the attack as the most brilliant battle incident he ever witnessed. "The flashing musketry along the side and from the crest of the hill, the cheering of our men as they mounted, the call of the bugles, the roar of our guns reverberating in long echoes from one side to another of the deep ravine at the bottom —all was martially fine and grand."

Pushing steadily on, in four days, with many bloody combats, Soult was driven back across most difficult country, as far as Sauveterre; and finally, destroying all the bridges on the Adour, the French general planted his headquarters at Orthez. While thus fixing Soult's attention on his left, Wellington was preparing to throw a stupendous bridge over the Adour, far to his right. The navy was to help in carrying out this plan. Forty large sailing boats of about twenty tons burden were collected at St. Jean de Luz, and loaded with materials for the huge structure. Accompanied by some gunboats, they were to appear at the mouth of the Adour on the morning of the 23rd. At the same moment Hope, with two British and two Spanish divisions, some cavalry, and twenty guns, was to make his appearance on the bank of the Adour, and throw over, by means of boats and rafts, a sufficient number of men to silence the French guns on the right bank, and to hold that bank till the great bridge was flung across the stream.

On the morning of the 23rd, Hope, with the 1st division, a rocket battery, and some guns, appeared on the left bank of the Adour as agreed upon. But the sea has incalculable chances. The flotilla of gunboats and sailing craft was far off, fighting its way up from St. Jean de Luz against a hard gale. The sea-line showed no gleam of sail. Hope, the most resolute of soldiers, however, did not hesitate. He would cross the Adour without the help of the flotilla! His eighteen-pounders were suddenly run to the river's edge and opened fire on the French flotilla. Three gunboats were sunk, and the rest were driven up the stream. Then a pontoon, carrying sixty men of the Guards, was rowed across. The men, leaping ashore, drove off a French picket; a hawser was drawn across the river, and pontoon after pontoon, crowded with squads of the Guards and of the 68th, with a rocket battery, were dragged to the farther bank. Less than 1000 men in this manner had crossed when two French battalions came up hurriedly to the scene of action.

But they hesitated to close; the rockets opened upon them, and their novelty was terrifying to the French. Wellington had hitherto despised this new weapon. "I don't want to set fire to any town," he said, "and I don't know any other use for the rocket." But the rockets played a great part in this action on the right bank of the Adour. A French sergeant, a veteran of twenty years, who was taken prisoner, admitted to his captors that he had never really known the sensation of fear till these strange rushing missiles, with their roar and flame, broke upon his battalion. One rocket, it seems, had passed through the knapsack on his back!

All night Hope continued to pass his men in driblets across the Adour. On the morning of the 24th, the flotilla was off the bar, the boats of the men-of-war leading. The French had removed the buoys which marked the true channel, and the boats saw nothing before them but a tumult of tossing breakers. The sailors, with characteristic reckless-ness, took their chances, and dashed at the bar. The first boat sank, the second, a six-oared cutter, shot safely through; but the tide had by this time fallen, and the flotilla had no choice but to draw off, and hang, like a flock of wind-driven seagulls, on the rough seas in the offing, till the tide rose again. Meanwhile the weather darkened. There was peril of tempest seaward and peril of surf and bar land-ward. When the tide had turned, Bloye, of the *Lyra*, led in, and was swallowed up, boat and crew, in the breakers. Then, wheeling round to right and left, like a covey of frightened seabirds, the flotilla drew off again.

Presently a keen-eyed naval officer, in command of the *Woodlark's* boat, caught a glimpse of the thread of quieter water which marked the channel, and putting up his helm, ran daringly through the

surf.   Boat after boat came following, and with slanting decks, torn canvas, and dripping crews, reached
the broad river beyond.   But out of the flotilla eight
boats with their crews perished.

Then began the construction of the great bridge,
one of "the prodigies of war."   The river at that
point ran, in a breadth of 800 feet, within huge retaining walls.   Twenty-six two-masted vessels were
fastened like beads on a thread to five great parallel
stretches of thirteen-inch cables, and drawn across
the stream.   The cables were kept by blocks of wood
at an equal distance of two feet apart, forming a
swinging pathway nearly ten feet wide.   The vessels
were moored lengthways at a distance of forty feet
from each other, and thus gave a swaying support
to the cables.   The ends of the cables were carried
over the retaining walls on either side, fastened to
a great wooden framework which was buried deep in
the ground, and kept firm by gigantic piles of sand-
bags.   Provision had to be made for raising and
lowering the swinging bridge of cables, as the tide
ran out or flowed back.   Across the parallel cables
planks were fastened so as to make a passage way,
and a gigantic floating boom protected the bridge
from attacks of the French above.   Thus was im-
provised a slender, swaying, yet perfectly secure
bridge, across which the artillery and supplies of an
army might safely pass.   The whole work was completed on the 26th.   It opened up to Wellington the

direct road to Bordeaux, turned the flank of Soult's
defences, and made the abandonment of Bayonne
imperative.   This bridge, it may be added, constructed with a speed as of magic, by the skill and
daring of the British engineers, remained in use till
the end of the war.

While Hope completed the investment of Bayonne,
Wellington moved forward to attack Soult at Orthez,
where he stood at bay, hoping to stay the tide of
invasion setting northwards.   The position where
Soult awaited battle was of great natural strength.
The Garonne flows along the southern flank of
Orthez, and Soult had destroyed every bridge across
it, save the ancient bridge of Orthez itself, which was
held in such strength by the French that any direct
assault upon it was hopeless.   Hill, with his corps,
was left to watch the Orthez bridge, and, if possible,
break through when the defence beyond the river
had been shaken by the assault on Soult's front.
The other two British columns, under Beresford and
Picton, crossed the Garonne by pontoons some miles
down its course, and, moving up the right bank,
found themselves in front of Soult's position.

The curving range of hills he occupied, as depicted
on the map, resembles nothing so much as the head
of a gigantic ant, with two long diverging antennæ
running out on either side of the head.   The open
rounded hill, looking westward, which forms the
head of the "ant," was Soult's centre; the two

antennæ formed his right and left wings. The left antenna was a narrow ridge, rough with rocks, rising sharply, with battery after battery of guns frowning above each other, and barring the narrow front with their fire. The steep and narrow ridge called the St. Boes Hill, which formed the right horn or antenna, was equally difficult. It was crossed by a village strongly held. Behind the village the track narrowed to a ravine, and Soult's reserve batteries swept the whole pass as with a tempest of fire.

The tips of these hilly antennæ were about a mile and a half apart, the interval betwixt them being an almost impassable marsh. Midway betwixt these diverging ridges was an old Roman camp, where Wellington placed the Light Division as a reserve, and took up his own position. Wellington's battle line thus practically consisted of two disconnected wings and no centre. Beresford was to attack the St. Boes ridge, which formed the French right, Picton the corresponding ridge on the French left, and each general had an almost impossible task.

At nine o'clock Cole, with the 4th division, was launched at the village of St. Boes. He carried it with splendid valour. But when the British emerged from the village and tried to deploy on the open face of the hill beyond, they came under the stroke of Soult's great reserve battery on the crest above, in addition to the batteries scourging them on either flank. Nothing could be more daring than the

British onfall. Five times Ross led his brigade out into the open, and struggled up through the ravine, tormented with a deadly fire on flank and front; and five times the reeling, scattered British regiments were driven back to the shelter of the village, leaving

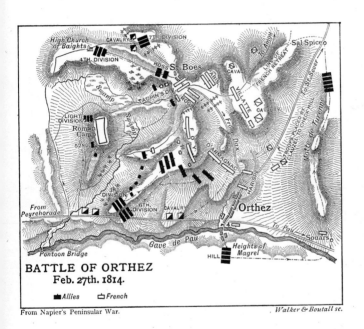

BATTLE OF ORTHEZ
Feb. 27th. 1814.

■ *Allies*   ⌂ *French*

From Napier's Peninsular War.   *Walker & Boutall sc.*

the narrow crest of the ridge strewn thick with their dead.

On the British right, Picton, with the 3rd and 6th divisions, fared as badly. Hill stood idly opposite the bridge of Orthez, while the roar of the battle

swelled and sank on the ridges beyond; and Soult,
looking down the battlefield from his central hill,
saw both Wellington's attacks falling back in confusion. On the British right, indeed, even the hardy
4th division had yielded the village it had won so
desperately and held so long. And this was the
result of a struggle which had lasted three hours.
Soult, it is said, as he gazed on that strange spectacle
of British columns falling back on both his flanks,
smote his thigh in excitement, and said, " At last I
have them," and put all his reserves in motion.

Wellington, however, was a captain of ready and
measureless resource. Watching the fight from the
Roman camp in the centre, he suddenly changed
his plan of battle. He organised a threefold attack
on the St. Boes ridge. The 7th division, with
Vivian's cavalry, moved up on the farther side of
that ridge; Ross's brigade, supported by Anson's,
renewed the direct attack on its crest ; and when
the tumult of the fight awoke again there, the 52nd,
under Colborne, was sent across the swamp to take
the French, who were holding the ridge against Ross
and Anson, in flank and rear.

The veterans of the 52nd—soldiers, as Napier is
never tired of saying, " who never yet have met
their match on the field "—pressed through the marsh
wading in mud to their knees, sometimes almost to
their waists ; but nothing shook their coolness and
order. They reached the hard ground at the foot

of the ridge. For a moment the muddied lines stopped and steadied themselves; then, with a far-heard shout, and volleys that sounded like the blast of heavy artillery, they went up the ridge at the double, and broke through betwixt Foy and Taupin's divisions. The battalions in their path were wrecked; General Bechaud was killed, Foy desperately wounded; Reille's whole wing was shaken. The French went staggering back, the 7th division and Vivian's cavalry broke in upon the other face of the ridge. Soult's entire order of battle was loosened; Picton's column drove back its left, and won the central ridge, and thus Wellington's two wings were united.

As Soult fell back, Hill forded the river above the bridge of the Orthez, and moving behind the town, threatened to cut off the Frenchman's retreat. The French columns were falling back across the heathy hills behind Orthez, and Hill's regiments, eager to play a part in the battle which they had watched so long, pushed fast along a parallel ridge to head them. The goal of the rival columns was the wooden bridge of Soult de Navailles, which crossed a stream five miles distant. On both ridges the swiftly marching columns redoubled their pace, the leading companies quickened into a run. Many of the French broke from their ranks and spread, a flood of dis-ordered soldiers, across the plain, and the British cavalry rode through these, slaying and capturing.

But the French reached the bridge first, crossed it with the loss of six guns, and destroyed it.

The battle cost Soult in killed, wounded, captured, and in stragglers, not less than 7000 men. The British loss was not quite 2500! And Soult's defeat would have proved a still more crushing disaster but for the fact that late in the fight Wellington himself was wounded in the hip by a grape-shot, and temporarily disabled, so that the pursuit was not urged with the keenness and vigour that might have been expected. The French fought with signal valour at Orthez, and Soult showed the skill of a great commander. Perhaps no troops but Wellington's hardy Peninsular veterans could have driven the French from the strong position they held with a courage so high.

CHAPTER V

SOULT fell back towards Tarbes, and in this way he drew near Suchet, hoping to still keep the field of war on the flanks and in the valleys of the Pyrenees. But his movement left open the road to Bordeaux. Soult calculated that Wellington would not advance to that city leaving Bayonne uncaptured in his rear; but Wellington understood how serious would be the political effect of seizing that great city, and making it the centre of a Bourbon rising, and on March 12 Beresford with 800 cavalry entered Bordeaux. The scene which followed was very striking. The mayor of the city, with a great body of citizens, met Beresford. The mayor wore the tricoloured scarf and the cross of the Legion of Honour, while the municipal guard about him had the Imperial eagle in their caps. Beresford explained his instructions. If the municipal authorities wished to proclaim the Bourbons, they were at liberty to do so, but it must be their own act, and done at their own risk. Whereupon the mayor made a short speech, tore the tricoloured scarf dramatically from his shoulders and the cross from his breast, and producing a white cockade and scarf, adorned himself with these symbols of Bourbon rule. Every citizen in the crowd apparently had a white cockade in his pocket, and promptly followed the mayor's example. The guard tore the eagles from their caps, the white flag was hoisted on every spire, and shouts arose of "A bas les aigles." "Vivent les Bourbons!" The Duc d'Angoulême made his appearance on the scene, and Louis XVIII. was proclaimed.

As the Bourbon Duke rode in the crowd, the citizens thronged to touch him, to kiss his boots, his trousers, or even the skin of the horse he rode. Shopkeepers were busy in painting out all varieties of the word "Imperial" from their signs. The scene was very curious and very French. One patch of France at least had, in this dramatic way, renounced Napoleon. Soult relieved his feelings by issuing a manifesto in which he swore at large at the English, and swore even more furiously at such Frenchmen as had hoisted the white flag. The English, Soult declared, "have in view to reduce Frenchmen to the same servitude as the Portuguese, Spaniards, and Sicilians, who groan under their dominion." As for all Frenchmen who favoured their insidious projects, Soult solemnly consigned them to "opprobrium and execration." "To arms!" he cried; "revenge the offence in blood."

On March 20 Soult was driven roughly from the

position he held at Tarbes, and finding Wellington
was not to be allured back to the shaggy flanks
of the Pyrenees, the French columns were pushed
forward at great speed, marching thirty miles in a
single day, to Toulouse, where Soult was to make his
last stand for Napoleon. He was moving on a wide
curve to Toulouse, and it seemed as if Wellington,
advancing along the string of the arc, might have
outmarched his opponent and reached that city first.
His cavalry, as a matter of fact, did harass Soult
sorely; but on the 24th the French had reached
Toulouse, having broken down all the bridges in
their rear.

Wellington only came up two days later. Incessant rains were falling, the rivers were flooded,
and Wellington, moving through strange country,
and unwilling to expend his troops unnecessarily,
advanced but slowly. Perhaps the single visible blot
in Wellington's generalship is found in a certain lack
of whirlwind energy in pursuit of a beaten foe. The
art of war, said Napoleon, is to march twelve leagues
in a single day, overthrow your enemy in a great
battle, and then march twelve leagues more in
pursuit. Wellington could satisfy the two first
conditions of good generalship as thus defined; he
sometimes failed in the third.

Toulouse had a population of 50,000; it was the
chief military arsenal of the south of France, and
commanded the principal passage of the Garonne.

For Soult himself, Toulouse was almost as a native city, and he was perfectly familiar with the country about it. Wellington's slowness in making his appearance before the city gave the French general a golden opportunity for increasing its defences, and at that task he laboured with magnificent energy day and night. Toulouse lent itself splendidly to purposes of defence.

The Garonne, flowing northwards, makes a sudden and deep curve to the east, and in the curve thus formed stands the suburb of St. Ciprien. This formed the western face of the town, its massive and ancient brick wall being covered by a zone of field-works. If the suburb were carried, the Garonne had then to be crossed in the face of new defences on the farther bank. On the west, that is, Toulouse was practically unassailable. Its northern front was covered, as by a vast wet ditch, by the great canal of Languedoc, which curved round the eastern face of the city, and then ran southward to the sea. The north face of the town, covered thus by the great canal, was almost as unassailable as the west face. Beyond the canal, and parallel with it, ran the steep ridge of Mont Rave, serving as the eastern defence of the city. Its outer face, sloping down to the river Ers, was rugged, its three highest points had been turned into formidable redoubts. Soult, indeed, had employed the whole male population of Toulon in making Mont Rave impregnable. If it were carried, the great canal yet flowed betwixt the assailants and the city.

Toulouse was most open to attack on the south, but the Garonne—swift and broad and swollen by

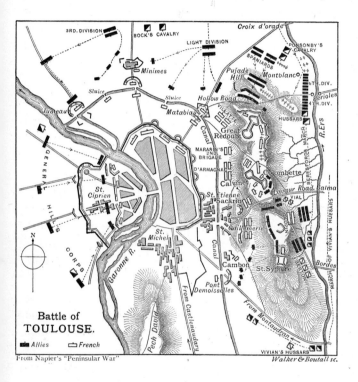

Battle of
TOULOUSE.

■■ *Allies* ▭ *French*

From Napier's "Peninsular War"   *Walker & Boutall sc.*

rains—barred the English advance. On the night of March 27, Wellington's engineers tried to throw a bridge of pontoons across the river, but the attempt failed. The river ran at flood-height; there were too few pontoons to reach the opposite bank, and that fatal lack of half-a-dozen pontoons cost the British dearly in gallant lives.

The rains still fell incessantly, the snows melting in the high Pyrenees kept the Garonne at flood-height, and by the impassable roads and the ever-falling rain, Wellington was kept day after day inactive. Soult, in fact, had no less than seventeen days in which to reorganise his broken troops, perfect his defences, and make an assault on the city almost hopeless. On April 3, Wellington threw a bridge across the river below Toulouse, and Beresford crossed with three divisions and some cavalry. Then the river suddenly rose, swept away the bridge, and from the 4th to the 8th Beresford's forces lay isolated, exposed, without possibility of succour, to the attack of Soult, who could throw all his force upon this dislocated wing of Wellington's army. It was a position which might well have tried the nerves of any general; but Wellington declared afterwards he never slept sounder in his life than on those three nights! He trusted to the fighting quality of his men ; he understood, moreover, Soult's limitation as a general. With all his great qualities as a captain, Soult lacked the faculty of lightning-like decision, and of lightning-like attack, which was needed to turn to profit the chance at that moment offered him. Napoleon, with an enemy's dissevered wing lying under his stroke, would have smitten it with the impact and the suddenness of a thunder-bolt. But Soult for seventeen days had bent every energy to preparations for fighting a defensive battle in Toulouse itself. He lay rooted in his entrench-ments; he could not suddenly invert his strategy ar 1 march out for an audacious and overwhelming stroke of offensive war.

It was on this occasion, Wellington used to say, that his face saved his life. In the early dawn, with a couple of officers, he got into a small boat and rowed over to ascertain how Beresford was faring. An Irish sentry covered the boat with his musket as it approached; both Wellington and his com-panions had forgotten the countersign, and the soldier was on the point of firing. Looking along his musket barrel, however, in the act of taking aim, he recognised Wellington, and brought his musket to the salute, crying, "God bless your crooked nose; I would sooner see it than tin thousand men!" Wellington used to say that was the greatest compli-ment ever paid him!

On the 8th the English bridge was restored, and on the 10th the great battle was fought. Wellington's plan was simple. He attacked at three points, but two of his attacks were mere feints. Hill, with two divisions, menaced St. Ciprien to the west; Picton, with the 3rd and Light Divisions, was to attack the bridge-head of Jumeau crossing the canal on the north. This assault was intended to serve as a mere distraction, as the position threatened was of commanding strength. Picton, however, understood nothing of "feigned" attacks. Once engaged, his blood took fire, the dogged fighting strain in him kindled, and mere "pretence" was quickly changed into bloody reality. Wellington understood Picton's limitations, and his orders were given to him formally in writing, and enforced verbally with energy. But when the thunder of the guns awoke, Picton, whose fierce temper was admirably reflected in the hard-fighting ranks of his own division, pushed his attack stubbornly home, with the loss of many brave men.

Wellington's single serious attack was on the eastern face, and seldom has a general attempted a more hazardous stroke of war. Beresford, with the 4th and 6th divisions, Ponsonby's horse, and three batteries of guns, was to defile for two miles betwixt the craggy heights of Mont Rave, frowning with a hundred guns on his right flank, and the river Ers on his left, till he reached the southern extremity of the French position. He was then to wheel to the right and storm the southern shoulder of the long ridge. Freire's Spaniards, 9000 strong, were to attack the Pujade hill at the northern extremity of Mont Rave, and forming the angle betwixt the northern and eastern faces of the town.

The path of Beresford's divisions lay along a real "Valley of Death." On their left was the river Ers, on their right ran the rugged slope of Mont Rave, its black lower slopes red with darting musketry volleys, and its crests white with the smoke of heavy artillery. The track over which Beresford's troops toiled was so marshy that their guns stuck fast and had to be abandoned. Yet for two miles, torn thus by a cruel flank fire, Beresford's stubborn columns plodded on till they reached the point where they were to become the attacking party.

A disaster in their rear meanwhile seemed to tumble Wellington's whole battle into ruin. Freire took his Spaniards, 9000 strong, gallantly forward to the assault on the northern extremity of Mont Rave. Nothing could well be finer than the Spanish advance. A French brigade in their path was trampled out of existence, and up the steep shoulder of the hill went the Spaniards. But from the frowning redoubt on its crest came a crushing artillery fire, some great guns from a redoubt on their flank opened on them from a still nearer distance; and so terrible was the cross fire that the Spaniards seemed to crumble beneath it. Their leading battalions, indeed, with the great guns on their flank smashing the files behind them, ran forward and leaped, as if for shelter, into a deep hollow road in front of the French defences; but their second line turned and fled to the rear.

Wellington, who watched the solid Spanish columns crumble up and take to flight in this fashion, offered the dry comment, "Well, d—— me, if ever I saw

10,000 men run a race before!" He added a grim doubt as to whether the Pyrenees themselves would stop the flying Spaniards. This was hardly fair to Freire's men. Freire's first line at this moment was filling the hollow road in front of the French defences, and was faring cruelly there. The French poured from their redoubts, lined the crest of the road, and opened on the struggling mass of Spaniards beneath a terrible fire. Freire rallied his second line, and brought it up again, but when it reached the crest of the hollow road the spectacle of slaughter offered was so terrible, and the fire on front and flank so fierce, that the Spaniards broke and fled once more, and Wellington had to check the eager pursuit of the French with his reserve of artillery, and by a flank fire from the Light Division. It was the spectacle of this flight of the Spaniards, and the exultant pursuit of the French, which helped to harden Picton's temper, and made him throw his strength on the massive works which covered the bridge of Jumeau. The men of the 3rd actually tried to carry its lofty counterscarp by standing on each other's shoulders, and only drew back when 500 of their number had fallen.

Wellington's advance had thus failed at three points; there remained only Beresford's column, and at this moment Beresford himself was in imminent danger of a deadly counter-attack. He was without guns, two miles from his supports, a bridgeless river in his rear, a steep hill with a slope a mile long swept by the fire of a dozen redoubts in his front. And Soult, with the eye of a great captain, seeing Beresford's isolated position, had brought up Taupin's division, with D'Armagnac's in support, and sent its battalions in solid column, with the *pas de charge* loudly sounding, against Beresford's extended and slender line. As he wrote afterwards to the French Minister of War, he was sure that "under such a stroke 7000 or 8000 English and Portuguese could hardly fail to be taken or destroyed."

Taupin's division came on gallantly; clouds of cavalry skirmishers were on either flank; the guns from the hill summit above bellowed loudly over their heads. The French officers, running to the front with waving hats and brandished swords, led the charge with great fire. From the great column coming thus down the slope rose a shrill and confused clamour, a fierce human treble heard above the deep-voiced diapason of the guns. The aspect of Taupin's attack was so formidable that it might well have shaken ordinary troops into ruin. But Beresford's men were not ordinary troops, and British soldiers lack utterly the nervous imagination which can be impressed by mere noise and gestures. The English skirmishers, running forward, shot coolly into the advancing mass; the 79th and 42nd—Highlanders all—who formed the long British front, poured in a sustained fire that struck down most of the French

officers leading the column, and then dropping their
bayonets to the charge, the Highland regiments
went forward at the double, sending up one wild
stern Gaelic battle-cry. Just when the hostile lines
seemed about to touch, the French gave way, their
close-linked battalions dissolved into fragments, each
scattered atom being a flying soldier. Taupin himself was slain ; some squadrons of French cavalry,
riding fiercely to the help of Taupin's reeling column,
were wrecked by a volley from the 79th. The British
won the crest of the hill, and their skirmishers
followed the flying French down the reverse slope.

Captain Ford, of the 79th Highlanders, gives a
vivid account of the manner in which his regiment
repelled the attack of the French cavalry. The
French horse suddenly made their appearance from
a fold of the hill, and, falling into rank on the road
along which the 79th were moving in threes, prepared to charge. "The colonel of the 79th immediately formed a hollow square, ordered out Ensign
Balfour with the regimental colour to the front as
a directing point, and then gave the word, 'March.'
We thus continued our march in the original
direction. To see Balfour, some distance in front,
marching erect, pointing his toes with as much precision and care as if at a formal parade in England,
with the colour inclined forward, which required
strength of arm (for we had no shoulder belts to
support them), and the French leisurely walking

their horses towards us, was a beautiful sight, and reminded me of what I had read of the days of Marlborough, when such slow movements were common." The square was halted, Balfour called in, and a volley fired by the right face, and the enemy immediately wheeled about and slowly retired.

Beresford halted till his guns came up, and then, at three o'clock in the afternoon, proceeded to sweep along the summit of Mont Rave northwards. The four Highland regiments—the 42nd, the 71st, the 79th, and the 92nd—played a gallant part in the close fighting which followed. The 42nd, which led the assault on the great Calvinet redoubt, carried that strong post, but was almost destroyed in a counter-attack by Harispe. Anton, who served in the 42nd, in his "Retrospect of a Military Life," describes the onfall of the regiment. The colonel of the 42nd kept his men under a dreadful fire, while he made a leisurely and complicated re-arrangement of its order, the men meanwhile growing mad with wrath at their losses and with eagerness to charge. Then came the order, "Forward! Double quick!" which let the regiment loose. The men had to cross a sloping field that had been roughly ploughed, and many a charging Highlander tripped over the furrows, and the man behind him in turn fell over him.

It was thus, with loosened and broken ranks, that the 42nd, charging through the very flames of the guns, reached the French redoubt. "In a minute," says Anton, "every obstacle was surmounted, the enemy fled as we leaped over trenches and mounds, and we frightened them more by our wild 'hurrahs' than by ball or bayonet." The gallant Highlanders held the redoubt stubbornly, pelted with fire on every side. Presently Harispe's strong column came down the slope, its drums beating the *pas de charge*, to recover the work. "Two officers," says Anton, "and about sixty of inferior rank, were all that now remained without a wound of the right wing of the regiment that entered the field in the morning. The flag was hanging in tatters, and stained with the blood of those who had fallen while carrying it. The standard, cut in two, had been successively placed in the hands of three officers, who fell as we advanced: it was now borne by a sergeant, while the few remaining soldiers who rallied around it, defiled with mire, sweat, smoke, and blood, stood ready to oppose with the bayonet the advancing column, the front files of which were pouring in destructive showers of musketry among our confused ranks."

Ford claims that his regiment alone carried the Calvinet redoubt, and lost one half its own numbers in doing it. The light company of the 61st was skirmishing in front of the 79th as they mounted the hill, and a French column in close files and beautiful order descended the hill to meet them, its colonel, in advance, leading them. A soldier of the 61st, Ford says, coolly doubled out in advance of his regiment, stood in the path of the approaching French column till it came within a few yards, then lifted his musket and shot its colonel dead. Immediately the French column halted, turned to the right-about, and fell back, checked by a single musket!

But Beresford's hold on the crest was too stern to be shaken, and finally Soult abandoned Mont Rave, and withdrew his whole army behind the Languedoc Canal. In the murderous fighting of that day the French lost five generals and 3000 rank and file; the allies, as they were the attacking party, suffered still more cruelly. Their killed and wounded amounted to 4600 men and officers, 2000 of these being Spanish. And all this, it turned out, was wasted blood; for Napoleon by this time had abdicated, and the war was over!

CHAPTER VI

THE CLOSE OF A GREAT CAMPAIGN

ON the night of the 11th Soult abandoned Toulouse, with his hospitals and magazines, and on the 12th Wellington entered the city in triumph. As the British marched through the streets a strange scene caught their eyes. A colossal statue of Napoleon in white marble stood on the pediment of one of the public buildings of the city. A rope had been placed round the neck of the statue, and hundreds of French hands were busy dragging enthusiastically at the ropes, till at last the great statue gave way and fell, smashed into a hundred fragments, on the pavement. This was a French testimony to French feeling about Napoleon! At five o'clock that afternoon two staff officers arrived from Paris with the news of Napoleon's abdication. They had been detained by some petty official on the road, and that delay splashed the rough slopes of Mont Rave red with the blood of gallant men. Wellington sent in the tidings to Soult, who lingered sullenly until direct official intelligence reached him.

But on the 18th a formal convention for the suspension of hostilities was made.

Four days after the bloody and unnecessary struggle at Toulouse a similar waste of valour and human life took place at Bayonne. At three o'clock on the morning of April 14, Thouvenot, who commanded the French garrison in Bayonne, broke out in the darkness on the British outposts. Hope, on the previous evening, had sent in the news of Bonaparte's abdication, but Thouvenot affected disbelief, and merely said the British would "hear from him on the subject before long." A French deserter brought the news of the intended sortie a little after midnight; but Hay, who commanded the outposts that night, could not understand the deserter's French, and took no precautions. At three o'clock 3000 French sallied from the citadel, broke through the English pickets, carried with a rush the whole village of St. Etienne, with the exception of a single house, stubbornly held by a party of the 30th, and swept along the road behind the village. General Hay was slain, Colonel Townsend of the Guards was captured. There was danger of the whole right wing of the British being destroyed. The British pickets fought stubbornly, but in the darkness all order was lost. The fighting was bayonet to bayonet, sword to sword, and no man knew whether it was friend or foe he struck. Above the wild struggle of that obscured battlefield roared the great guns of the citadel.

Hope hurried to the scene, rallied a retiring British picket, led it back to the fight, and was himself struck by a couple of bullets, fell, and was captured. When day was breaking Howard brought up the reserve brigade of the Guards, and drove back the French with a bloody bayonet charge into their works. The French lost a general and more than 900 men, the British nearly as many; and it was all wasted slaughter.

Hay had fought all through the Peninsula, and survived a hundred perils. As he went the round of the pickets that night, he said to his men with glee, "No more fighting, my lads! Now for our homes, wives, and sweethearts!" Three hours later he himself lay slain.

With the last sullen shots of that desperate night sortie the Pensinular war came to an end. It was a great struggle, begun with a noble purpose, and maintained on a great scale and at an heroic cost. As a mere chapter of war it is scarcely to be paralleled in British history. It is absurd to say that the war in the Peninsula on the French side was not also planned on great lines and waged with splendid energy. An oft-quoted saying of Henri IV. of France declares that in Spain "large armies will starve and small armies will be beaten." But Napoleon's genius at least disproved that platitude. He poured enormous armies into Spain, and they were not starved. He scattered his forces over the whole area of the Peninsula, and, as far as the Spaniards were concerned, they were not beaten.   Hardier or more gallant soldiers than the French showed themselves in the Peninsula are not to be found in the history of war. "To them," says Napier, "winter and summer were alike.   They endured terrible toils and privations: and for their daring and resource a single fact recorded by Wellington will suffice.   They captured more than one strong place in Spain without any provision of bullets save those fired on them by their enemies, having trusted to that chance when they formed the siege!"

And these were the soldiers, led by captains trained in Napoleon's school, that the English, "a nation of shopkeepers," yet drove out of the Peninsula! The scale on which Great Britain maintained the war in the Peninsula is not easily realised.   She spent £100,000,000 on her own operations; but she also fed, armed, disciplined, and led to battle the armies of Spain and Portugal.   Into one sentence of stately and sonorous prose Napier—who was an actor in the strife, as well as its historian—condenses the story of what Great Britain accomplished: "Her land forces fought and won nineteen pitched battles and innumerable combats, made or sustained ten sieges, took four great fortresses, twice expelled the French from Portugal, preserved Alicant, Carthagena, Tarifa, Cadiz, Lisbon; they killed, wounded, and took 200,000 enemies, and the bones of 40,000 British soldiers lie

scattered on the plains and mountains of the Peninsula."   And the end—won at such a cost—was noble
and adequate.   It was not merely the freedom of the
Peninsula: it was the freedom of the civilised world.
"The Spanish ulcer destroyed me," said Napoleon;
and it was the wealth, and strength, and valour of
England which made the struggle in the Peninsula
fatal to Napoleon.

CHAPTER VII

FROM MOSCOW TO ELBA

THE struggle in the Peninsula represents only one aspect of that black cloud of war, shaken with the thunder and gleaming with the lightning of mighty battles, which lay across Europe during the early years of the century; and events in the Peninsula and on the Continent profoundly affected each other. It was, as we have already seen, the preoccupation of Napoleon in the struggle with Russia which gave Wellington his chance in Spain. On the other hand, the shattering blows with which Wellington struck down Napoleon's marshals in the Peninsula, one after another, shook Napoleon's whole military power in the Continent, and hardened the purpose of the Allies against the common enemy. And it has a curious effect to set in juxtaposition the eddying changes of these two great parallel streams of battle.

On October 15, 1812, Napoleon began the great retreat from Moscow. On April 11, 1814, with crown lost and empire vanished, he left Fontainebleau for Elba. Betwixt those two events there were only eighteen short months; and in that brief period the greatest Empire of which history has any record fell !

If Napoleon had succeeded in his Russian campaign, it is curious to reflect on the change it would have made in history. This Corsican soldier would have been master of the planet, save where the fleets of England still held him at bay. And not even England, solitary and unhelped, could long have maintained the struggle against a consummate soldier, who had gathered into the palm of his hand the strength of all other civilised nations. But Napoleon failed in Russia, and he had practically failed even before the fires of Moscow were kindled. He was defeated by the unmanageable scale of his own hosts, and by the natural conditions against which he had to contend. His intellect, at this stage, seems to have lost its hard sanity; his vision the sense of perspective. A strain of megalomania ran through Napoleon's schemes. He planned on a scale too great for sober execution. His strategy was in conflict with the hard facts of the world, and he expected facts to accommodate themselves to his plans. But Nature is inexorable: against the iron logic of facts even the plans of a Napoleon dash themselves in vain.

Napoleon crossed the Niemen on June 23 with a vast and many-tongued host, such as modern war had never yet witnessed. The columns under his personal command numbered 380,000; the armies he drew into his combinations amounted to over 600,000 men. Five days after, on June 28, he entered Wilna, the capital of Russian Poland, and already he had 25,000 men in his hospitals, while 30,000 stragglers were scattered along the roads behind. Nearly one-fifth of Napoleon's army had thus melted away without a battle, in fine weather, and at the first stage of the great expedition! By September 7 more than a third of Napoleon's great host was dead, missing, or in hospitals. He reached Moscow, and saw it break into flames about him, but it was not the ascending smoke of the burning city which drove Napoleon into retreat. More than 2000 houses were still standing when the French columns turned their back on Moscow to face the long 600 miles of their homeward march. Russia, like Spain, to quote Professor Sloane, "had the strength of low organisms." Its vitality was not centred in a single organ. It could lose a capital and survive. Napoleon had captured Moscow, and seen it turn to ashes in his grasp, as he lingered five planless, loitering, and amazed weeks, "killing time" with idle debates and vile pleasures, and waiting for some unknown chance to arrive. Then famine lifted its menacing visage. Napoleon could no longer find food for his soldiers. To stay in Moscow meant starvation or captivity.

So he began that retreat which is one of the most memorable tragedies in human history. "It was a *sauve qui peut* at a funeral pace," wrote Sir Robert

Wilson. The passage of the Beresina on November 28 is perhaps the climax of that tragedy. How many perished in the black and icy waters, or beneath the fire of the Russian guns, cannot be told. It is said that when the ice of the Beresina melted away on the return of spring, over 30,000 corpses were found in its bed! The frost on the night succeeding the passage of the Beresina was almost as fatal to Napoleon's weary and hunger-wasted troops as the river itself. The Old Guard, after the desperate fight for the bridges across the Beresina, numbered only 3500; and 1500 even of those war-hardened veterans lay dead, slain by mere cold, when, white with falling snow, the next morning dawned.

The Beresina destroyed the Grand Army as a military body. The passage of the Niemen a fort-night afterwards, on December 13, almost put an end to that procession of frost-bitten stragglers which still stumbled on towards the friendly shelter of Wilna. Only six months earlier nearly 400,000 men had crossed that river under Napoleon's eyes. Its reinforcements amounted to not less than another 100,000. But of that half million of gallant men only 20,000 re-crossed the Niemen on December 13. "Two kings," says Mitchell, "one prince, eight marshals, nine guns, a few hundred men of the Old Guard still in arms, together with 20,000 famished and rag-covered objects, hardly retaining the appearance of human beings, were all that remained of the once mighty host."

In the last stage of the retreat even the rear-guard dissolved, and every one remembers the story of how Ney led the last survivors of the Grand Army across the bridge at Kowno. General Dumas tells how he was sitting at breakfast in Gumbinnen, "when a man in a brown coat, with long beard, red eyes, and weather-beaten face, entered saying, 'At last I am here. Dumas, do you not know me?' 'No, who are you?' 'I am the rear-guard of the Grand Army. I have fired the last musket-shot on the bridge at Kowno. I have thrown the last of our arms into the Niemen, and have come here through the woods —I am Marshal Ney!'" That proud and gallant host had vanished like an army of phantoms! In the hands of the Russians as prisoners were 170,000 of the soldiers who had been the terror of Europe; the rest had perished, slain not so much by the spears of the Cossacks or the musketry of the stubborn Russian infantry, as by hunger, tempest, snow, and exhaustion.

Napoleon, meanwhile, had issued the famous 29th bulletin, in which, for once, he told at least part of the truth. The instinct for dramatic effect was too strong even for the impulse to deceive, and he recited the tale of his wrecked army in sentences which horrified the world. At the very same time he told Caulaincourt, "All that has happened goes for nothing; a mere misfortune for which the enemy can claim no merit." He reached Paris on December 18, where he found that Malet's conspiracy had well-nigh robbed him of his throne and crown. "The Revolution is not yet dead," said Napoleon, when he realised how nearly the conspiracy had succeeded; "my dynasty has not yet taken root amongst even the members of my Council."

In four months Napoleon, however, practically created a new army, and on April 25, 1813, he was able to put 140,000 men, perfectly equipped, in line of battle on the Elbe. It is true the veterans of so many campaigns had perished. Napoleon's new troops were mere conscripts in uniform, gallant enough, but soft-fibred and undisciplined. As Napoleon complained, brutally, they "choked his hospitals with their sick, and strewed his roads with their dead carcases." Nevertheless, it was a great feat to improvise an army of any sort in a space of time so brief. But Napoleon used that terrible engine, the conscription, with ruthless energy. The blood-tax he levied again and again upon France is a sufficient condemnation of his rule. No less than 600,000 men were demanded, and granted, in two months to repair the waste of the Great Retreat. From September 1, 1812, to the end of 1813—in not quite sixteen months, that is—Napoleon's successive conscriptions amounted to 1,260,000 men, and this in addition to 800,000 under the eagles

at the beginning of that period. The military age
was reduced to seventeen, the standard of military
height to five feet one inch. France herself was
being exhausted by these monstrous levies. Twenty
years of the "glories of war" had utterly drained
her strength.

In many districts the fields lay untilled because
the entire adult male population had perished on
far-off battlefields. Whole villages had no other
inhabitants than women, old men, and boys. The
conscription failed to yield recruits, for the conscripts themselves fled to the hills to escape military
service. Even so early as August 6, 1805, Napoleon
writes to Fouché, "The conscription in the department of the Eure is a complete failure. All the
conscripts have deserted. It is also a blank in the
Eastern Pyrenees. . . . Take measures to have all the
conscripts arrested and marched off." How much
more bitter must the revolt against the conscription
have become in 1813? In fourteen years Napoleon
drew into his camps from the villages and homes
of France alone 2,500,000 men; and this leaves un-
reckoned the almost equally vast multitudes he
raised amongst subject nations outside France.

Meanwhile Europe was rising against Napoleon.
He had hitherto, as Wellington said, ruled one half
of Europe directly, and the other half indirectly,
but now one nation after another shook off his
yoke, and hastened to swell the host of his enemies.

Prussia hardened her heart, took her fate in her hands, and joined Russia against the common enemy, declaring war on March 17. Austria was still neutral, but beneath her mask of "neutrality" was a resolute purpose to repair the losses of Marengo and of Austerlitz. "A year ago," said Napoleon himself, "all Europe marched with us; at present it all marches against us."

May witnessed the battles of Lützen and of Bautzen; victories, in a sense, for Napoleon, but bloody and barren, and utterly unlike the fruitful triumphs of Jena and of Friedland. They yielded the victor no trophies; they left the vanquished unsubdued. As Napoleon himself rode over the corpse-strewn field of Bautzen he exclaimed, "What! no results after all this carnage! Not a gun, not a prisoner! These people will not leave me a single nail!" The war waged against Napoleon now was not one of kings and their mercenaries against an aroused people. It was an uprising of nations, contending for all that men count most precious, against an intolerable tyranny. So the war had quite a new temper.

On June 4 an armistice, on the proposal of Austria, was agreed upon. It was to last for seven weeks, and was more fatal to Napoleon than many defeats. Napoleon agreed to the armistice, as he calculated it would give him time to bring up Eugene's columns, and thus enable him to overawe Austria. He did not

consent to it with the hope of peace, or as a prelimi-
nary to peace. He wanted no peace which did not
leave him the Dictator of Europe. He merely wished
for time to concentrate his scattered columns. But
the armistice served his enemies better than it served
Napoleon. The slow-marching Russian reinforcements came up, the Prussian ranks were filled;
English subsidies flowed into the treasuries of the
allied sovereigns.

On June 21 Wellington fought and won the
history - making battle of Vittoria, and the news
decided the wavering plans of the Allies. On June
30 it was agreed that a Congress should assemble
at Prague to negotiate for a general peace, with
Austria as mediator. If Napoleon refused the terms
offered, Austria was pledged to join the league
against him. It was on the day after this treaty
was signed that the news of the battle of Vittoria
reached Dresden, and it hardened the purpose and
added an edge to the courage of the Allies. But
the terms offered to Napoleon were still most generous. They gave him Italy, Switzerland, Flanders,
the left bank of the Rhine to the sea, and left him
the Protector of the German Confederation. This
would have given Napoleon a greater France than
that of which Louis XIV. dreamed.

But Napoleon despised such a peace. "What!"
he exclaimed with scorn to Metternich, "give up
half Italy, restore the Pope, abandon Poland, Spain,

Holland!" The treaty, he declared, would be "one vast capitulation." He would accept no terms. He loitered, he evaded a decision, till the armistice itself expired. The term fixed for Napoleon's decision ended at midnight on August 10. The representatives of the Powers sat waiting silently round a table till the clock struck; then they told Metternich their powers had expired, and called upon him, as the representative of Austria, to carry out the compact agreed upon and declare war on France. Before daybreak on August 11 the beacon-fires on all the hills of Silesia proclaimed that war had awoke again. It was the fatal and long-remembered blunder of Napoleon's career that he rejected the magnificent terms offered to him at Prague.

In the battles which followed, it is said that the generals of the Allies adopted the plan of always falling back before Napoleon himself, and always attacking the armies commanded by his marshals. It is certain that Napoleon's generals suffered defeat everywhere, while Napoleon himself found it difficult to bring his enemies to battle. They fell back whenever he advanced. "These creatures have learned something at last," was Napoleon's bitter comment on the generals whom he despised, but whom he could not bring to a decided combat.

On August 26–27, Napoleon won the battle of Dresden, and might have made the Emperors of Russia and Austria and the King of Prussia prisoners,

and so ended the war, had he pushed on the pursuit
with the overmastering energy of his earlier years.
He failed to do this. He abandoned the pursuit, and
sent back his Guards, leaving Vandamme to be destroyed at Kuln. Wolseley finds in that sudden
arrest of the pursuit after Dresden a proof of the existence of the mysterious malady which, it is asserted,
in his later years afflicted Napoleon. Some subtle
paralysis of brain, some strange collapse of nervous
energy, left him for the moment inert. But it is at
least doubtful whether Napoleon suffered from any
such mysterious illness the day after Dresden. Baron
Odeleben, quoted by Mitchell, says Napoleon was "in
high spirits," full of animated talk on the afternoon
and evening when he returned to Dresden, instead of
pursuing the broken Allies.

While Napoleon was triumphing at Dresden,
Oudinot was being crushed by Bernadotte at Gros-
beren, and Blücher had overthrown Macdonald on
the Katzbach. Three of Napoleon's marshals thus
were smitten into ruin, with a result that cancelled
Napoleon's own triumph at Dresden. In the twelve
days betwixt August 18 and 30, Napoleon,—to sum
up the result of so much bloodshed,—had lost 100,000
men, and had won no forward step. On September 6,
again, Blücher inflicted a crushing defeat on Ney
at Dennewitz, and Ney wrote to his master, "The
spirit of the generals and officers is shattered."
"The foreign troops," he warned Napoleon, "would

turn their arms against France on the very first
opportunity." Napoleon's army, it was clear, was
crumbling into ruin.

October proved a yet more fatal month for Napoleon. Bavaria fell from him. The Allies crossed the
Elbe on October 3. On October 7, Wellington had
forced the Bidassoa, and the invasion of France from
the south had begun. Napoleon had fallen back to
Leipsic, and on October 16–19 came the three days'
struggle known as "The Battle of the Nations."
In scale, in slaughter, if not in results, this was the
mightiest battle of even the Napoleonic era. The
total number of British killed and wounded in all the
land battles from 1793 to 1815 is reckoned at 85,500;
the losses on both sides at Leipsic reached 80,640.
The slaughter of this single battle was thus almost
equal to the losses the British sustained in actual
fighting during the whole twenty years' war! It
was an ominous sign, too, that in the very height
of the struggle at Leipsic the Saxon troops, 35,000
strong, deserted the French eagles. They were Germans, compelled to fight for France against Germany;
and they seized the opportunity to array themselves
on the side of men of their own speech and blood.

The retreat from Leipsic was a tragedy almost as
great as the passage of the Beresina. The single
bridge over the Esler, across which lay the French
line of retreat, was blown up, and the French rear-
guard, with an immense mass of fugitives, was cut

off. Napoleon himself had ascended to the upper storey of a mill to watch the wrecks of his army flowing past, and, curiously enough, had fallen asleep with the tumult of the retreat filling earth and sky about him. Suddenly a great blast shook the mill and awoke the slumbering Emperor. The mine beneath the bridge had been by accident exploded prematurely, and 15,000 of Napoleon's troops had to lay down their arms. In killed, wounded, and prisoners, Napoleon lost within three days 70,000 men with 200 guns. There remained to him less than 80,000 of the great force of 400,000 gallant soldiers with which he had opened the campaign six months before. And with these discipline was lost, courage was broken, supplies were exhausted.

A deadly hunger-typhus was kindled in the blood of Napoleon's raw conscripts. They died in thousands, and their bodies strewed the roads along which their columns marched. They infected whole villages with their plague. Napoleon himself bitterly described his forces as "a set of scoundrels going to the devil." At the rate in which they so inconsiderately persisted in dying, he grumbled, "I shall lose 80,000 men before I get to the Rhine!" Gratitude to the peasants who marched and fought and died for him was not one of Napoleon's virtues.

A fortnight after Leipsic, Napoleon crossed the Rhine with his scattered forces, and all Europe was falling from him. The Princes of the Confederacy

of the Rhine joined the Allies. Jerome fled from
Westphalia. Even Murat was preparing to make a
profitable change of allegiance, and on January 19,
1814, he turned his arms against Napoleon, issuing
a furious proclamation against him. "Soldiers," he
cried, "there are but two banners in Europe. On
the one are inscribed Religion, Morality, Justice,
Law, Peace, Happiness; on the other Persecution,
Falsehood, Violence, Tumult, War, and Mourning to
all nations." Napoleon had raised this son of an
innkeeper to a throne, and it seemed odd that
Murat should have fought for so many years under
the banner of Napoleon without having earlier discovered what was inscribed upon it.

From Frankfort on November 9 the Allies once
more offered peace to Napoleon. Even after Leipsic
they were willing to concede Belgium, Savoy, and
the Rhine; but they demanded the acceptance or
rejection of their terms by the end of November.
But Napoleon would neither accept nor reject these
offers, and on the last day of 1813 the Allies crossed
the Rhine, first issuing a proclamation in which
they declared their war was not against France, but
against the despotism which Napoleon imposed on
all the nations.

It is, perhaps, open to doubt whether the Allies
were very sincere in their Frankfort proposals. It
is certain Napoleon would have strangely perplexed
his enemies had he accepted their terms. His

MARSHAL JOACHIM MURAT

GRAND DUKE OF CLEVES AND OF BERG, KING OF NAPLES

From an engraving

acceptance, indeed, might have been the signal for the rupture of the great alliance. Alexander would have despised success which was not crowned by an entry into Paris. England would have been indignant with a peace which gave Napoleon Antwerp; and the Prussians had Jena and Berlin to avenge. Metternich, in his "Memoirs," admits that the Frankfort terms would never have been offered to Napoleon had any one believed he would have accepted them. This only makes more plain Napoleon's fatal blunder in not frankly, and at once, closing with these proposals.

But Napoleon was haunted with the sense that France—even the France of the dreams of Louis XIV.—could never be a secure kingdom for him. France endured him because the shadow of his power stretched across Europe. His true crown was the nimbus round his brow, reflected from so many victories. But, thrust back, a defeated soldier, into France, with the halo of all his victories quenched, it was certain that even the French throne would not long be his; and, with the spirit of a gambler, Napoleon risked everything on his last stake. He must be the Dictator of Europe or nothing.

The Allies issued a proclamation to France in which they declared they warred not with her, but with the despot whose restless ambition forbade the world to be at peace. They guaranteed France "an extent of territory such as she had never had

under her kings;" but it must be France without
Napoleon. In this proclamation the famous edict
of Fraternity recoiled on France. Twenty years
before, the Directory appealed to all the peoples of
Europe against their governments. Now the allied
sovereigns, marching to invade France, appealed to
her citizens against Napoleon.

On December 2, Napoleon sent a letter to Metternich, accepting the terms offered at Frankfort,
whether sincere or not; but it was too late. In the
negotiations of 1813–14, indeed, Napoleon repeated
again and again the fatal blunder of postponing
the acceptance of offered terms till the offer had
been withdrawn. His diplomacy is but the fable of
the Sibylline leaves translated into modern shape.
At Prague, at Frankfort, at Chatillon, terms were
offered which steadily shrank in scale, but any one
of which would have left Napoleon the monarch of
a great and powerful France. Napoleon trifled with
each offer; loitered till it was withdrawn—and then
accepted it! And the terms offered grew harsher
with each renewal.

Napoleon calculated that winter would bring an
arrest of hostilities, and he would thus have breath-
ing-time, and the opportunity of improvising new
armies of boy-conscripts. But the Allies, urged on
by the pride of Alexander and the impetuous daring
of Blücher, resolved to give Napoleon no pause or
rest. They crossed the Rhine on the last day of

1813 with hosts numbering 265,000 men. "We must march to Paris," said Blücher, in blunt, soldierly speech: "Napoleon has paid his visit to every capital in Europe, and we can do no less than return the compliment."

Napoleon had prepared for many contingencies, but not for an actual invasion of France. Its cities were without defences, its fortresses without garrisons. Napoleon, too, had made the fatal mistake of leaving his best troops scattered and useless in scores of fortresses along the German frontier. In the fortresses on the Oder and the Vistula were French garrisons numbering in the aggregate 150,000 men, most of them veterans. Napier, indeed, contends that Napoleon allowed his veterans to stand idly in scattered and remote garrisons as part of a strategy so vast, so original, and so hardy, that nobody except Napier himself has ever yet guessed it! Napoleon's intention was to march down the Elbe, re-cross that river, appear in the rear of the Allied forces, seize Berlin, gather up his garrisons on the Oder and the Vistula, and thus appear in resistless force on the communications of his astonished enemies.

This great plan—if it ever existed—failed because the Bavarians betrayed him. Leipsic was a defeat so shattering that Napoleon was flung backwards upon France without being able either to use his garrisons or to withdraw them. Whether, indeed, Napoleon had any such far-reaching strategy may be doubted.

It is certain that this division of his forces, which left his best troops standing idly on a distant German frontier, while he himself was fighting for existence and for empire in front of Paris, was one of the blunders that destroyed Napoleon. In the nine weeks' campaign of 1814—the only defensive campaign that Napoleon ever waged — again and yet again the fortunes of the contending hosts were so nicely poised that the presence of those 150,000 formidable but wasted veterans would have turned the scale in favour of Napoleon.

CHAPTER VIII

A FALLING EMPIRE

IT is impossible to follow in detail the marches and battles of those nine weeks, while Napoleon was being slowly pushed back from the Rhine to Paris. Napoleon's generalship flames out in these conflicts as brightly as in the days of Lodi and Arcola, of Austerlitz and of Friedland. He flung himself on one column or the other of his slowly converging enemies in turn, with lightning-like speed, and with strokes that had the impact of thunderbolts. And wherever Napoleon was present in person his conscripts won. There was bad generalship, of course, on the side of the Allies. There were too many kings in their councils of war, and too few generals. Schwartzenberg was too slow, and Blücher too quick. Again, and yet again, the bewildered Allies doubted whether they ought not to offer terms to their terrible opponent. "He had beaten us all one after the other," writes Langeron. "We were always frightened by the daring of his enterprises, the swiftness of his movements. Scarcely had we formed a plan than it was disconcerted by him."

But if the campaign of 1814 adds to Napoleon's fame as a general, nothing more absolutely cruel and selfish on his part than that campaign can be imagined. He could have made peace for France at the sacrifice of his personal ambition; but his own fame and pride were dearer to him than the blood of his boy-conscripts. In the words of Lord Wolseley, "He deliberately preferred to trust his luck and to expose his country to the likelihood of a mortal blow, rather than accept any terms which should injure his future renown as a ruler and a conqueror. To satisfy his craving for immortal fame, the fair fields of France must be given over to the ravages of infuriated Cossacks and her capital occupied by revengeful Prussians."

Slowly, clumsily, at the cost of seas of blood and many disasters, the huge columns of the Allies pushed Napoleon back foot by foot towards Paris. At last, on March 3, came the fatal surrender of Soissons, which defeated Napoleon's plans for the destruction of Blücher. Wolseley, with the judgment of a practical soldier, declares that "Napoleon's star set when Soissons surrendered. The last great opportunity of the campaign had vanished." When Napoleon could no longer oppose the direct advance of the Allies upon Paris, he adopted the daring policy of marching eastward past their flank and falling upon their communications. This left Paris open to the Allies, but Napoleon reckoned that when they found him breaking like a thunderbolt across

their communications they would fall back from
Paris, and the seat of war would be transferred to
Lorraine. It would be a violation of all orthodox
military principles if the Allies still marched Paris-
wards when their communications with the Rhine
were destroyed. The slow, faltering, and divided
generalship of the Allies was incapable, Napoleon
believed, of such a stroke of audacious war.

Yet the Allies falsified all Napoleon's calculations.
A letter from Napoleon to his wife was intercepted,
in which he explained his plan and its reasons. " I
have resolved," ran the letter, "to betake myself to
the Marne, in order to draw off the enemy from
Paris." ." This movement," added Napoleon, "makes
or mars me." A Cossack brought the intelligence
that "the enemy was retreating, not on Paris, but
on Moscow." The intercepted letter of Napoleon
to his wife made the Emperor's strategy almost super-
flously clear, but still the allied generals hesitated.
The ablest head amongst them, Barclay de Tolly,
declared in favour of following Napoleon. This was
exactly what Napoleon desired; but wiser counsels
prevailed. Napoleon was left to march into space
while the Allies grasped Paris, which lay a defenceless
prize under their hands.

Napoleon himself afterwards at Elba described to
the Austrian commissioner there his surprise. " I
marched on St. Dizier," he said, "because twenty
experiments had convinced me that I had only to

send a few hussars on your line of communication in order to spread dismay amongst you. On this occasion I stood on it with my whole army, but you never took any notice of me. It was because the devil had possession of you."

That decision of the allied generals was fatal to Napoleon. On the morning of March 24, the Emperor Alexander sat in his saddle on the roadside as the columns began their march. Stretching out his hand, he said, "Let us all march on Paris." And moved for the first time in this campaign on the line of a clear and daring strategy, the allied columns pushed on. The Empress, with her son and the chief functionaries of State, fled to Blois. Marmont fought a gallant battle in front of Paris and was defeated. On March 28, from the heights of Belleville the Allies looked down on the city which for so long had been an earthquake centre for all Europe. A battery opened fire on the streets. "So, Father Paris, you must now pay for Mother Moscow," a Russian gunner said as he laid and fired his gun.

Marmont sent out a flag of truce. Paris, the city of pleasure, was no Saragossa, willing to perish in its own ruins rather than submit to its enemies. Terms of surrender were agreed upon, and, to quote the words of Mitchell, "the setting sun beheld Paris, whence proclamations of eternal war against thrones had so often gone forth, now humbled at the feet of victorious kings."

On March 31, the Allies entered Paris. First came some squadrons of Cossacks, next the Prussian cavalry of the Guard, then the Austrian grenadiers, the Russian and Prussian footguards, some batteries of Russian guns, &c. It is curious to remember that Paris welcomed her conquerors with a sort of rapture. A crowd is always fickle. A French crowd is a mere bundle of caprices; and a Parisian crowd, with feline energy, can both kiss and scratch the same object in turn, with equal facility, and at the shortest interval of time. The allied troops were hailed with frantic shouts as liberators. The Parisians pressed forward to kiss the boots, the swords, the very horses of the allied cavalry. Parisian dames begged to be given a place on the saddles of their conquerors. Shouts arose for the Bourbons. French hands were already busy trying to pull down the statue of Napoleon from the column in the Place Vendôme. The column was too solid to be shaken, but the mob covered Napoleon's statue with a white sheet, so as to save it from offending their virtuous eyes. The Allies had to interfere and save the effigy of Napoleon from Parisian wrath. A proclamation was issued declaring "the monument on the Place Vendôme is under the special safeguard of the magnanimity of the Emperor Alexander and his allies." The Allies announced they would treat no more with Napoleon Bonaparte or with any of his family; and a proclamation was issued calling on the French Senate to form a

Provisional Government and prepare a Constitution for France.

Meanwhile Napoleon had discovered that the Allies were marching on Paris. He knew its defence-less condition, and how fatal to his cause would be its capture, and he pushed on at his utmost speed to its rescue. Napoleon himself told Campbell at Elba that when pressing hard on the heels of the Allies towards Paris, "never were he and his friends more gay. He knew that all the workmen of Paris would fight for him, and what could the Allies do against such a force?" This alleged gaiety of Napoleon and his generals, when they found the Allies marching in advance of them on Paris, may be taken as a mere flight of mendacious imagina-tion; and certainly not a workman in Paris was willing to fire a shot in the cause of Napoleon.

On March 29, Napoleon with the Imperial Guard reached Troyes, after a march of forty miles. The roads behind him were sprinkled with fainting and worn-out stragglers. On the 30th he drove furiously onward in his carriage, leaving his wearied cuirassiers behind, and sending courier after courier in advance to bear the tidings of his approach. Towards even-ing the low, faint sound of heavy guns over the horizon told that Paris was being attacked. At ten o'clock at night the Imperial carriage stopped for a moment for a change of horses. Some straggling soldiers called out, "There is no need for haste;

Paris has capitulated." "These men are mad," cried Napoleon; "bring me an officer." An officer rode up and confirmed the news. For once Napoleon's coolness was shaken. Great sweat-drops ran down his white face. "Miserable wretches that they are!" he cried to his generals. "This comes of employing fools and cowards. And Joseph ran off too! My very brother!" He insisted on still driving onward, and only when assured repeatedly that Paris was held by 120,000 allied troops did he consent to return to Fontainebleau.

Exactly a year before Napoleon had told the French Senate that "he would not abandon a single German village if the enemy were encamped at Montmartre." Now he sent forward Caulaincourt with authority to accept any terms—to surrender the fortresses and pay a huge war contribution— to secure peace. But it was too late. The allied sovereigns, in consultation with Talleyrand and some leading members of the French Senate, had already determined upon their policy. Talleyrand was the governing spirit of that conference. "Napoleon," he said, "was impossible; and what could they give France in his stead?" "A soldier?" asked Talleyrand. "We want no more soldiers." "A Regency? The Empress as Regent? This would be but a mask for Napoleon."

There remained only the Bourbons. "A Regency," argued Talleyrand, "represents an intrigue, the

Bourbons represent a principle;" and they represented the principle of the divine right of kings,
which, to the allied sovereigns, was the very founda-
tion of society, the alpha and the omega of all
politics! It was determined not to negotiate with
Napoleon. France must find a new dynasty or
re-accept her ancient one. And France, it must
be admitted, showed no reluctance to part with
Napoleon. Never was a more expeditious revolution
than that which substituted the Bourbons for
Napoleon. The Municipal Council of Paris had
already issued an abusive proclamation against
Napoleon. On April 1 a Provisional Government
was formed by the Senate, with Talleyrand as its
President. On April 2 a decree was issued declaring
Napoleon dethroned. To the army the proclamation
of the Senate ran: "See what you have suffered from
the tyranny of Napoleon. You were once a million
of soldiers. Almost all have perished under the
sword of the enemy, or, without food, without hospitals, they have perished of misery and famine.
You are no longer the soldiers of Napoleon. The
people of entire France have absolved you from your
oaths."

The address to the nation was even more epi-
grammatic. "Frenchmen," it ran, "on emerging
from civil dissension, you chose for chief a man who
appeared on the theatre of the world with an air of
grandeur. You reposed in him all your hopes; these

TALLEYRAND

From an engraving

hopes have been deceived. On the ruins of anarchy he has founded only despotism. He was bound at least in gratitude to have become a Frenchman with you; he has not done so. He has never ceased to undertake, without end or motive, unjust wars, like an adventurer who is impelled by the thirst for glory. In a few years he has devoured at once your riches and your population. Every family is in mourning; all France groans. He is deaf to our calamities. . . . He believed in no power but that of force; force now overwhelms him, the just retribution of insensate ambition."

Napoleon, meanwhile, at Fontainebleau, was drinking the last bitter dregs of the cup of defeat. He oscillated betwixt fits of the deepest depression and wild schemes for renewing the war. He would march on Paris; he would begin a campaign beyond the Loire. But his marshals were tired of fighting. At Elba Napoleon said he owed his ruin to the fact that he had not left his marshals unemployed and sought for younger chiefs amongst his other generals and colonels. His marshals had reaped every reward war could give. They were hungry for ease and safety. "Are we," asked Ney, "to sacrifice everything to one man? It is time to think a little of ourselves, our families, our interests." Napoleon was bluntly told that his marshals would not follow him in an attack on Paris, Ney again being their harsh spokesman.

On April 4 Napoleon abdicated in favour of his son,

with the Empress as Regent; but it was impossible
to trust Napoleon. "A Regency of the Empress and
her son," said Alexander, "sounds well, I admit; but
Napoleon remains. There is the difficulty. Some
fine day he will put himself at the head of the
Regency, or in its place, and all Europe will be on
fire." His marshals once more put pressure upon
Napoleon to extort from him an unconditional abdication. Ney told him sternly that France, the army,
and the cause of peace demanded his abdication. He
was offered, he was told, the sovereignty of Elba.

Growing impatient of their leader's hesitation, the
marshals hastened to make their own peace with the
Allies. Marmont set the example. He wrote to the
Czar, declaring he was ready to march in with his
troops, the vanguard of Napoleon's army, on certain
specified conditions. His regiments were to be allowed
to retire into Normandy, and Napoleon's life and
freedom were to be guaranteed. These terms were
accepted. With adroit management, Marmont's
troops were marched into the lines of the allied forces.
Marmont thought he was the Monk of the French
Restoration. His act certainly shattered the last
chance of winning a regency for the Empress in favour
of Napoleon's son; and neither Napoleon nor France
ever forgave him. "Marmont," said Napoleon, when
he heard the news, "has struck me the final blow."
It was plain that when the vanguard of his army,
under his most trusted marshal, had marched peace-

fully to the allied lines, the cause of Napoleon was lost beyond hope.

On April 6 Napoleon signed a document of a dozen lines declaring that for himself and his heirs he renounced the throne of France and Italy. The document, with its scrawling characters and blotted surface, is a mute and unconscious witness to the agitation of that hour, when Napoleon, under the rough pressure of his own army chiefs, signed away his empire. Then followed a general flight of such of his officers and the dignitaries of his court as had still lingered near Napoleon. His generals fled from him; his servants plundered him. Even the faithful Berthier left his chief without a sign of farewell. The Bonapartes themselves were flying to all points of the compass. His mother and his uncle, the Cardinal Fesch, made for Rome, the ex-King of Holland for Switzerland, the ex-King of Spain for America. Napoleon's wife proved faithless to him, her excuse being that he had been repeatedly and notoriously faithless to her. Her French guards were dismissed, Cossacks took their place, and after a few days she set out for Vienna taking with her her son, the King of Rome, and neither wife nor son ever saw Napoleon again.

CHAPTER IX

" I SAW before me a short, active-looking man, who
was rapidly pacing the length of his apartment,
like some wild animal in his cell. He was dressed
in an old green uniform, with gold epaulets, blue
pantaloons, and red top-boots, unshaven, uncombed,
with the fallen particles of snuff scattered profusely
upon his upper lip and breast."

This is the picture drawn of Napoleon by Sir Neil
Campbell, when, on the morning of April 17, 1814,
he waited upon him at Fontainebleau as the English
Commissioner appointed to accompany the fallen
Emperor to Elba. Napoleon had nothing in him of
Roman fortitude; and during those agitated days
at Fontainebleau, when his empire was tumbling in
ruins about him, his marshals were deserting him,
and his capital was in the possession of his enemies,
he was torn with varying paroxysms of wrath and
despair. He framed the wildest plans. He would
commit suicide; he would fling himself on Paris
with the faithful remnant of his Guard; he would
kindle the war afresh beyond the Loire. Sometimes

he sat as in a stupor, looking into vacancy, unconscious of persons about him, while in fantastic
vision all the scenes of his strange history rose before
him. Then he would pace to and fro in his chamber like some caged animal. He talked of bygone
battles, of comrades long dead. He swung from one
extreme of passion to another.

Constant, his valet, relates how he noted that his
agitated master "tore his thigh with his nails, so that
the blood came, without his being conscious of it."
His valet in alarm removed his pistols, and it seems
clear that once at least the fallen Emperor did
attempt suicide. "Suicide," Napoleon once said,
"must be left to weak heads and souls badly
tempered." Yet in the despair kindled by his ruined
fortunes Napoleon himself turned to the refuge of
dull heads and weak souls! He carried round his
neck a little packet of deadly poison, which his
physician had prepared for him during the retreat
from Moscow, in case he should fall into the hands
of Cossacks. On the night of April 12 Napoleon
rose from his bed, emptied this poison into a glass,
and swallowed it; but the dose did not prove fatal.
Napoleon had not the temperament of the suicide.
When reproached afterwards for not having put an
end to his life, he said calmly that his death in that
fashion would have been an injury to his friends and
a delight to his enemies.

As a matter of fact, this hero of so many battles,

who had sent such myriads to a bloody death without a sigh, showed a very unheroic anxiety for his
own safety; and he shrewdly suspected that safety
to be more in peril from the hands of his former
subjects than even from those of his victorious
enemies.   It gave him the utmost pleasure to learn
that Campbell, the English Commissioner, was to
accompany him to Elba.   He begged that an English
frigate, instead of a French corvette, might transport
him thither; and he frankly admitted that he desired this to "avoid any unpleasant observations"
which might be offered by a French crew.   He
wished, indeed, to be allowed to reside in England.
"It is a great nation," he said; "I am sure I should
be in security."   But when he reflected that English
ships of war would patrol round the island of Elba,
he added, "I shall be as safe in it as if in a street in
London"—at that moment his ideal of safety!   It
was perhaps the mere desire to flatter Campbell which
made him say to him, "The English are the only
people in the world; the rest are so many popu-
laces;" but it is certain that he could trust English-
men with his safety where he could not trust his
own former subjects.

On April 20 Napoleon left Fontainebleau.   The
story of his farewell to his Guards is historic.   A
handful of the grenadiers of that famous body stood
drawn up in the great courtyard at Fontainebleau.
They formed a double line leading to Napoleon's

carriage, and the fallen Emperor stopped, looking
haggard and bloated, to say a few agitated sentences
to these veterans. "For twenty years," he said, "I
have found you ever brave and faithful. . . . You are
my children," he continued; "I cannot embrace you
all, but I will do so in the person of your general."
Whereupon he fell upon General Petite's neck and
kissed him on both cheeks. The general took the
Imperial eagle from one of the officers and presented
it to Napoleon, and he, says Campbell, who watched
the scene, "embraced it for half a minute." Then
he entered his carriage, the cavalry guard closed
round it, and at a gallop Napoleon set off towards
the sea-coast. The guard which was to accompany
him to Elba, 400 infantry and 150 cavalry—all
volunteers from the Old Guard—had set off in advance. Drouot and Bertrand alone of Napoleon's
generals accompanied him. Just before he stepped
across the threshold of Fontainebleau, the fallen
Emperor stopped, put his hand to his head, and said,
"It is all like a dream."

Napoleon's journey to the sea-coast was a very
agitating experience. Near Valence Marshal Augereau
was met. Augereau cherished the utmost contempt
for his fallen master, principally because he was
fallen. Only five days before he had issued a proclamation telling his soldiers that the Emperor "had
not known how to die as a soldier, after sacrificing
millions to his ambition." Campbell, who was riding

ahead of Napoleon's carriage, met Augereau first, and told him that Napoleon was coming on, whereupon that general broke out, "He is a coward! I always knew it. He ought to have marched upon a battery and put an end to himself;" and he showed Campbell how he had flung away all the decorations Napoleon had bestowed upon him. When Napoleon's carriage came up, the Emperor dismounted and embraced his grumbling general, who received his fallen sovereign's salutation with ostentatious contempt.

But before Napoleon reached Elba he had to undergo still more distressing experiences. A tempest of popular wrath gathered round him as his carriage rolled southwards. He was pelted with epithets, and was in danger of being assailed with still more dangerous missiles. At Organ, his own effigy, smeared with blood, was held up at the window of his carriage. "We'll do no harm to the monster," the crowd shouted; "we only want to show him how much we love him."

Napoleon's nerve broke down strangely under the disgusts and perils of his journey. He disguised himself in an Austrian uniform and mounted the white cockade; he assumed alternately the names of the two English Commissioners. At La Calade he escaped the mob by getting out of a back window and riding on in advance of the party with a huge white cockade in his hat, and attended by a single courier. There are not many examples of the satire of history more curious than this spectacle of Napoleon disguising himself with an English name, an Austrian coat, and a Bourbon cockade, in order to escape the wrath of a French crowd!

On April 27 he arrived at Frejus, and stood on the very beach where, a little more than fourteen years before, he had landed on his return from Egypt. What other human being ever, in an equal space of time, passed through such amazing alternations of triumph and despair as, for Napoleon, filled those fourteen years since last he had stood on that strip of sandy beach at Frejus! It is curious that when safely on board the British frigate *Undaunted*, which was to take him to Elba, Napoleon rose into a mood of high spirits. He declared he had never felt in better health, and his officers confessed that they had never seen him more at his ease. "It seemed to me," said Campbell, "that one great source of his happiness and satisfaction arose from the security of his person." He felt that he was safe at last under the protection of the British flag. He showed the curiosity of a child in the routine of the ship's service; talked incessantly and about everything, and exhibited already that transcendent capacity for colouring the history of his own career which he carried to such a sublime height afterwards at St. Helena. On May 4 the *Undaunted* cast anchor in Porto Ferrajo, and Napoleon landed in his tiny kingdom.

The Allies had dealt with fallen France with

what might not unfairly be described as magnificent
generosity.   England gave her back nearly all her
colonies.   France was allowed to keep her limits as
they stood on January 1, 1792; nay, for the sake of
adjusting her boundaries, territory with a population
of 450,000 was added to those limits.   Two-thirds of
the great fleet at Antwerp were restored to France.
No contribution was laid on the country, and French
museums, crowded with the spoils of half the capitals
of Europe, were allowed to keep their booty.

But with Napoleon himself the Allies showed little
generosity, and still less wisdom.   It was the irony of
revenge to put Napoleon, with the spacious title of
"Emperor of Elba," on a little, half-savage islet off
the shores of Italy, a mere tangle of hills and
marshes, with a circumference of sixty miles and a
population of 13,000.   This was to imprison an eagle
in the cage of a canary.   And it was madness to
leave the eagle, with wings unclipped and beak and
talons undestroyed, within a flight so short of its
ancient nest !

Castlereagh, the representative of England, urged
the peril of leaving Napoleon so near to France.
Already St. Helena, as a safer prison, was mentioned.
But the allied sovereigns looked on Napoleon as
politically dead.   Elba would be a grave rather than
a prison for him.   The Congress of Vienna was busy
drawing up the new map of Europe.   Campbell relates how, on February 18, he met Cook, the English

Under-Secretary of State, who had just come from Vienna, and he bade him tell Napoleon that "in that Congress nobody thinks of him at all; he is quite forgotten, as much as if he had never existed." The allied sovereigns, it is clear, were living, as far as Napoleon was concerned, in a fool's paradise. Within a week of that meeting with Cook, Napoleon was on his way to Paris again. In less than a month he was supreme once more in France, and the Congress of Vienna found its occupation suddenly gone.

Amusing descriptions are given of the part Napoleon played during the ten months betwixt May 5, 1814, when he landed on the isle, and February 26, 1815, when he left it on his way to the Tuileries— and to Waterloo. Never was an astonished islet more energetically over-governed. Napoleon's activity was something phenomenal. He was still only forty-five years of age, short, thick-necked, deep-chested; with pendulous cheeks, indeed, and gross stomach, but possessed of amazing physical vigour. Campbell, who was familiar with the vigorous life of the soldier, declared he had never seen a man in any situation of life with so much restless personal activity. "He appears to take pleasure in perpetual movement, and in seeing those who accompany him sink under fatigue. I do not think it possible for him to sit down to study."

Perhaps Napoleon's restless spirit was seeking relief in physical exertion from the sharp tooth of

memory, the anguish of defeated ambition. He had
four residences in different parts of the island, and
rushed incessantly from one to the other. He began
making roads and never finished them. He invented
new taxes, passed innumerable laws, inspected everything, meddled with everybody. Ancient habits kept
all their tyranny over him. The day after he landed
he framed a plan for enlarging his dominions and
took possession of a small uninhabited island about
ten miles off the coast of Elba. "All Europe will
say," he added with a laugh, "that I have made a
conquest already." He was as despotic at Porto
Ferrajo as he had been at the Tuileries. He manœuvred his little army of 1600 men as though it
were the host that conquered at Austerlitz.

Napoleon at Elba, it must be confessed, had some
wrongs and many temptations. By solemn treaty
France was to pay him a pension of 2,000,000
francs per annum; but his pension, after the
fashion of French pensions of the period, was left
unpaid, and Napoleon was reduced to unkingly straits
for want of cash. His wife had been encouraged
to abandon him. Whether he loved his infant
son, the King of Rome, very much may, perhaps,
be doubted. He used to refer to him as "*le
pauvre diable!*" Domestic affection was not exactly
Napoleon's characteristic. But at least it gave him
the pretext of a grievance that his faithless wife kept
his son from him. Meanwhile France lay almost at

his touch, fermenting with discontent and restless under the rule of the despised Bourbons, with many eyes turning to the figure of that gloomy and terrible soldier in Elba. Louis XVIII., a gross-bodied and helpless old man, dressed in semi-English costume, who had the Bourbon faculty of forgetting nothing and learning nothing, was by no means the man to efface the memory of Napoleon; and he had advisers about him more stupid than even himself. France, with the shame of a great defeat yet upon it, and more than 300,000 old soldiers—the released garrisons from the fortresses of Central Europe and the prisoners of war sent back from Russia—without occupation or support, was rich in all the elements of discontent.

Wellington, with cool shrewd judgment, guessed that the great drama of Napoleon's career would not end at Elba; but it is curious to note he found the probability of change not so much in Napoleon's restless genius as in the character of the French nation. In a letter to his brother dated December 17, 1814, he declares his belief that "the French people are so completely ruined by the Revolution, and are now suffering so severely from the want of the plunder of the world, that they cannot go on without it, and they cannot endure the prospect of a peaceful government." So, in Wellington's judgment, if not the old Napoleon, a new one would emerge on the stage of France to trouble the peace of the world.

Much political good disappeared, curiously enough, with Napoleon, and much political evil returned. The restored monarchy attempted at a hundred points to re-establish the feudal system, which had disappeared before the breath of the French Revolution as ice melts before the south wind. The little German princelets restored the very pigtails and powder of their soldiers. In Hanover, torture was reintroduced in the law-courts. In Spain, Ferdinand brought back the Inquisition, strangled the press, made the priest once more the master of the bodies as well as the souls of men. In France, the army was, in a sense, the last hold of the democracy, and it was ruthlessly Bourbonised. Fourteen thousand officers and sergeants were dismissed; the Tricolour, splendid with so many victories, was banished. The image of the Virgin Mary was escorted through the streets of Paris in solemn procession, Marshal Soult and other ex-Jacobins acting, with smileless faces but unspeakable thoughts, as candle-bearers. A ruler of genius might have failed in the task of holding in order a nation in such a mood.

But the Bourbons committed every possible blunder. They. alarmed all interests; they embittered all resentments. Louis XVIII. dated his return as the twentieth year of his reign, treating all that had happened since the head of Louis XVI. fell in the Place de la Grève as non-existent. He issued a charter conferring on France, as his free gift, the constitution the Senate had already shaped. This made all institutions to depend on the royal will; and the caprice which had given to-day might take away its gift to-morrow. If there had been no legal Government in France since the death of Louis XVI., what title remained to the millions of peasant proprietors who now tilled what were once the national domains? The returned nobles were arrogant; the restored priesthood was intolerant; the soldiers were soured by the new colours they had to wear and the new officers they had to obey.

The titles and decorations won under Napoleon became crimes. And the Bourbons were as eager in creating new and worthless distinctions as in abolishing those which were old and precious. The Legion of Honour alone was allowed to survive, but its cross was sold at a market rate ranging from about £10 to £12, 10s. And more of these purchasable distinctions were issued in five months of Bourbon rule, from August to December 1814, than during the whole twelve years of the Empire, and more patents of nobility than during two hundred years of the monarchy before the Revolution!

Well nigh half a million of disbanded soldiers, moreover, for whom the industries of peace were insipid, if not hateful, found themselves without occupation, and in peril of starvation. The Bourbons were, for these soldiers, the symbol of defeat, while in the very syllables of Napoleon's name the echoes of a hundred triumphant victories lingered. And Napoleon himself, with his subtle Italian intellect, a plotter by genius, in communication with all parties, and admirably served by his private agents, watched this strange welter of passions, resentments, and disgusts with which France was filled. He still had faith in his "star." The Congress of Vienna counted Napoleon as dead. The Bourbons forgot his existence. But wherever, at least, his old soldiers wandered, there began to run a whisper that, with the violets of the coming spring, Napoleon would return to France. Napoleon cherished the keenest intellectual contempt for the Bourbons. With cynical shrewdness he summed up their chances. " The French," he said, " will be enthusiastic for them for six months; then cold for three; and at the end of the year will bid adieu to them." He believed he had but to land on French soil and armies would gather round him as if by magic. Elba was for him a prison, a political grave. He determined to risk the great adventure.

On the night of February 26, 1815, Napoleon's sister, Pauline, gave a ball at Porto Ferrajo. Napoleon, when the ball was at its height, slipped quietly out; his guard was already standing on the beach in silent ranks. The embarkation on the sloop of war—the flagship of his modest fleet of seven vessels—was quickly effected, and when morning broke this microscopic expedition—an army of 1100 men with 80 horses—was on its way to conquer a kingdom with a population of 30,000,000. France was reached, not without some adventures, on March 1. Once, in the short voyage, a French sloop of war bore down on the brig that carried Napoleon. Its captain hailed the *Inconstant*, and having learned that it was from Elba, asked "How the Emperor was." "Il se porte à merveille," answered Napoleon himself coolly, whilst his soldiers lay flat on the deck to escape notice. The little band stepped ashore on French soil as the sun was setting on March 1. Within three weeks, without a shot having been fired, the Bourbons were in flight, and Napoleon was once more in the Tuileries.

The story of those three weeks is the strangest romance. Till he reached Gap on March 7, Napoleon's recruits amounted to exactly four persons. The peasants were stolid, the inhabitants of the towns critical. After marching a hundred miles into France, the success of the expedition was as doubtful as when Napoleon stepped ashore. The crisis came when, on the evening of March 7, Napoleon came face to face with a battalion of royal troops despatched from the garrison at Grenoble to bar his progress. The royal troops stood impassive, while their officers shouted "Fire!" Napoleon sent an officer forward waving a white handkerchief to parley, but he was sternly warned back. "We have been deceived," said Napoleon to Bertrand, "but no matter now. Forward!"

The battalion, sullenly barring the road, but uncertain of its own purpose, saw a familiar figure in grey coat and cocked hat separate itself from the adventurous band in front. A thrill ran through the ranks of the royal troops. They wore the Bourbon uniform, but in heart they were the soldiers of Napoleon. And Napoleon himself, in the cocked hat and grey coat of history, was walking steadily up to the points of their bayonets. He threw open his greatcoat, showing on his breast the star of the Legion of Honour. "Comrades," he said, "do you know me again?" Then, in sharper accents, "Soldiers, do you know your general?" Then, in accents yet more imperious, "If there is one among you who desires to kill his Emperor, let him do it now. Here I am!" Comrade! General! Emperor! There was magic in these words. In a moment, with tears in many cases running down their cheeks, and with shouts of "Vive l'Empereur!" the Bourbon soldiers were round Napoleon vowing allegiance. France was practically won. "As far as Grenoble," said Napoleon long afterwards, "I was an adventurer; at Grenoble I was a prince." But he was more; he had met the soldiers of Louis XVIII., and they had refused to fire upon him, and that fact decided the fate of the expedition.

At Lyons Napoleon assumed all the functions of

an Emperor. He summoned a popular Assembly;
he published decrees which banished the returned
nobles, confiscated the Bourbon estates, and unfolded
a new policy for France. His old generals rallied
round him. Ney was despatched from Paris in command of the forces to repel this new invasion, and,
as he kissed the King's hand on taking leave, he
assured him he would "bring back Napoleon in an
iron cage." He met Napoleon at Auxerre, but it was
only to vow service to him. "Embrace me, General,"
was Napoleon's greeting; "I want neither explanations nor justifications." The soldier in Ney over-
came the politician, and even the man of honour.
"I know all we have to fear," he said to his soldiers,
"but I would rather be braized in a mortar by
Bonaparte than humiliated by fellows who never
fought."

The unfortunate Louis XVIII. issued proclamations
which nobody read, and delivered himself of appeals
to which nobody listened. Nobody would fire a shot
in his cause. To despatch columns against Napoleon
was only to supply him with recruits. The wits of
Paris ridiculed him. A mock letter, addressed
"Napoleon to Louis XVIII.," was fastened on the
railing round the Vendôme column. "My good
brother," it ran, "it is useless to send me any more
troops. I have enough."

On March 19 Napoleon had reached Fontainebleau,
and Louis XVIII. fled from Paris to establish his

court at Ghent. Never was a king more ignobly driven from his throne. He was dismissed, as it were, with a gesture. Chateaubriand, indeed, tried to kindle some spark of warlike resolution in the mind of Louis XVIII. Let Paris, he urged, shut her gates and barricade her streets, and the King prepare to fight for the Tuileries. "The spectacle of the King standing, pike in hand, on the threshold of that classic building," Chateaubriand declared, "would awaken a universal enthusiasm." "If His Majesty must die," the orator added uncomfortably, "let the last exploit of Napoleon be the murder of an old man. Louis XVIII., in sacrificing his life, will gain the only battle he has ever fought." But Louis had no aspirations for martyrdom. He was content to leave other people to do the fighting while he waddled comfortably off to Ghent.

For one agitated day Paris was without a king, but at nine o'clock on the night of March 20 Napoleon drove in an open carriage to the gate of the Tuileries. He passed through the streets of Paris without kindling any enthusiasm. Perhaps it was that, in the Parisians, the very capacity for emotion was exhausted. Napoleon himself, with his keen, quick vision, noted the careless indifference of the streets. "They let me come," he said bitterly, "as they let the others go." But as Napoleon stepped from his carriage at the gate of the Tuileries he was caught up in the arms of the officers and veterans that waited for him there, and swept with exultant shouts up the staircase and from landing to landing. That was for Napoleon a moment of triumph for which it was almost worth paying the price of Waterloo and of St. Helena.

CHAPTER X

THE STRATEGY OF THE FOUR DAYS

"BEHOLD," said Napoleon as he stepped on the beach at St. Juan,—"Behold the Congress dissolved!" But he was deceived. As a matter of fact, the touch of Napoleon's foot on French soil saved the Congress from dissolution.

The Congress of Vienna has become a term of opprobrium on the lips of mankind, and the Treaty of the Holy Alliance, which was part of its work, is now looked upon as a slightly profane jest. That treaty was the work of a Czar who compounded with his conscience for a gross private life by much zeal for religion in public affairs. The Treaty of the Holy Alliance was, in fact, the Beatitudes translated into political terms and declared to constitute the politics of the civilised world. It became a jest when to a document with such an ideal were attached the names of such eminent authorities on religion and morals as Ferdinand of Spain, Louis XVIII. of France, the Czar of Russia, and the Emperor of Austria. But the Congress itself had some virtues and did some wholesome work; though it was due to the obstinate, if somewhat inarticulate British conscience that the prohibition of the slave trade found a place in its agreements.

But at the moment Napoleon landed from Elba the Congress was perishing of mere strife amongst its own members, strife bred of unsatisfied greed and fast kindling jealousies. Russia claimed Poland, Prussia Saxony; and England, Austria, and France had bound themselves by a secret treaty to resist both demands. On reaching Paris, Napoleon found that treaty in the French Foreign Office, and sent it to the Czar, hoping it would turn him against his former allies. It was the sudden reappearance of Napoleon that hushed all strife in the Congress of Vienna, and revived at a breath the League of Chaumont, the pledge of the five Great Powers to make common cause against Napoleon as the enemy of the peace of the world.

The news that Napoleon had left Elba, took eight days in trickling through to Vienna. Metternich was roused from sleep on the night of March 6 to be told that Napoleon had left Elba on February 26. Wellington, to whom the news of Napoleon's landing in France first came, has described the effect the intelligence produced on the Congress. It kindled instant and inextinguishable laughter, the Czar laughing loudest of all! The Congress cannot be suspected of possessing any very lively sense of humour; but it stirred the sense of the

ridiculous, in even so many elderly and cynical
heads, to realise how instantly all their mutual jealousies had grown pallid and insignificant in the
presence of this new fact.

The Congress, however, acted with decision. Napoleon had disappeared from Elba; he was at large somewhere in France, and what might be his fate there
could not yet be guessed. Lord Castlereagh touched
the heart of the question when he asked "Can the
Bourbons get Frenchmen to fight for them against
Frenchmen?" No one imagined they could. The
Powers, therefore, acted as though Napoleon were
once more master of France. They signed a declara-
tion on March 13, declaring him beyond the pale of
civil and social relations. It was impossible to keep
terms with him, and, as a common enemy and dis-
turber of the peace of the world, he was "delivered
over to Public Justice." On March 25 the League
of Chaumont was formally renewed, the four Great
Powers binding themselves to contribute 150,000
men each, and not to lay down their arms without
joint consent, and only when Bonaparte should be
unable to give further trouble. All the smaller
States added themselves, one by one, to this League,
Great Britain taking its familiar office of paymaster,
and agreeing to subsidies amounting in the aggregate
to £11,000,000.

Napoleon, on his part, issued a mellifluous proclamation thrilling with flute-like cadences. His

"sweetest hope," he declared, was to see universal
peace established. He yearned for nothing else but
"the felicity of nations;" and he offered to join
with the other Powers in "a noble emulation to
that end." He gave no other guarantee for the
offer, indeed, than his own word; and that, unhappily, was of the moral value of a gambler's
loaded dice.

The Allies were deaf to Napoleon's flutings. His
couriers were turned back; his letters remained unopened. The Great Powers would discourse with him
only from the iron lips of cannon. Napoleon thus
found himself alone against banded Europe. Murat,
it is true, took arms in his own cause and that of
Napoleon; but he was crushed with almost laugh-
able expedition. Napoleon had no other resources
than such as he could find in France itself; and even
here his sky was dark. Civil war awoke in La
Vendée. In Paris itself Napoleon discovered that
his new royalty had by no means the magic and
authority of his old empire. Politicians tried to
fetter him with the cobweb filaments of a liberal
constitution, and, for a while, Napoleon had to play
the tame part of a constitutional monarch. "The
taste," he told Benjamin Constant, "is all for con-
stitutions, debates, harangues. I have no objection
to them. I am no longer a conqueror. I am growing old, and I have need of repose. The rest of a
constitutional king suits me." The lion, in brief, was

prepared to roar like a sucking dove—until the time came for resuming its natural voice.

Meantime Napoleon exerted his matchless energy in reorganising the military resources of France. Paris and Lyons were fortified. The veterans were summoned back to their regiments. A new conscription was ordered, though it yielded scanty conscripts. Napoleon was a master in the art of war, and he created a great army with magical speed. When active operations began in the early days of June, he had a force of 240,000 of the line, and nearly 30,000 of the Imperial Guard. For immediate action under himself, on the frontier facing the Netherlands, he had a fighting force of 123,000 men of all arms, with 343 guns.

The preparations of the Allies were naturally on a much vaster scale. The forces at their command approached, roughly, 740,000 men; but they were scattered over Europe and under divided generalship. Slowly their plans crystallised into a definite strategy. Three great armies were formed, or to be formed; one on the Upper Rhine, of 265,000, under Schwartzenberg; a second, of 155,000 Prussians, under Blücher, on the Lower Rhine; a third, under Wellington, of 106,000, a mixed multitude of British, Nassauers, Belgians, Hanoverians, &c., in the Low Countries. Yet a fourth was to be organised, a great Russian army, 170,000 strong, as reserve to the other three. The whole

European landscape was, so to speak, streaked with vast bodies of armed men converging on a common centre—Paris.

But these great columns were, for the most part, remote, and all were slow-moving. Months must pass before their converging march actually threatened the French capital, and each month would add tens of thousands to Napoleon's strength. Napoleon's wisdom lay in striking at the enemies nearest to him before these huge and distant columns had reached the scene of action. And close at hand, near enough to strike and to be struck, were the two most formidable captains opposed to him—Blücher and Wellington. If, say, Schwartzenberg and Kutzoff, with their timid strategy and loitering movements, had commanded in the Netherlands, the outlook would have been very different for Napoleon. But just across the French frontier, with an army of 117,000, was Blücher, the fiercest fighter of even that fighting age. Blücher was described by Napoleon himself as "that old devil" who "always attacked me with the same vigour. If he was beaten at night, he was as ready as ever the next morning for the fight!" And by the side of Blücher was Wellington with an army of nearly equal scale: a captain as great as Napoleon himself, if of a different type. It is the fact that the two fight-ing generals of the Allies were within thirty miles of the French frontier, which explains why the

campaign reached its crisis—and its close—almost
at a breath.

The campaign—the great and final act in Napoleon's career — practically lasted only four days.
Napoleon crossed the Sambre with 128,000 men on
June 15; on the night of June 18 the Grand Army,
in the tumult of flight and in utter wreck, was pouring
back across that river.   The events of those four days
have been studied for three-quarters of a century as
with a microscope, and have furnished the text for
measureless controversy.   Much blood was spilt in
making the history of those four days, but almost as
much ink has been expended since in writing that
history, or in wrangling over it.   Time, indeed, has
lost one of its familiar offices with regard to this
chapter of history.   It has scarcely cooled the controversies kindled by it, or cleared the horizon in
which they are set.   We are too near those times
to write a true history.   Wellington told Napier
that he could not tell the whole truth about Waterloo without doing as much mischief as Bonaparte!
All that the writer of to-day can do is to listen to
all the witnesses, balance all the opposing arguments, and then tell the story in the plainest fashion
he can.

Napoleon left Paris on June 12.   He reached Laon
at nightfall, took over the command of the army next
morning from Soult, making him the chief of his staff,
and pushed on to Arbesnes.   His strategy was simple,

but marked by great audacity. He had before him the armies of Blücher and of Wellington, each, roughly, as strong in numbers as his own. They could oppose, that is—counting troops actually available—213,000 men of all arms, with 496 guns, to Napoleon's force of 128,000 men and 344 guns. These two armies stood on guard betwixt the Sambre and Brussels, the great road from Charleroi to Brussels marking the line where their forces touched. If that host had been under a single captain, either Blücher or Wellington, Napoleon might have flung himself against it in vain. But it was two armies, not one, and in its divided generalship lay Napoleon's opportunity.

And there were many elements of weakness in the allied forces beside their bifurcated generalship. They had separate and sharply diverging lines of communication; that of Blücher running westward to the Rhine, that of Wellington northward to Antwerp. To an army its communications are what the spinal cord is to the body. To have them snapped means paralysis. Napoleon calculated that if either of these two armies, under the shock of attack and defeat, had to fall back, it would move on the line of its own communications and diverge from its sister army. The line where two hosts, allied in their cause, but diverse in language, in speech, blood, method, and generalship, meet, is sure to be the line of relatively least resistance. At that line information will, somehow, be arrested. It lends itself easily to fissure.

If Napoleon had moved to turn Wellington's right, he would have pushed the English and Prussians together; and they numbered in all 230,000 men. To merely thrust himself, again, betwixt the two armies would be to give both the opportunity of a combined attack, which must crush him. Napoleon moved on the point where the two armies touched each other; but it was with the calculation of falling on Blücher and on Wellington separately, and of destroying each in succession before the other could come up. So he did not aim merely to seize Quatre Bras and Sombreffe, and to cut the nerve which connected the two armies. He gave express instructions above all *not* to occupy Sombreffe. Napoleon's plan, in a word, was to fight Blücher before Wellington could come up, not merely to cut off Blücher's communications with Wellington. This seems to settle the much-debated question as to whether Napoleon gave Ney orders to actually occupy Quatre Bras. The presumption is he did not; as, if Wellington had promptly collected his forces this might have involved fighting two great battles, instead of one, at the same hour.

That Napoleon did not aim to provoke an equal battle with Wellington while he was engaged in crushing Blücher, explains why Ney, the most daring of soldiers, did not push resolutely on and seize

Quatre Bras. His temperament must have suggested that course, but his orders were against it. Yet, amid all the contradictory evidence on this point, Mr. Horsbury brings out the curious fact that Napoleon's bulletin for June 15, published in the *Moniteur* on June 18, reports that Ney's headquarters that evening were actually at Quatre Bras! This, of course, was not true; yet it seems to show that Napoleon expected it to be true, and the occupation of Quatre Bras was included in his orders.

Napoleon's plan, then, was to thrust in fiercely betwixt the junction of the two armies opposed to him, drive them apart, outstrip each in speed of movement, and crush each separately, and so march in triumph to Brussels. And it was clear that victory here would have far-reaching political effects. It might, Napoleon thought, in his ignorance of English politics, bring about a change of Ministry in that country, and call into power a new Cabinet bent on making peace. It would probably arrest the march France-wards of the slowly gathering armies of Russia and Austria. These Powers might well hesitate before marching across Europe to meet the victor who had just overthrown both Blücher and Wellington. There were other circumstances favourable for Napoleon. The forces of the two generals in his immediate front were scattered over a vast area, from Liège on the west to Hal on the east, from Charleroi on the south to Brussels on the north, a district 100 miles long by

40 broad. Even a force of 200,000 men, sprinkled over so wide a district, must offer many penetrable points.

It was also in Napoleon's favour that Wellington believed he had guessed Napoleon's plan, and stuck obstinately to his guess. And his guess was wrong! He was persuaded that Napoleon would strike at Brussels by Mons and Hal, not by Charleroi and Genappes. The road by Mons was the shortest and easiest; moving by it, Napoleon would cut Wellington off from his base. So it became a fixed idea with Wellington that Napoleon would move on the Mons road. To the day of his death he held that Napoleon ought to have moved on that line. He was convinced that not his left flank, where he touched Blücher, was in peril, but his right flank, resting on Hal. Wellington, accordingly, held the Charleroi road lightly and with his worst troops, keeping his strength to guard his right.

Napoleon thus was about to strike at the point where he was least expected and could be most feebly resisted. There were qualities, too, in the character of Blücher, and facts in the experience of Wellington, which, no doubt, entered into Napoleon's subtle calculations. Ziethen's army corps lay nearest the frontier. If Napoleon struck at it, Blücher, all the hussar in him taking flame, would rush to the aid of his threatened division. Wellington, whose Peninsular experiences had trained him to be sus-

picious of foreign allies and sensitive about his communication with the sea, would, on the other hand,
be anxious about his right flank and slow to move.

Napoleon at St. Helena told Sir Pulteney Malcolm
that, in determining the strategy of the Waterloo
campaign, he "took into consideration the character
of the two generals.   One was an hussar; the other
an officer of method who would not move his army
without reflection nor without his supplies.   If he
had first attacked the English the Prussians would
have been on him at full gallop.   He thought it best
to begin with the Prussians, believing the English
would be somewhat slower."   That was character-
istically subtle generalship on the part of Napoleon,
and facts exactly justified Napoleon's calculations.

With incomparable secrecy and speed Napoleon
drew his forces together, until, on the night of
June 14, he had 128,000 men at Beaumont, Philippeville, and Sobre, all, roughly, fifteen miles from
Charleroi.   He had shrouded the movements of
his troops with the most subtle art.   Wellington's
spies, indeed, told him that there was a great French
force on the Sambre, and that Napoleon had left
Paris to join it.   But the British general was at
Brussels, thirty-four miles from Charleroi, watching
Hal, nearly thirty miles distant from the point on
which Napoleon was about to break.   Ziethen, who
commanded Blücher's most advanced corps towards
the Sambre, was startled by a strange red glare in

the night-sky above the hills on the French bank of the Sambre. Napoleon had directed that his troops should bivouac in the rear of these hills, so that their fires might escape the notice of the Prussian vedettes. He forgot that these night-fires would still be reflected from the sky; and that crimson sign hanging in the heavens was, to the Prussians, the first signal of the tempest of war about to break on them.

It is impossible not to admire the skill of Napoleon's strategy, and no one can deny to it the quality of daring in the highest degree. But, in a sense, it was the strategy of an adventurer or a gambler. He was risking everything on a single chance. With 128,000 men he was thrusting himself betwixt two armies, each almost equal to his own in strength. He calculated to divide them and beat each in turn. But if he failed to divide Blücher and Wellington— and each was a great master in the art of war—then Napoleon himself must be crushed. He would be attacked on both flanks at once; exactly, as a matter of fact, what happened. Napoleon thus was putting his hand betwixt the hammer and the anvil, hoping to pluck it back, with victory in its grasp, before it could be crushed.

CHAPTER XI

THE ACTORS IN THE NEW CAMPAIGN

NAPOLEON himself was still in the prime and vigour of life, unsurpassed in resource and subtlety as a general. But the campaign is full of evidences on his part of what may be called an exhausted will; of an imagination which could frame vast plans, but lacked sustained force to execute them; of a brain that worked with the speed, and sweep, and exactitude of a supernatural machine up to a certain point, and then suddenly grew inert; a brain that lost its grasp and vision, its power to remember, to co-ordinate, to command; that went mysteriously to sleep at inopportune times. "This," said Vandamme after Ligny, "is not the Napoleon we used to know;" and that was certainly true.

Wolseley says, the Napoleon of the Waterloo campaign "was no longer the thin, sleek, active little man he had been at Rivoli." A French writer describes him in 1815 as having a pallid face, huge, pendulous cheeks, and "an abdomen which protrudes so much as to cause his shirt front to ruck up above his waistcoat." He was only forty-seven years

of age, but his swollen unwieldy body was no longer
the willing and fit instrument of his vehement will
and piercing intellect. "I do not know him again,"
said Carnot. "He talks instead of acting, he the
man of rapid decision; he asks opinions, he the imperious dictator, who seemed insulted by advice; his
mind wanders, though he used to have the power of
attending to everything when and as he would; he
is sleepy, and he used to be able to sleep and wake
at pleasure." "In some of the most critical and
terrible moments of the Waterloo campaign," says
Seeley, "he seems to have been scarcely able to keep
himself awake."

Napoleon's army is commonly, and quite truly, described as being, for its numbers, the most formidable
he ever led into battle. It was, in the main, an army
of veterans; even the raw conscripts of Lützen and of
Bautzen had by this time become hardy soldiers.
And the spirit of the army was in the highest degree
exultant and daring. It had a passionate faith in its
leader; and a sense of personal interest gave edge to its
courage. The reign of the Bourbons, it was realised,
meant an end to the career of the soldier, and
Napoleon's forces in this campaign felt they were
fighting for, not merely a dynasty, or for a political
theory, but for every personal prize in life worth
having. Foy, in his Journal, on June 14, wrote:
"The troops exhibit not patriotism, not enthusiasm,
but an actual mania for the Emperor and against his

enemies." Against the Prussians, indeed, the spirit of the French was one of murderous hate. They had great humiliations to avenge.

Yet Napoleon's army had, as a matter of fact, some

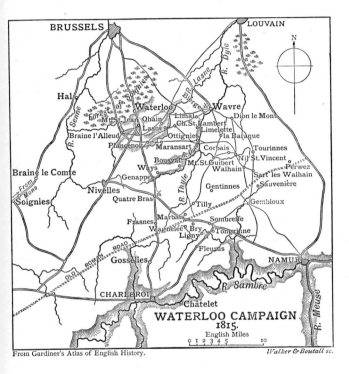

From Gardiner's Atlas of English History.

WATERLOO CAMPAIGN 1815.

English Miles

Walker & Boutall sc.

serious weaknesses. It had, in a sense, no patriotism. Its soldiers were not Frenchmen fighting for France; they were adventurers fighting for a captain and for booty. The army did not represent a nation or a

cause, but only a man.   France was tired of war.   To
use a much-quoted phrase, " The mothers had joined
the priests of all the churches in resistance to war."
The 128,000 soldiers who took part in the campaign
across the Sambre had thus no flame of genuinely
patriotic sentiment behind them ; they were more the
followers of a great adventurer than the soldiers of a
nation.   As Maurice puts it, " The struggle was a contest of a great soldier, and of his personal adherents,
against Europe in arms.   Everything depended on
the genius of Napoleon, on the personal activity of
Napoleon, on the enthusiasm of his men for Napoleon.
There was no other link, not even that of discipline,
which held together that strange army."   And the
mood of Napoleon's soldiers towards their own officers,
it is to be noted, was one of jealous suspicion—
a suspicion that found half-tragical, half-absurd expression.

Again and again, as Napoleon rode past his columns,
some eager private would step from the ranks to
warn him against some one or other of his generals
—Soult, or Ney, or Grouchy, or Gerard.   French
soldiers are always apt to believe they have been, or
are about to be, betrayed by their leaders.   Napoleon
himself, it may be added, so systematically deceived
his soldiers, that they were never quite sure they
were not being fed with lies ; and, as most of their
superior officers had worn the Bourbon cockade only
a few weeks before, an enthusiastic belief in their

loyalty was not very possible. And a French soldier in a suspicious mood about those who lead him is a military factor of very uncertain quality.

Blücher was, in some respects, a general very unfit to cross swords with Napoleon. He was not a scientific soldier. Muffling, who had fought and marched by his side, and knew him perfectly, gives an unconsciously amusing sketch of his general and his limitations. "Old Prince Blücher," he says, "who had passed his seventieth year, understood nothing whatever of the conduct of war; so little, indeed, that when a plan was submitted to him for approval, even relating to some unimportant operation, he could not form any clear idea of it or judge whether it were good or bad." More scientific brains, those of Gneisenau and of Muffling himself, shaped the strategy of Blücher's campaigns. Blücher, it will be remembered, once in a London drawing-room declared jestingly he was the only man in the room who could kiss his own head, and thereupon went up to Gneisenau and bestowed a sounding kiss upon his face!

But Blücher was the one rough-tongued, hot-blooded, hard-fighting battle-leader of his army, who could march with the privates, and bandy rough wit with them, and whom the privates would follow to the very cannon's mouth. His men, as he rode by the column, says Chesney, would grasp his knee joyfully with a soldier's salutation, "Good work to-

day, father." His familiar title amongst his soldiers
of " Marshal Vorwärts " tells Blücher's character as a
soldier. And Blücher had a quality of dogged loyalty
which proved of supreme importance in the coming
campaign, and which, in fact, made Waterloo possible.
" You may depend upon this," Muffling told Wellington, " when he (Blücher) has agreed to any operation
in common, he will keep his word should even the
whole Prussian army be annihilated in the act." That
was simple truth ; and it was a happy circumstance
for Europe that two such loyal and high-minded
soldiers as Blücher and Wellington stood together in
the path of Napoleon in this campaign.

In the Vienna Congress, when the news came
that Napoleon was once more at the Tuileries, the
Emperor Alexander put his hand on Wellington's
shoulder, and said, with a touch of emotion, " It is
for you to again save the world." Alone, amongst
European generals, Wellington had met and defeated,
and with greatly inferior forces, the marshals and
armies of France. He had beaten Junot at Rolica
and Vimiera ; Victor at Talavera ; Massena at Busaco ;
Ney after Torres Vedras ; Marmont at Salamanca ;
Jourdan at Vittoria, and Soult in the Pyrenees and
at Toulouse. He alone could meet Napoleon with
something of equal fame.

But the army of Wellington was a very composite
and polyglot body. Including his garrisons, it consisted of 106,000 men, of whom roughly one-third

were British, one-third German, one-third Nassauers,
Dutch, and Belgian troops. The Belgians and the
Nassauers were poor soldiers at best, and their
fidelity was even more doubtful than their courage.
Many of them had served under the French eagles,
and still wore the French uniform, with a Dutch or
Belgian cockade added. The Belgians were French
by custom, language, and bias. Wellington's Germans,
especially the King's German Legion, were good
soldiers, but his British troops were themselves of
very mixed quality. His Peninsula veterans, the
men of Vittoria and of Toulouse, were in America,
or on the sea returning from it. His present regiments were largely composed of second battalions,
crowded with recruits from the militia, and still
wearing the militia uniform. Of his purely British
troops not above 6000 had yet seen a shot fired in
battle. Three out of every four, that is, were half-
drilled and wholly untested recruits. "I never saw
such a set of boys, both officers and men," was the
comment of one disgusted general after inspecting a
battalion of the 14th at Brussels: fourteen officers
and 300 men were below twenty years of age.

But a British soldier never fights better than in
his first battle; and the gallant lads, fresh from the
public schools and cricket-fields and the farm-lands
of England, who held commissions in the regiments
that fought at Waterloo, were as good fighting leaders
as any soldiers could desire. In its higher ranks the

army suffered greatly from the absurd nepotism then in vogue. Wellington's staff was crowded with youths of good blood and family, who had zeal, dash, pluck, and gaiety in ample measure, but who utterly lacked experience and knowledge. Muffling was shocked with their jests and alarmed at their ignorance, but filled with admiration at their horsemanship. "Mounted on the best horses of England's famous breed," he says, "they made it a point of honour, whenever the Duke added 'quick' to a message, to ride across country three German miles (twelve English miles) in the hour."

It would, perhaps, be unfair to judge the army that held Quatre Bras and won Waterloo by Wellington's comments upon it. "I have got," he wrote, "an infamous army, very weak and ill-equipped, and a very inexperienced staff." "The worst army I ever commanded," he says again. "I really believe," was his disgusted summary, "that with the exception of my old Spanish infantry, I have got not only the worst troops, but the worst-equipped army, with the worst staff, ever brought together." Twenty-five years after Waterloo was won, Wellington repeated his judgment that it was "an infamously bad army, and the enemy knew it. But, however," he added on reflection, "it beat them." That, after all, is sufficient virtue in an army! "I might have expected," he grumbled to Lord Bathurst, three weeks before Waterloo was

fought, "the generals and the staff formed by me
in the late war would have been allowed to me
again; but instead I am overloaded with people I
have never seen before." He describes himself as
"commanding a very small British army with a very
large British staff, to which my superiors are making
additions every day." He begged the War Office to
send him some more soldiers instead of sending him
so many generals.

Wellington, it must be admitted, was accustomed
to talk somewhat wildly on the subject of his
soldiers. It is possible to quote the most contradictory opinions on the subject from his lips. The
English soldiers of that period, he once said, "were
the mere scum of the earth; they have all enlisted
for drink." But in another mood he was accustomed to say that he owed all his success to his
soldiers. "Their soldiers," he said, "got the French
marshals into scrapes; mine got me out." Of his
Peninsula troops Wellington was justly proud. Once
after Waterloo, at a dinner party, the quality of
English soldiers was being discussed. Sweeping the
table energetically with his closed hand, Wellington
said, "Had I had at Waterloo the army that broke
up at Bordeaux, I should have swept him [Napoleon]
off the face of the earth in two hours!"

A proof of how commanders were thrust upon
Wellington by mere Court influence is found in the
fact that the Prince of Orange, who had been an

aide-de-camp in the Peninsula, was put in command
of Wellington's first corps. He was a gallant youth,
only twenty-two years of age, with exactly the
virtues required in an aide-de-camp. Colborn describes him as "a growing lad." And he was given
command of an army corps, and was technically
Wellington's second in command! At Quatre Bras,
and again at Waterloo, he simply destroyed a fine
regiment by a rash and foolish order.

The history of the campaign just beginning bristles
with disputed points, debates that turn on minute
questions of time or of distance, and about which the
experts are in a state of violent civil war amongst
themselves. A mere recital of the unsettled prob-
lems of the Waterloo campaign would stretch through
pages. They include such questions as "What was
Napoleon's real plan, and was that plan, in a military
sense, justifiable?" "Had Blücher and Wellington
agreed on a common strategy in case Napoleon advanced against them?" "Was Wellington justified
in his long delay in concentrating his troops?"
"Ought he to have concentrated at Nivelles or
at Quatre Bras?" "Did Napoleon give Ney express orders to seize Quatre Bras?" "Was Wellington right in maintaining his headquarters so
long at Brussels?" "Did Blücher fight Ligny re-
lying on Wellington's unfulfilled promise to come
to his help?" &c., &c. The literature of the four
days' campaign is of amazing abundance. The

list of "Waterloo" books given by Ropes stretches through ten pages, and might easily be trebled.

The latest writer on the story of the Waterloo campaign has, of course, one advantage over his predecessors. He hears all the witnesses. He listens while—to quote English writers alone—Chesney replies to Hooper, Maurice to Chesney, and Ropes to Maurice. And with every new volume issued some error is corrected, some surviving delusion exploded. It might almost be said that the farther off in point of time the critic of Waterloo stands, the greater is the chance of his learning its real story. For, in the keen acid of criticism, one blunder after another is in turn dissolved.

A study of the Waterloo literature, it is true, tends to shake the student's faith in the accuracy of history in general. Nowhere else can be found such a procession of examples of the shortness of the human memory, the bias of the human reason, and the impish qualities of the human imagination. Less than a year after Waterloo, Wellington described the battle as "one of the most interesting events of modern times," and added that "he entertained no hopes of ever seeing an account of all its details which shall be true." "I am really disgusted and ashamed," he wrote again, "with all accounts that I have seen of the battle of Waterloo."

It is unnecessary to dwell upon Napoleon's St. Helena fictions. His most friendly critic can only suggest that in writing them he honestly mistook his imagination for his memory. But Wellington himself, the most resolutely accurate of men, has contributed many errors to the literature of the great battle. He wrote the history of the campaign in his despatches, and while the echoes of the guns of Quatre Bras and Waterloo had scarcely died into silence. Twenty-seven years afterwards he dictated a series of notes on the campaign, in reply to the criticisms of Clausewitz ; and the notes contradict the despatches on the gravest points, and both alike are at many points demonstrably wrong. And if Wellington proved unequal to the task of giving an accurate account of the campaign of Quatre Bras and Waterloo, what wonder is it if every one else has failed ?

CHAPTER XII

THE CURTAIN LIFTS!

NAPOLEON'S columns were in movement towards the bridges across the Sambre at three o'clock on the morning of June 16. By noon the river was crossed and Ziethen's outposts struck. Ziethen showed so bold a front against the overwhelming masses converging upon him, that for a while he checked their march. The Prussian general, however, made two blunders; he failed to destroy the bridges over the Sambre, and he failed to send word to Wellington of the French advance. He sent the news promptly to Blücher, and "Marshal Vorwärts" acted with all the impetuosity on which Napoleon calculated. On learning, indeed, of the reflection of the French watch-fires in the night-sky above Charleroi twenty-four hours before, he gave orders for all his corps to be in readiness to move. On the afternoon of June 15 he transferred his own headquarters from Namur to Sombreffe, and three of his corps were pressing at speed towards the point of concentration at Ligny. Bülow's corps, it is true, was at Liège, fifty miles distant, and failed to reach

the scene of action in time. But on the night of the
15th, Blücher had 60,000 men in or near to Ligny;
on the morning of the 16th he had 80,000. It was
not for nothing that Blücher has been described as
"a hussar general." Within twenty-four hours of
Napoleon's crossing the Sambre, Blücher stood in his
path ready to give battle with 80,000 men.

Napoleon reckoned that Blücher could not concentrate his full strength in less than forty-eight
hours, and that space of time was, for Napoleon,
his supreme opportunity. Ziethen's corps stood in
his path, and must meet, almost unsupported, the
first onfall of Napoleon's converging columns. But
Ziethen, as we have seen, stubbornly fighting, fell
back and escaped undestroyed, a fact due to the
seemingly trivial circumstance that the French
fourth corps, under Gerard, started late, and so
failed to come up in time to fall on Ziethen's flank
as the Prussians fell back before D'Erlon and Reille.
The active campaign began before sunrise on June
15th. "The hour of five o'clock on the afternoon
of the 16th," says Horsbury, "marks the turn-
ing-point when the fortunes of Napoleon began to
decline." By that hour it was clear that Ziethen
had escaped Napoleon's stroke, and that Blücher
would be able to effect at least a partial concentration of his army. So soon did fortune declare
itself! Yet Napoleon last and least of all men
discerned this. He was full of confidence—a con-

fidence which encouraged mere loitering and ruinous delay.

Great events in war sometimes turn on strange trifles, and all the accidents of the campaign were not friendly to the Allies. Blücher's despatch to Bülow on the 15th, directing him to bring up his corps, reached Hermut, Bülow's headquarters, when Bülow himself happened to be at Liège. His chief of staff judged the despatch from the look of its envelope to be of no consequence, and neither opened it nor forwarded it. It lay at Hermut unopened till Bülow himself found it there at ten o'clock the next day! That blunder involved the loss of ten hours to Bülow's corps. If it had not happened, Ligny would have had another issue, and Waterloo might never have been fought!

Wellington was much slower than Blücher, a fact due to many causes. It was only betwixt five and seven o'clock on the evening of the 15th that he sent orders to his scattered divisions to stand in instant readiness to march. At ten o'clock on the same evening he sent orders to them to move eastward. It is asserted—and denied—that more definite orders were sent a little later—orders which still remain unverified and undiscovered. But it is known that early in the morning of the 16th he did send decisive orders for his troops to concentrate at Quatre Bras. Blücher thus had practically assembled 80,000 men at Ligny, and was ready for battle, when Wellington had only despatched the orders for his far-scattered columns to march on Quatre Bras.

It was by an accident, indeed, independent of Wellington's volition, that Quatre Bras was held at all by his troops on the morning of the 16th. Prince Bernhardt, when he realised that the French were moving in the direction of Charleroi, had marched with his brigade to Quatre Bras without orders. The strategic value of that position was plain. The road from Charleroi to Brussels intersects at Quatre Bras the road running from Nivelles to Namur. The French, moving from Charleroi, would be sure to seize it; and if seized, Wellington's communications with Blücher were fatally broken. Prince Bernhardt's outposts, as a matter of fact, were attacked by Reille's advance about 5 P.M. on the 15th, but held their ground. At 11 P.M. that evening, Wellington's five o'clock order from Brussels came, directing the division to which Prince Bernhardt's brigade belonged to collect at Nivelles. The divisional commander, however, in view of the facts before him, disobeyed that order, and pushed his whole division on to Quatre Bras.

Thus Quatre Bras was occupied on the afternoon of the 15th, and held up to eleven o'clock that night, not only without orders from Wellington, but contrary to his orders. Had Wellington's instructions been obeyed, when Ney came up on the morning of the 16th, he would have found Quatre

Bras empty of troops. Prince Bernhardt did what Wellington would have done had he been on the ground, not what Wellington ordered from a distance of thirty-three miles. To quote Chesney, "At dark, thirty hours after his first warning, Wellington had only present at Quatre Bras three-eighths of his infantry, one-third of his guns, and one-seventh of his cavalry. Truly, in holding his own, the great Englishman owed something that day to Fortune!"

But Wellington was cruelly served by both his allies and his own staff in the matter of news. The French columns from early dawn on the 15th had been pressing through Charleroi; for eleven hours Prussians and Frenchmen had been contending in the valley of the Sambre, within ten miles of the British outposts at Frasnes, and within less than forty miles of Wellington's own headquarters at Brussels. Yet Wellington, ill-served by his own staff, and left without news by the Prussians, was peacefully unconscious of it all! "Napoleon has humbugged me, by G——!" he said to the Duke of Richmond on the night of the famous ball. "He has gained twenty-four hours' march on me!" But it was not so much that Napoleon had "humbugged" him; his own allies and staff had failed him.

It is curious to note that all three armies suffered tragically from the defective quality of their staffs. It was a blunder of Blücher's staff which robbed him of the aid of Bülow's corps at Ligny. Ney can hardly

be said to have had a staff at Quatre Bras; he had
only a single aide-de-camp when Napoleon put him
in command of his left wing and bade him cross
weapons with Wellington at Quatre Bras. It was a
blunder on the part of an officer of his staff which
cost Napoleon the services of D'Erlon's column at
the battlefields of Ligny and of Quatre Bras. It was
the defective quality of the staff again which, after
Ligny, left Napoleon in ignorance both of what had
happened to Ney and whither the Prussians had
gone. "It is most curious," says Maurice, "that
within the few days of this short campaign almost
every blunder that a staff ought to avoid seems to
have been committed by some one of the three
staffs." And yet these staffs were composed, not of
amateurs, but of experts!

A curious picture of the state of ignorance of the
enemy's movements which prevailed at the British
headquarters is given in the letters of Sir A. Frazer.
Frazer was in command of the British horse-artillery,
and attached to headquarters, and so was within the
inner circle of affairs; but writing at Brussels on June
15 at 10 P.M., he records how he had just learned
from General Kempt that the enemy was moving on
Mons! He had found on his table an invitation from
Wellington's chief of staff to dinner next day. "All
depends," he says, "on the news which may arrive in
the night. . . . It is now half-past eleven." Seven
hours afterwards, at 6 A.M on June 16, Frazer

writes again, "I have just heard the Duke moves in half-an-hour. . . . Nothing can be done to-day." Yet this was the day of Quatre Bras! Later still he writes, "Our army is concentrating at Braine l'Aleud." At the moment when Frazer was writing those lines Napoleon was across the Sambre, there had been eleven hours' fighting between Charleroi and Fleurus, and Blücher's three corps were concentrating at Ligny. The great fight of Quatre Bras was almost beginning! Yet, with such great events transpiring at a distance so short, there was this curious state of ignorance and uncertainty at Wellington's headquarters.

But, apart from the lack of intelligence by which Wellington was perplexed, it is easy to see inside his brain, in a sense, and to understand why he acted so slowly where Blücher moved with such swift energy. He held, with Napoleon, that "war is not a conjectural art." A good general will be sure of his facts before he moves. Wellington was stubbornly preoccupied by the conviction that Napoleon would move by Mons to turn his right; and till he knew definitely that Napoleon was advancing, in mass, along the Charleroi road on his centre, Wellington would not stir. He was perplexed, that is, betwixt two possible movements on the part of his great antagonist, and would not stir till that perplexity was solved. Blücher had no such conflict of anxious alternatives to perplex his brain. His left was covered by the steep, bare, cold plateaux of the Ardennes. If Napo-

leon struck at him at all, it *must* be on his right. So
when, early on the 15th, Blücher heard that the
French were crossing the Sambre, no divided purpose
paralysed his movements.   He was able to act swiftly
and with energy.

Wellington heard the news that Napoleon was
advancing towards Brussels twelve hours later than
Blücher.   There remained the doubt whether he
would advance by Mons or Genappes.   Was Wellington's right, or his left, threatened?   Had Wellington's own headquarters been at Nivelles, instead
of at Brussels, his doubt would have been quickly
ended, and it seems plain that the British general
erred by not being himself earlier at the front.   But
even when Wellington found he must concentrate
on his left, there yet remained the question whether
he should concentrate at Nivelles or at Quatre Bras.
It was perilous to fix the gathering point of his
troops too near the enemy's stroke.   Maurice argues
with great force that Wellington never intended to
concentrate at Quatre Bras.   Napoleon did not
expect him to concentrate there.   "And," says
Maurice, "when Wellington and Napoleon are both
entirely agreed on a question of war, he is a bold
man who traverses their opinion."   Quatre Bras, in
a word, was too near the enemy to be a safe gathering
point for Wellington's scattered forces.   It seems
clear that, for this reason, Wellington meant at first
to concentrate at Nivelles.   This explains the first

set of orders issued at ten o'clock on the night of the 15th. The British divisions were to march to their left; the final point of assemblage was not fixed; Wellington was hesitating betwixt Nivelles and Quatre Bras. Then came the news that Blücher was standing to deliver battle at Ligny, and this determined Wellington to take the risk of concentrating at Quatre Bras.

Maurice's theory is the most rational. Before going to the historic ball of the Duchess of Richmond, Wellington had fixed 4 A.M. as the hour of parade of the troops. Later and fuller news coming, he issued a new set of orders, fixing 2 A.M. as the time of the parade. These orders, it is true, are not preserved. De Lancey, Wellington's deputy quartermaster-general, was slain at Waterloo and his papers lost; but this theory of a double set of orders fits into the facts and explains them.

The fact that not a few officers at the famous ball did not change their dress on joining their regiments, but marched and fought in pumps and silk stockings, is easily explained by this change of orders. The order fixing 2 A.M. had been sent to their quarters, and their orderlies had packed up their baggage. Hence, on going to their rooms, expecting to parade at 4 A.M., these officers learned the change of hour, found their baggage gone, and had to follow in ballroom rig. The Duke long afterwards said that he refused to postpone the ball out of regard for what might prove its effect on public opinion in Brussels. "It was a thing desirable in itself," says Lord Ellesmere, "to postpone to the last the inevitable moment of alarm."

The ball has been made immortal by Byron's glowing lines; but it is not the accident that a poet's genius has wedded it to imperishable verse which has given the ball before Waterloo so secure a place in human memory. Never before or since was the gaiety of a ball so closely linked to the pathos of a tragedy. The bugles had sounded before the orchestra ceased. Before the evening of the following day many of the Duchess's gilded *corps de ballet* were stretched bloody corpses in the rye at Quatre Bras. The list of the guests is preserved, some 220 in all; and it is pathetic to note for how many gallant soldiers that ball was the brief prelude to a bloody death. The ball-room itself has been identified by the care of Sir William Fraser. "The windowed niches" of "that high hall" are entirely due to Byron's imagination. The room in which the ball was held was a narrow low-roofed apartment, only thirteen feet high. It was once a coach-maker's depôt; it is now a brewery!

A new bit of evidence on the question of Wellington's orders on the night of the 15th has emerged since Mr. Ropes' careful study of the question. In his "Diary of a Cavalry Officer," Tomkinson records that Alten, then at Mons, sent an aide-de-camp on the night of the 15th with a special report to Wellington; this messenger arrived at Brussels about three on the morning of the 16th, and going to the Duke's house, requested to see him. He was shown into his room, where the Duke was lying down in his clothes. He told him all he had heard and delivered his letter. The Duke said, "Then it is your opinion it is their intention to attack us?" He replied it was his opinion they would. The Duke then said, "Ride immediately to Waterloo, where you will find Sir Thomas Picton with his division, and order him to turn the troops out at once." He did so, and five minutes after he arrived the Duke himself rode up, and directed the troops to move on Quatre Bras. This seems to fix the moment at which the order to concentrate at Quatre Bras was given.

Wellington, it may be added, in other respects than the collection of news, was badly served by his headquarters staff. On the night of the 15th his chief of staff supplied him with a memorandum showing "the disposition of the British army at 7 A.M. on the 16th June." That "disposition" represented not actual facts, but only the sanguine calculations of Wellington's chief of the staff. The "disposition," as it happened, was in hopeless quarrel with facts. Wellington, on the evidence of his own senses, might have known that the statement supplied him by his quartermaster-general was wrong. He had himself, on his ride to Blücher's headquarters on the morning of the 16th, passed Picton's division halted at Waterloo, where it was to wait for orders to advance to Nivelles or Quatre Bras. Yet, according to his quartermaster-general, that division was at that very moment beyond Waterloo, marching to Genappes, where it would arrive at noon!

Yet Wellington somehow accepted the official report in good faith, and set out from Brussels on the early dawn of the 16th with a cheerful though quite mistaken impression, as to the nearness of his troops to the threatened point. He embodied this mistaken return in a letter to Blücher, and that unfortunate letter, exhumed and printed more than fifty years afterwards, has been made the basis of the charge that Wellington deliberately deceived the Prussian staff in order that, expecting help from the English which could not be given, Blücher might stand and fight at Ligny, and thus give the English time to concentrate in safety. There is evidence that Wellington himself keenly resented the blunder into which his staff had betrayed him, and his bitter references years afterwards to the very bad staff with which he had to work the Waterloo campaign refer to this incident. His staff had put his personal honour in peril by making him the vehicle of untrustworthy information.

Napoleon, just outside Charleroi, was joined by

Ney. That gallant and ill-fated soldier had been out of favour; but, when entering on an adventure so desperate, Napoleon could not leave the bravest battle-leader in France idle, and he had summoned Ney to his side. Ney, with the help of borrowed money and horses, and accompanied by a single aide-de-camp, reached the bridge at Charleroi just as Napoleon crossed, and was at once put in command of Napoleon's left wing, consisting of the corps of Reille and D'Erlon and some cavalry brigades, and ordered to push towards Quatre Bras. Napoleon himself took the Fleurus road on the tracks of the retiring Prussians.

When night fell on the 15th, Napoleon, with 100,000 men, was thus within striking distance of Blücher, who had only three corps out of four assembled. His left wing, under Ney, had before it the road to Brussels barred by only a single Belgian brigade at Quatre Bras; while Wellington had not set a single division in movement towards the threatened point. The night of the 15th, in a word, found Napoleon a satisfied and happy strategist. Yet, as a matter of fact, Napoleon was already wandering in a realm of delusions. He believed there were only 40,000 Prussians before him. He could easily crush, he calculated, the force in his path, and then join Ney to destroy Wellington and seize Brussels.

CHAPTER XIII

QUATRE BRAS

MUFFLING relates how, at midnight of the 15th, Wellington came into his room. He knew now that Napoleon was aiming at Charleroi. Orders, he said, for the concentration at Nivelles and Quatre Bras had been despatched. "Let us go," he said, "to the ball of the Duchess of Richmond; after which, about five o'clock, we can ride off to the troops assembled at Quatre Bras." So he attended that famous gathering, the echoes of whose music are still audible in the cadences of Byron's noble lines.

A little after seven next morning Wellington was riding to Quatre Bras. From Quatre Bras, where all was quiet, he rode to Ligny, and in a mill at Bussy he held a memorable interview with Blücher. On the way he met Hardinge, the English Commissioner on the Prussian staff, who, on the part of Blücher, was seeking Wellington to ask his co-operation. "How are they forming?" asked Wellington abruptly, as Hardinge turned his horse to ride back to the Prussian lines. "In column, not in line," was Hardinge's answer; "the Prussian soldier, Blücher says, will not stand in line." "Then the artillery will play upon them, and they will be beaten damnably," said Wellington; and that somewhat profane sentence is a sufficiently accurate forecast of the battle of Ligny.

From the window of the mill at Bussy, Blücher and Wellington watched Napoleon's forces taking up their positions for battle. It was agreed that Wellington, after pushing the French in his front aside, should advance to where he could join hands with Blücher. "Well," said Wellington, as the brief debate closed, "I will come provided I am not attacked myself." Before the generals parted Wellington said to Blücher, "Well, every general knows his own men, but if my lines were drawn up in this fashion, I should expect to get beaten." And to his own staff, as he rode off, he said, "If Bonaparte be what I suppose he is, the Prussians will get a —— good licking to-day."

That interview in the mill at Bussy is picturesque as showing how completely Napoleon had failed in his strategy, and how unconscious he was of his failure. He had hoped to separate Blücher and Wellington, but at that moment they were in the mill of Bussy together, watching the French columns deploy, and agreeing on the strategy which led to Waterloo. But that interview also settles the question whether Blücher fought Ligny, as Wellington two days later fought Waterloo, in reliance upon promised help from his brother general. The

plain facts we have recited are decisive. The famous
interview in the mill of Bussy took place between one
and two o'clock on the 16th. The French columns
were deploying at that very moment for attack.
Blücher's army was in battle order, and committed to
the engagement. According to Muffling's account of
the interview the Duke asked, "What do you want me
to do?" With some difficulty the part Wellington
might take was settled; but Wellington only agreed
contingently: "All right! I'll come if I'm not myself
attacked." He was attacked. When he reached
Quatre Bras he found the fight already raging, and
the struggle held him fast till nightfall. But Blücher
had committed himself to battle before that con-
tingent agreement was made, and independently of
it; though, no doubt, he calculated on some form of
help from Wellington.

Wellington reached Quatre Bras and found the
great fight begun. Ney, it is true, had loitered long,
had failed to concentrate his forces, and was even
now attacking with only 18,000 bayonets and sabres
and 38 guns, when he might have attacked with
double those numbers. But Quatre Bras was held
at that moment by less than 7000 Dutch-Belgian
troops with 17 guns, and when Wellington rode
up the position was on the point of being carried.
Muffling says that in the presence of a crisis so deadly
and sudden Wellington took "a resolution worthy of
a great commander." He tried, in homely language,

a magnificent game of pure bluff. With loud beating of drums, he led out his left wing to attack the French, and as the fields were deep with bearded corn, the real weakness of Wellington's attack was concealed.

The French halted. That clamour of martial sound, that vision of mounted officers and of regimental flags above the yellow corn seemed to threaten an overwhelming attack. A pause in the fighting took place, and presently far up the low ridge north of Quatre Bras were visible deep red masses of troops. It was Picton's division! The men had left Brussels at five o'clock in the morning, had halted to cook their dinners at noon, when news came to the resting troops of the peril at Quatre Bras. They flung away their dinners, fell into column, and pressing forward, reached Quatre Bras a little after three o'clock, having marched twenty-one miles practically without food.

Quatre Bras consisted of three or four houses at the junction of four roads, the Brussels road, which ran north and south, being crossed at an inclined angle by the road from Nivelles to Namur. The field of battle was a slope of hedgeless farm-lands on which the ripening wheat stood thick and deep. The road to Charleroi ran straight down the slope, an isolated house standing beside the road about 250 yards in advance of Quatre Bras. Here the Duke of Brunswick was killed. Some 600 yards farther was the farmhouse of Gemioncourt. On the western side of the Charleroi road, and diverging from it, stretched the wood of Bossu; another wood defined the eastern side of the battlefield. And on that triangle of golden wheat-field, framed on either side with dark forest, with the gentle ridge 1000 yards distant on which stood Ney's batteries, raged for five heroic and desperate hours the battle of Quatre Bras.

The French had at the outset an overwhelming advantage in numbers; all through the fight their guns overpowered the British, and their superiority in cavalry gave them complete command of the attack. They had early seized the cluster of buildings at Gemioncourt, with a corresponding cluster some 800 yards eastward, and they quickly gained possession of the Bossu wood. They were thus able, in perfect safety, to form their columns for a rush on the British centre, and, under the screen of the wood, could scourge with their fire the British right. Wellington, in a word, with every disadvantage of situation, had to fight horse, foot, and artillery with his infantry alone, and of his infantry the greater part being Dutch-Belgian, either could not fight or would not. Kincaid, for example, in his "Adventures in the Rifle Brigade," describes how Barnard tried to persuade a battalion of Belgian infantry to advance in skirmishing order. "As often as the word 'march' was given to this battalion, it stood stock-still, and broke into wild firing into space;" a firing which smote the nearest British, but was quite harmless to the distant French. After repeated experiments, it was found that these extraordinary troops were more dangerous to their allies than to

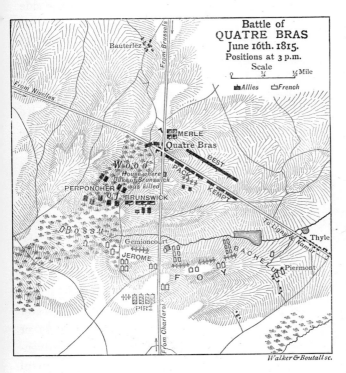

the enemy, and they were allowed to stand back from the line, silent and safe; their contribution to the struggle consisting merely in "the moral effect their presence might have on the French!"

Wellington's peril thus lay in the fact that he had a weak artillery, no cavalry, while of his infantry half was either poor in soldiership or of doubtful loyalty.   At half-past two the French were three to one in numbers; and though successive reinforcements by the time the battle ended transferred the advantage in numbers to Wellington, yet the manner in which the reinforcements arrived—at distant intervals, in small bodies, and nearly all exhausted with long marches—told greatly to the disadvantage of the British.   The French superiority in cavalry enabled them to keep the British infantry constantly on the defensive and in squares; and in that formation the French guns, firing at short range, wrought immense slaughter.   Ney, it may be added, had reserves within easy reach which would have doubled his fighting force and enabled him, beyond all doubt, to have driven Wellington back.   That he failed to use his reserves, and fought Quatre Bras with 20,000 troops, when he might have put 40,000 in battle-line, is the true secret of the French failure.

Just as Picton's division came up, the French had carried Gemioncourt on the Charleroi road, and a cluster of houses called Piermont, a mile eastward of that road.   The 95th was sent to retake Piermont, and the 28th to drive the French out of Gemioncourt, but both regiments failed in their attack.   A brigade of Dutch-Belgian cavalry, which covered their retreat, broke, and galloped from the field, and the strain of the battle fell upon the dogged British regiments. Two great French columns now advanced across the open plain eastward of Gemioncourt on Quatre Bras, and Wellington sent Kempt's and Pack's brigades to meet them with the bayonet. Picton led the attack, and through the wide stretch of rustling corn the hostile lines, edged with darting musketry fire, steadily approached each other. The interval between them narrowed. Presently the French line slackened its march. It was cruelly wasted by the rolling volleys of the British; it wavered, paused; the bayonets in the British line fell to the charge, and with a shout Picton's men ran in. Then the French broke, and the disordered mass was swept down the slope in disordered retreat.

The Duke of Brunswick, in command of some Brunswick battalions, was holding the position betwixt the wood of Bossu and the Charleroi road. He kept his young troops steady by coolly riding to and fro in front of them, smoking his pipe. A French column, under Foy, moved up to the attack, and the Duke led a charge of the lancers against the advancing column. The lancers rode forward, but presently began to draw rein. They visibly shrank from the steady line of French muskets, and, turning, they galloped back in disorder to the ridge, and swept the Brunswick troops away in their rush, the Duke himself falling mortally wounded while trying to rally them. Lancers and Brunswickers, a flying

mass, with the French chasseurs riding exultantly
and slaying fiercely in their rear, crashed upon the
front of the 92nd Highlanders, holding the Namur
road as it forms an angle with the Charleroi road.

The Highlanders coolly wheeled one company
back, let the confused mass through, then swiftly
re-forming their line, poured upon the eager French
horsemen a deadly volley. As the French cavalry
drew off, a regiment of Brunswick hussars was
launched in pursuit. The French turned on their
pursuers, the hussars broke, and back once more on
the 92nd came the torrent of flight and pursuit. The
Duke of Wellington was caught in the rush, and
escaped by riding straight to the ditch lined by the
Highlanders, and leaping over the fence in their front.
He was personally attacked by a French officer, who
was shot by one of the Highlanders.

A brigade of French lançers rode through the
British line, swept past the flank of the 42nd and 44th,
and wheeling round with great cleverness, attacked
the rear of these regiments. The 42nd was caught
with its square half formed, and the lancers rode in
at a gallop upon it, spearing many. But a Scottish
square with one face destroyed, and a crowd of French
lancers storming in upon it, is yet a formidable bit
of fighting machinery. The inner faces of the square
poured a murderous fire on the reckless lancers, and
every Frenchman was shot or bayoneted. But the
colonel of the 42nd was slain, his lieutenant-colonel

and major were wounded, and when the regiment, after that wild struggle, shook itself into shape again, its command had changed hands no less than four times in less than ten minutes. It would be difficult to find in the records of war another example of a square half broken by cavalry which unaided had yet succeeded in destroying its attackers and recovering its own formation.

The 44th was caught by the swift lancers almost at the same moment as the 42nd, for the deep corn hid the horsemen till they were close at hand. The colonel of the 44th showed cool judgment and quick decision. There was no time to "form square." "Rear rank, right about face," came the sudden order. The rear rank turned, the men held their fire till the horses were nearly touching them, and then their sudden shattering fire wrecked the charge. Some daring lancers who survived the bullets rode furiously on to the very line of the 44th. One grey-haired veteran, charging straight at the colour party, drove his lance through the face of the ensign carrying the flag, and strove to seize the colour. The wounded ensign, however, staggering from the dreadful thrust of the lance, flung the colour on the ground, and threw himself on it to protect it. The desperate Frenchman strove to pick up the colour on the point of his lance, and was bayoneted in the attempt. Pack's brigade lost in the furious fight of that day 800 men out of 2200, and the 42nd and 44th were so

reduced in numbers that late in the struggle they had
to join in making a single square.

A French column during this struggle had seized
the solitary house in advance of Quatre Bras.   The
92nd, led by General Barnes, stormed the building
and drove out the Frenchmen; but every second man
in the 92nd was killed or wounded.   Kellerman, perhaps the finest cavalry leader next to Murat in the
French army, had, by this time, come up with the
11th heavy cavalry division, and Ney galloped up
to him and told him that " on him depended the fate
of France." He must charge and break through the
stubborn infantry that held Quatre Bras.   Kellerman,
with two regiments of cuirassiers, each 400 strong,
came at a trot along the Charleroi road, swung to the
right on the open slope, and rode at speed on the
British line, and his cuirassiers flung themselves in
turn upon the 42nd and the 44th.   Picton, as he had
no cavalry, took the Royals and the 28th in single
column down to the fight, infantry attacking cavalry!
Deep into the tumult of horsemen he led his column
till near enough to the sorely-pressed squares of the
42nd and 44th to cover them with his fire; then he
suddenly flung the Royals and the 28th into square.

The French horsemen rode again and again on to
the steady British front.   The squares stood in rye so
deep that only the bayonets of the men were visible
above it, and the charging horsemen, as they rode
down on the squares, seemed to be wading through a

sea of grain.   The French resorted to the device of
sending down a single lancer at speed to plant a lance
in front of a British square, and form a point upon
which they could ride.   This wild combat of cavalry
and squares raged for a considerable time, a picture
in little of the still greater contest of sabre against
bayonet which was to take place two days later on the
ridge at Waterloo.

The two brigades of cuirassiers, led by Kellerman
in person, had one stroke of good fortune.   Halkett,
who had brought up his division to the fight, despatched the 69th to the assistance of Pack's brigade.
It was in the act of forming square when the Prince
of Orange rode up and bade it stand in line.   Its
colonel, Morice, said he expected the French cavalry
to be upon them in another minute, but the Prince
scornfully declared that no attack was to be feared.
At that moment Kellerman, riding at the head of
800 cuirassiers, came at speed up the road.   With
the glance of a born cavalry commander, he saw the
69th was unready.   Wheeling his squadrons sharply
to the right, he rode in on the ill-fated 69th, and
well-nigh destroyed it.   In less than ten minutes
every fourth man in the regiment was wounded or
killed.   One of the colours of the 69th was captured,
and the survivors of the wrecked regiment escaped
by taking refuge under the bayonets of the nearest
British square.   As an actor in the scene describes
it : "Suddenly the ridge in front grew dark with

huge straight-sworded, steel-clad horsemen, and through the tangled rye swept Kellerman's cuirassiers. Before this rush of horses no men in line could stand. From right to left the regiment became a shapeless wreck, and the triumphant cuirassiers rode onwards, leaving 150 dead or dying men in the blood-stained rye, and bearing with them a single British colour."

The lancer brigade on the east of the road attacked three faces of the 28th simultaneously. The men of the 28th have numbers on both the back and the front of their hats, in commemoration of their exploit in Egypt in 1801, when the regiment was attacked in rear and front, and the rear rank facing about, repelled the enemy. At the moment when the shaken square at Quatre Bras was attacked on three faces at once, Picton steadied it by shouting in his deep lion-like voice, "28th, remember Egypt!"

Kellerman's mail-clad squadrons rode into the very heart of the British position, but a battery, which Wellington had placed in the line of the charge, smote their front, the unshaken lines of British infantry on either flank raked them with steady volleys, and the cuirassiers found themselves riding in a blinding tempest of fire. Kellerman's horse was shot, and when their leader fell, the cuirassiers wheeled, broke, and galloped in tumult back. Kellerman himself threw his arms across the necks of two of his soldiers' horses, and was carried off the field with the flight of his men. That flight went far. The mass of disordered cuirassiers, as it still stormed rearwards, caught in the whirl of its rush the lancer brigade; it next broke a brigade of chasseurs. The tumult of maddened horses and disorganised men, two miles from the field, swept on another body of French cavalry, 2500 strong, moving up to the fight, drew it away in its stampede, and never pulled rein till it reached Frasnes!

Odd gleams of humour flit occasionally, even across the grim visage of war. The Rifles, in the crisis of the fight at Quatre Bras, were moved to a position along the Namur road. The men were brought up by a thick quick-set hedge. The French were just beyond; and the Rifles were cheerfully willing to face the point of their bayonets, the flash of their musketry. But the prickles of a Belgian hedge were a more serious thing. The men halted in disgust; the hedge, indeed, did what a line of French bayonets could not have done—it stopped them. While they halted a youthful and impetuous lieutenant solved the difficulty. "Seeing the check," says the regimental record, "he went back a few paces, and, rushing at Sergeant Underwood, hit him on the knapsack and butted him through. Both rolled on the ground on the other side, which was much lower; but they soon sprang to their feet, and, the gap once made, the men poured through."

Ney, meanwhile, had despatched urgent orders for

D'Erlon's corps to come into the fight. As it happened, however, that column, 20,000 strong, was at that moment marching towards Ligny, with its back turned to Quatre Bras. Napoleon, fighting desperately at Ligny, had sent an aide-de-camp with peremptory orders to Ney to send D'Erlon's corps to join in the fight there, as soon as he had carried Quatre Bras. The aide-de-camp, riding to Quatre Bras, fell in with D'Erlon's corps on the road, showed his orders, and persuaded its commander instantly to begin his march towards Ligny.

D'Erlon's own account is that Labédoyère, the chief aide-de-camp of the Emperor, showed him a pencil note he was carrying to Ney, directing the march of D'Erlon's corps on Ligny. Labédoyère had already shown the order to Durutte at Frasnes, and D'Erlon's columns had begun their ill-fated march. D'Erlon sent his chief of staff to tell Ney what had been done, and that exasperated general found that, just when his own fate depended on D'Erlon's corps, that body had marched beyond his reach. Halkett's brigade had joined Wellington; the Guards under Cooke were coming up, and Ney sent back D'Erlon's chief of staff with peremptory instructions to that general to instantly return. D'Erlon was within sight of the fighting at Ligny when that order reached him. He obeyed it, no counter-order reaching him from Napoleon, and marching back, reached his disgusted general at 9 P.M., when the battle was

over and the defeated French had fallen back to
Frasnes.

The arrival of the Guards decisively turned the
scale in favour of the British. The French were
thrust roughly out of Gemioncourt and Piermont,
and the exhausted British bivouacked on the bloody
slope they had held with a courage so high and at a
cost so great. Wellington's loss in killed and wounded
reached 4463, and of these one-half were British.
Most of the British troops that took part in the
fight at Quatre Bras, it may be added, had marched
and fought for seventeen successive hours, and this
under a heat so great that even from the hardy ranks
of the Rifles men fell slain by the sun. Some of the
English Guards, on reaching the wood of Bossu, fell
exhausted on the ground, while their comrades went
on into the fight. The writer of "The English Army
in France" tells an odd story illustrating Wellington's
coolness. Once during those five desperate hours at
Quatre Bras, he saw the Duke lie down upon the
ground with the back of his head resting upon his
hands, and his eyes fixed upon the heavens; aides-de-
camp and others brought him intelligence incessantly,
and in that quiet posture he gave his orders!

Quatre Bras supplies another example of Wellington's amazing faculty for throwing off the burden of
great affairs at will. At the close of the long and
bloody fight, a British cavalry regiment came up
under the command of Ponsonby, who was on terms

of personal friendship with Wellington. Ponsonby relates how he found the Duke "reading some English newspapers which had just reached him, and joking over their contents." That he should have found time to read London newspapers and laugh at London jokes in the interval betwixt nightfall at Quatre Bras and the dawn of Waterloo is one of the most surprising proofs of the power of mental detachment which can be well imagined.

CHAPTER XIV

LIGNY

QUATRE BRAS was thus a French defeat, but it might easily have been a French victory. That it was not was due to Ney's failure in generalship, and to the mischance that robbed him of D'Erlon's help. Nothing could be finer than the courage with which Ney fought the battle in its later stages, and nothing more helpless than his failure to concentrate the forces under his command and use their full strength in the fight. Soult told William Napier that " Ney was the evil genius of the campaign. He neglected his orders at Quatre Bras, and again at Waterloo." Ney's orders, it is true, were vague, but he carried them out without intelligence or energy. He was to " unite the corps of Reille and D'Erlon with his cavalry, and beat and destroy any force that he might meet." Ney did not unite his corps; he left half his force (20,000 strong) at Frasnes, two and a half miles south of the cross-roads, till late in the afternoon of the 16th, when, by the impulse of a too energetic aide-de-camp, it was sent wandering off to Ligny.

Ney thus did not strictly obey his orders; he

did not act with energy; he appeared to doubt the
wisdom of pushing forward so far in advance of
the main body of the army. The truth is, Ney had
fought with the English in the Peninsula, and that
experience affected his tactics. He knew Wellington's
trick of keeping the main body of his forces out
of sight till the moment came for delivering a blow;
and his imagination, chilled by Peninsular memories,
pictured concealed masses of British infantry ready
to break out upon him from Quatre Bras and shatter
his battle-line.

The French horsemen fought magnificently. Tomkinson, himself a fine cavalry soldier, tells in his
"Diary" how he watched their charges; the lancers
with their glittering steel points, the cuirassiers in
their shining armour, and he describes them as riding
again and again with the utmost hardihood on the
front of the British squares. They were vanquished
by the cool and steady valour of the British infantry. The British private, it may be added, is of a
severely practical turn of mind. That night, when he
bivouacked amid the bodies of his slain foes and
comrades, he extracted an unexpected service from
Napoleon's much-vaunted cuirassiers. He discovered
that a dead Frenchman's cuirass forms a spacious
and delightful frying-pan; and at all the English
bivouac fires through the night which followed Quatre
Bras French cuirasses were being devoted to that
useful but inglorious office.

Meanwhile Napoleon in person had fought and won the great battle of Ligny. He lingered, strangely, all the early hours of the day, "when every hour of time," to quote Lord Wolseley, "was worth 10,000 men to the Allies." The hours of the morning went past, his troops mutely wondered at their general's inactivity, and fretted over the wasted minutes that flew by. Only at eight o'clock was Napoleon visible; not till two o'clock were his plans made up. He allowed more than seven hours of daylight in this fashion to be wasted. His apologists have urged that Napoleon was waiting for Ney to begin his attack at Quatre Bras; but Napoleon himself, who has explained many other mysterious or discreditable incidents in the campaign, has offered no explanation of this puzzle.

The truth is, Napoleon began the day with a delusion, or rather with a cluster of delusions. Only 40,000 Prussians, he believed, were in his path. Quatre Bras was unoccupied. Brussels lay defenceless under his stroke. Neither Blücher nor Wellington would stand in battle before him till their armies were concentrated. Nothing is more striking than the world of illusions in which Napoleon, whose intellect had usually the keenness as well as the hardness of a sword-blade, stood on the morning of the 16th. "The Prussians," he writes to Grouchy, "cannot oppose to us more than 40,000 men;" and at that moment Blücher stood with 90,000 men in his path! Ney, the Emperor was persuaded, had only a handful of troops before him; the business of occupying Quatre Bras was trifling. Napoleon himself expected to "reach Brussels to-morrow morning." On the morning of Ligny and Quatre Bras, that is, Napoleon anticipated neither battle. He was calmly reckoning on reaching Brussels without fighting any Waterloo!

All this, perhaps, explains Napoleon's fatal delay on that fateful morning. There was no need, he believed, for hurry. His soldiers had been marching and fighting for well-nigh sixteen hours, so he could give them a long morning's rest. And thus he loitered for so many fatal hours — from 3.30 A.M. to 1.30 P.M. In all this Napoleon fatally under-estimated both Blücher's energy and Wellington's fighting qualities.

At half-past two Napoleon began his attack, first sending orders to Ney to drive the English from Quatre Bras, and move to take the Prussians in the rear. The fight was waged with singular fury on both sides. In the streets of St. Armand French and Prussian fought hand to hand with the madness of Soudan dervishes. Gerard's troops four times carried the village of Ligny, were driven out of it thrice, and only held it when every house was blackened with smoke and splashed red with blood, and when the streets were choked with the bodies of the slain.

As Napoleon felt the strain of the battle, he became more urgent for the help he had arranged Ney should yield him. At a quarter-past three he despatched a letter to Ney urging him to manœuvre at once, so as to fall on the rear of the Prussian right wing. "The fate of France," he told Ney, was in his hands; the Prussian army was lost if he acted vigorously. He expected to see D'Erlon's corps make its appearance before six o'clock. At five o'clock Napoleon prepared for his decisive stroke. He strengthened the attack on St. Armand with the Young Guard; then with the Old Guard, Milhaud's cuirassiers, and the heavy cavalry of the Guard, he stood ready to break through the Prussian centre.

At that moment Vandamme, who was in command of the attack on St. Armand, sent word that a column of the enemy was only two miles distant, and was marching on Fleurus. Napoleon held his hand, and sent some cavalry to ascertain exactly what the approaching body was. It was D'Erlon's corps! The help he had expected had come.

Napoleon then resumed his postponed attack on the Prussian centre. Blücher had used up his last reserves, and was in no condition to resist an onfall so tremendous. The dark column of the French, in perfect array, swept up the slope, and broke through the village. Milhaud's heavy cavalry came on at a charging pace. Blücher, a "hussar general" to the last, led his remaining cavalry in one furious counter-

attack on the French. His horse was shot, and over
his fallen body the torrent of Milhaud's galloping
cuirassiers swept. Blücher's aide-de-camp saved his
general by concealing his body with his cloak till
the rush had passed. Presently the cuirassiers,
pushed fiercely by Prussian lances, ebbed back in
retreat; and Blücher, sorely bruised and shaken,
was picked up and carried off by his horsemen.

Nothing could resist the advance of the Old
Guard; but nothing could shake the obstinate long-
enduring courage of the Prussians. They were beaten,
but not broken, still less routed. Night fell, leaving
the French in possession of the battlefield, and under
the screen of night the sullen and still defiant
Prussian columns moved off the field. They had
lost 12,000 men and 21 guns; but the French loss
was only a little less, and though he had won the
battle, Napoleon had failed, though he did not yet
suspect it, in the end for which the battle was
fought. He had not crushed Blücher; he had not
torn the British and Prussian armies asunder.

As a result of the fighting on the 16th, it will be
seen that the French left wing failed at Quatre Bras,
its right wing succeeded—but hardly, and with vast
slaughter—at Ligny. Napoleon, however, missed by
the narrowest margin an overwhelming success at
both points. The fate of both battles was decided
by the wandering of D'Erlon's unhappy column.
Wellington might well have failed at Quatre Bras as

the result of his slowness in concentrating his troops. He must have failed had D'Erlon's corps come frankly into the fight at the cross-roads. Blücher, too, would have been destroyed beyond all power of rallying if, when Vandamme was fiercely pushing his right wing and Napoleon with the Old Guard and Milhaud's cuirassiers was breaking through his centre, Ney, with D'Erlon's corps, had at that supreme moment fallen upon his rear. But it failed to do this; and so Ligny was for Napoleon a quite illusive victory.

Great campaigns seem sometimes to turn on trivial incidents. It is picturesque to say that when that over-eager aide-de-camp showed to D'Erlon the order he was carrying to Ney, and persuaded him to act instantly upon what was, in fact, a mistaken reading of that order, the fate, not merely of Quatre Bras and of Ligny, but of Waterloo and of Napoleon, was decided. Yet, in a sense, that is true. Had Ney, indeed, kept a firmer grasp of the forces Napoleon put into his hand, these disasters would have been escaped. D'Erlon would have been fighting at Quatre Bras, and Wellington probably retreating, when Napoleon's aide-de-camp rode up. But the whole mischief of D'Erlon's undirected and helpless wanderings might have been remedied, again, by Napoleon himself when D'Erlon's corps came within the field of his vision. It is not clear why it took two hours to discover that the body of troops within sight was D'Erlon's corps, and not a British column marching

to the aid of Blücher. That inexplicable two hours'
delay cost Napoleon dearly. It postponed his victory
till darkness fell, and made that victory, if not worthless, yet barren. The great reproach on Napoleon's
generalship is the fact that he allowed D'Erlon
to drift on to the field of Ligny, and to drift away
again into space, without making use of him.

When all "explanations" have been offered, there
remain the plain facts of which plain sense can judge.
Napoleon allowed 20,000 men, the very force for which
he was waiting, and on which victory hung, to come
within sight and touch of his army, and then to
wander helplessly off into mere darkness and night.
He had no orders to give this corps, no use for it;
and yet its appearance was not a surprise. He had
planned for its appearance, searched the westward
running road with longing eyes for its coming, held
back his final stroke on Blücher till it came. It
arrived, like a lost and helpless sheep: it wandered
off again with sheeplike aimlessness. And Napoleon
suffered it to wander!

It is asserted vehemently, though on very doubtful
evidence, that Napoleon sent orders to D'Erlon direct,
bidding him march on Ligny. If this be so, it does
not remove the blame for the failure of the day from
Napoleon; it only shifts its incidence. For, on this
theory, after expressly ordering D'Erlon to march on
Blücher at Ligny, he allowed that general, when he
was within sight of the flashes of the guns of Ligny,

to turn round, and march aimlessly back to Frasnes. Napoleon, on this theory, had generalship enough to summon D'Erlon to his help, but neither the wit nor the purpose to make use of him when he had arrived.

In the great landscape of the fighting on June 16, while English and French charged and rallied amidst the golden wheat at Quatre Bras, and French and Prussian wrestled and slew each other amid the burning houses of St. Armand and Ligny, the strangest and most dramatic object, that which practically decided the fate of both battles and of the whole campaign, was this wandering column of 20,000 men, which looked on both battles and took part in neither !

CHAPTER XV

THE NIGHT BEFORE WATERLOO

NIGHT darkened over the two battlefields, little more than seven miles apart, strewn so thickly with the dead and the dying. Napoleon's left wing had failed at Quatre Bras; the stubborn English were not to be shaken. But Napoleon's centre and right wing had conquered at Ligny. Yet the blackened village of St. Armand—its narrow streets and wrecked houses, and the deeply trodden slope beyond literally packed with the fallen—showed how bravely the Prussians had fought, and at how deadly a cost the French had won. The French held the battlefield, but, as a matter of fact, they did not thrust an outpost beyond the Namur road.

On the high ground beyond Ligny, as their shattered and sullen battalions fell back, the Prussian staff held a brief consultation. . Blücher, sorely shaken by his fall in the last cavalry charge, could not be consulted, and Gneisenau—the brains of the Prussian army and its one strategist—had to decide on the line of retreat. On that decision hung the fate of the campaign. The communications of the

GENERAL VON GNEISENAU

From a lithograph after a drawing by F. KRUGER

Prussian and English armies diverged almost at right angles; those of the Prussians running eastward to Liège; those of the English northward to Antwerp. If each army clung to its own line as it fell back, every yard of retreat would widen the gap betwixt them. On this Napoleon calculated; and, had Gneisenau as he sat on his horse in the darkness, with the Prussian staff about him, spoken the word which turned the Prussian columns eastward, the course of history would have been changed.

He made a gallant choice, yet made it half unconsciously, and more than half reluctantly. He first gave the order to march on Tilly, a village some five miles distant. Then, finding that name not marked on the maps of his divisional leaders, Wavre was chosen. This gave a line of retreat almost parallel with that which Wellington must take when falling back towards Brussels. Wavre was a little over twenty miles from Ligny; when it was reached, less than ten miles of cross-roads would carry the Prussians to Waterloo, where it was probable Wellington would make a stand.

It seems clear that Gneisenau's order to retreat on Tilly—or, in its later form, on Wavre—did not necessarily involve the complete abandonment of the line by Liège, and did not represent a definite purpose to fight a combined battle in conjunction with the English at Waterloo. At Tilly the Prussian columns could still have wheeled eastward to Liège. It was

the fiercer spirit and more loyal purpose of Blücher
later which definitely carried the Prussian columns
to Waterloo.   Here Hardinge's story comes in.
Blücher was lying at the little village of Mellery,
a mile and a half north of Tilly; and here the debate was held which finally settled the strategy
which made Waterloo possible.   Hardinge was lying
with an amputated arm on a bundle of straw in the
room which led to that which Blücher occupied,
and all night long Gneisenau and other generals
were passing in and out of Blücher's chamber.   A
debate was raging as to the next move in the great
game of strategy, and keen arguments were urged,
with many guttural expletives, on both sides.   In the
morning Blücher burst triumphantly into Hardinge's
room crying, "Gneisenau has given way! We march
to join Wellington!"

Meanwhile both at Ligny and Quatre Bras the
night of the 16th and the morning of the 17th
brought a succession of events which cannot be
described otherwise than as surprising, even in war.
The Prussian army had vanished in the darkness, and
when the French stirred in their camp in the early
dawn of the 17th the dogged columns with which
they had wrestled for so many desperate hours had
disappeared like a procession of phantoms! Now an
army of 90,000 men, with its artillery and ammunition
waggons and its wounded, creeping heavy-footed
across country roads deep in mud, or wide plains

rich in tall crops, is not an object easily missed.   Its
pace is that of a sloth.   Its trail is scribbled deeply
across the very landscape.   This great, slow-moving
multitude, too, had vanished somewhere in the
triangle betwixt the two roads running eastward to
Liège and northward to Brussels, a perfectly definite
tract of country of quite limited area.   Napoleon had
at Ligny 10,000 of the most enterprising cavalry in
the world; their fierce squadrons might have hung
on the rear of Blücher's weary columns, harrying
them at will.   And yet the Prussians had been
allowed to disappear—whither was a mere guess, and,
as it happened, was, on Napoleon's part, wrongly
guessed.

Fourteen hours after the last guns at Ligny were
fired, Napoleon despatched Grouchy with 33,000
men to pursue these vanished Prussians in a direction
in which they had not gone!   That war is "not a
conjectural art" was a favourite saying of Napoleon's;
but on the morning after Ligny his whole strategy
was determined on a conjecture, and on a conjecture
that was wrong-headed and false.   He guessed that
Blücher had moved eastward to Namur and Liège,
and after a fatal delay he despatched Grouchy to
pursue him in that direction.   Neither Grouchy nor
Napoleon himself sent so much as a single squadron
of cavalry towards the Dyle, where Blücher's columns
were pressing on with tired feet in the direction of
Wavre and a junction with Wellington.   That

Grouchy did not encounter the Prussians, or even come across a trace of them within so small a space, is, says Thiers, almost a miracle—"a miracle of incomprehensible misfortune." But it was Napoleon who wrought that miracle of evil aspect and who was responsible for it. It was he who despatched Grouchy so late in pursuit, and who determined his line of march. His own fixed idea that Blücher was moving towards Liège was stamped as the governing impulse on Grouchy's movements. If Grouchy's cavalry scouts should have explored the country towards the Dyle, much more should those of Napoleon himself.

Thiers holds that Napoleon had, by his overmastering personality and his habit of fierce self-exaltation, destroyed in his generals the very faculty of initiative. It was dangerous for Napoleon's lieutenants to be too successful or original. One of their recognised uses was to serve as scapegoats for the Emperor. So Napoleon's generals learned to attempt nothing on their own account, scarcely even to use their own natural senses. They waited to see what Napoleon bade them see and do what he bade them do. As Napoleon sent out no cavalry to hang on the Prussian rear, no one else would stir. The mood of suspicion towards all the superior officers, which burned in the rank and file of the French army, still further disposed the French officers to attempt nothing on their own account. "If, on the night of the 16th or 17th," says Maurice, "an officer had been

seen to lead a patrol near enough to the Prussians
to detect their line of retreat, he would have been
suspected of deserting."

The inertness of Napoleon on the morning of the
17th is, indeed, one of the strangest features of this
strange campaign.   He rose late, the tired general
of a tired army.   He let the precious hours of the
morning slip past, while he wandered over the battlefield and discussed politics and metaphysics, and the
news from Paris, with his generals.   Yet it was the
crisis of the campaign, every moment of which was
charged with triumph or failure.   Napoleon had
defeated and driven into space the Prussian army;
there remained only the English.   Wellington, with
less than half his forces concentrated, and beyond all
reach of immediate help from Blücher, was within
a distance of eight or nine miles, with Ney in his
front and Napoleon on his flank.   Yet Napoleon
made no move !   Twelve hours after the last sullen
shot had been fired at Ligny, Napoleon wrote to Ney,
" The Prussian army has been put to rout: General
Pajol is pursuing it on the roads to Namur and
Liège."   Both those statements were inaccurate; the
Prussians had certainly not been " put to rout," and
they were moving, not on Liège, but on Wavre—and
Waterloo.   Pajol had before him, not Blücher's army,
but only his stragglers, and Napoleon mistook a
fringe of stragglers for three great army corps !

The same curious stupor seemed to lie on Ney as

on Napoleon.   Wellington, now thoroughly alert, was
riding along his outposts at Quatre Bras at three
o'clock in the morning; but all was quiet, and the
quiet was unbroken for hours.   In the middle of
the morning Wellington, after a keen scrutiny of the
French position through his telescope, turned to his
staff and expressed his amazement at the perfect
stillness which lay upon it, and began to speculate
whether Ney was not retiring—retiring from a British
army only equal to his own in numbers—while
Napoleon, with 90,000 good soldiers, was within easy
striking distance of the British flank!

Perhaps the most curious feature in the position of
affairs that morning was the absence of communications betwixt Napoleon and Ney.   Ney had fallen back
to Frasnes; Napoleon's headquarters were at Fleurus;
the two places were only nine miles apart.   Yet it
was eight o'clock on the morning of the 17th—eleven
hours, that is, after the last gun at Quatre Bras had
been fired—when a French officer rode into Fleurus
and brought to Napoleon the first tidings of how
the fight at Quatre Bras had ended.   And Napoleon
was as careless in sending news to Ney as in obtain-
ing news from him.   It was nearly ten o'clock in the
morning of the 17th before he sent to Ney either
intelligence or orders.   Many ingenious explanations
of this state of affairs exist; but no ingenuity of
"explanation" leaves it less than almost incredibly
strange.   Blücher, too, was slow in sending news of

his defeat and of his future plans to Wellington;
but the general of a beaten army, retreating through
the night, with all his wounded and stores, may be
forgiven for a touch of incidental forgetfulness.

The picture indeed offered by the rival armies
during the early hours of the 17th, is a curious
example of the uncertainties of war. Ney was
ignorant of what had happened to Napoleon. Napoleon knew nothing of what Ney had done, or whither
Blücher had gone. Wellington was groping for the
whereabouts of Blücher. Grouchy was pursuing a
phantom on the road to Gembloux. But the delays
of the 17th are even more wonderful than its
illusions. For twelve fatal hours Napoleon neither
undertook the pursuit of Blücher, nor joined Ney in
an attempt to crush Wellington. He could have
flung 50,000 good troops—the Guard and the 6th
corps—on Wellington's flank, while Ney, with 22,000,
attacked him in front, and Wellington had not 40,000
in hand. But for twelve hours Napoleon made no
sign. He was tired; he assumed that Wellington
had fallen back. As for himself, he went to bed and
gave instructions that he was not to be disturbed.
This was not the Napoleon of Arcola and of Austerlitz!

Meanwhile Wellington, with transcendent coolness
and audacity, was maintaining a bold front at Quatre
Bras, with Ney in his front and Napoleon on his
flank, while Blücher had vanished in the darkness

and given no sign. Frazer, his chief of artillery at
Waterloo, describes Wellington as "cold and indifferent; nay, apparently careless, at the beginning of
battles;" but, he adds, "when the moment of difficulty comes, intelligence flashes from the eyes of this
wonderful man, and he rises superior to all that can
be imagined." Those words almost exactly describe
Wellington in this campaign. If he had been "cold
and indifferent" in its opening hours, he was now in
a mood of hawk-like vigilance.

At daybreak on the 17th, his quick and watchful
eye detected French vedettes far along the Namur
road; he guessed from this Blücher had not driven
Napoleon back. His patrols soon brought him the
news that the Prussians were in retreat, and Colonel
Gordon was sent with a troop of the 10th Hussars,
to communicate, if possible, with Blücher. Gordon
overtook Ziethen in command of the Prussian rear-
guard, and learned from him full details of the result
of the battle and the march of the Prussians on
Wavre. Wellington seems to have been aggrieved
and uneasy that Blücher had sent him no direct
news. He had been left by his ally alone in the
presence of the French, and no word of intelligence
apparently had been sent to him. As a matter of
fact, a Prussian officer had been despatched with
news to Wellington. He fell in with a French
cavalry picket, was wounded, but reached the lines
of the Allies, and demanded to see some superior

officer to whom he could give his message. But his demand was neglected, and his message remained ungiven. At nine o'clock a second messenger brought direct intelligence from Blücher.

The story of how Wellington took the news is classic. Captain Bowles was standing beside the Duke at Quatre Bras on the morning of the 17th, when a Prussian staff-officer, his horse covered with sweat, galloped up and whispered an agitated message in the Duke's ear. The Duke, without a change of countenance, dismissed the messenger, and, turning to Bowles, said, "Old Blücher has had a —— good licking, and gone back to Wavre—eighteen miles. As he has gone back, we must go too. I suppose in England they will say we have been licked. I can't help it! As they have gone back, we must go too." And in five minutes, without stirring from the spot, he had given complete orders for the famous retreat to Waterloo. Wellington sent word that he would fight at Waterloo if Blücher would come to his aid with one corps. "I will join you," replied that fiery veteran, "not only with two corps, but with my whole army; and if the enemy does not attack you on the 18th, we will attack him together on the 19th."

But were these messages actually interchanged? Ropes argues, with great force of evidence, that Wellington did not receive that message till the morning of the 18th, when he was actually in position at Waterloo; and that, as a matter of fact, Wellington

accepted the risk of having to fight Napoleon single-
handed, and with inferior numbers, without any
definite promise of help from Blücher. There is,
indeed, the fact, or legend, that on the night of the
17th, Wellington mounted his famous horse, Copenhagen, and, accompanied by a single orderly, rode
over to Blücher's quarters at Wavre, and obtained the
assurance of co-operation, on the strength of which
he fought the battle of Waterloo.

It is possible to discover the most authoritative testimony both for, and against, that much-disputed interview. Wellington himself may be quoted on both sides.
He denied bluntly that the interview ever occurred;
and, at least, two witnesses independently declare the
Duke told them the story of how he paid the visit, and
the narrative has all the characteristics of Wellington's style; his bluntness, his off-hand English, his
terse detail, including the circumstance that when he
dismounted from Copenhagen, who had carried him
for ten hours, and ended up with a twenty-eight miles'
night-ride, he gave the horse a slap of approbation.
Whereupon, by way of expressing its sentiments,
Copenhagen did his best to kick the Duke!

The story must remain in the realm of things
doubtful, or at least of things unproved. It may be
taken as certain that Wellington would not have run
the tremendous risks of Waterloo without a perfectly
definite assurance of Blücher's appearance on the
battlefield. In his despatch to Lord Bathurst

after Waterloo Wellington says, "The Marshal had promised me . . . he would support me with one or more corps." Yet the most puzzling mystery exists both as to the form and the hour in which Wellington received the pledge of Blücher's help. The only letters in existence which contain such a pledge are one written near midnight on the 17th, and a second written betwixt seven and eight o'clock on the morning of the 18th.

The copy of the latter, preserved in the Prussian archives, bears a minute in Gneisenau's writing, suggesting that perhaps Wellington would not fight with resolution, but only "make a demonstration," and suggesting that the Prussian columns should not be thrown into the contest till Wellington was committed past the chance of recall. Maurice suggests that Wellington knew of the existence of this minute. He felt it was a reflection on his honour, and the dogged temper he showed at Waterloo, his own unusual self-exposure to danger there, his statement, "I and every Englishman here must remain to fight till we all lie dead upon the field," show that he felt his honour and loyalty had been challenged. But this is merely an ingenious conjecture, and it really remains still unknown on what exact evidence Wellington risked Waterloo in the expectation of Prussian help.

The truth seems to be that the combination betwixt Wellington and Blücher was of a loose, undefined, if not inarticulate sort. It was based on knowledge of each other's character and confidence in each other's loyalty, rather than on formal pledges to support each other at some given spot and at some given time. It is idle to seek for the evidences of their co-operation in official documents and carefully preserved letters. Each general understood the other and relied on the other.

At noon on the 17th, Napoleon sent orders to Ney to attack Wellington, and announced that he was moving on the English general's flank. Wellington, however, had watched the situation with keen and alert vision. The divisions in his rear were already moving towards Mont St. Jean; his infantry columns were falling back from Quatre Bras, while, with cool audacity, he still held his position at that place with his cavalry, his guns, and a battalion of Rifles. Every moment gained, of course, made surer the concentration of his forces at Waterloo. It was fine soldiership to hold on to the last moment, with Ney in his front and Napoleon moving on his flank, and then to fall back easily and coolly, and just evading his great opponent's stroke. There is no finer bit of soldiership, indeed, in the four days' campaign than Wellington's retreat from Quatre Bras.

It was past noon when, along the Namur road to Wellington's left, some crimson squadrons were seen moving, and behind them solid masses that gleamed with a curious metallic brilliancy in the June sun.

They were the red lancers of the Guard, with Milhaud's cuirassiers in support, coming on at speed. The 10th Hussars fell back skirmishing; Wellington's long cavalry line broke into columns; and, covered by the fire of his horse-artillery, the British general fell steadily back. Here was an army of 48,000 loitering apparently within the stroke of Napoleon, at the head of nearly thrice that number, and yet, by cool and skilful tactics, evading his stroke!

Napoleon himself drove in his carriage to Quatre Bras; here he leaped on his horse; the soldier awoke in him. He realised what an opportunity had been missed, and with what half - contemptuous skill Wellington was baffling him. He pushed on the pursuit in a fury of wrath. D'Erlon relates how, as Napoleon rode up to the head of his column, he cried, "They have ruined France!" But if France was "ruined" by the drowsy generalship, the loiter-ing delays of that morning, Napoleon himself was the chief cause of that "ruin." The pursuit, however, was now fierce enough. "It resembled," says a French officer who took part in it, "a stampede or a steeplechase," so eagerly were the guns pushed for-ward, so fiercely did the cavalry press on, Napoleon himself riding with the foremost files, and some-times dismounting to urge the gunners as they toiled at their pieces. But nothing shook Wellington's steady order, and his cavalry, under Lord Uxbridge, was magnificently handled, checking the too eager French with stern counter-charges, and then falling back with the speed and accuracy of a Hyde Park parade.

At Genappes a dashing cavalry fight took place. The 7th Hussars covered the British rear; they had cleared the narrow streets of the town, the red lancers following closely in pursuit; and Uxbridge, halting his heavy cavalry on the rise beyond Genappes, sent the 7th Hussars back at speed to smite the red lancers as they emerged from the narrow street. The French lancers, however, halted in the street itself. The street behind them described a curve, and the squadrons in their rear, crowding up, made a packed and solid mass which it was impossible to shake. The files in front dropped their lances to the level, making a complete front of shining points from wall to wall of the street, and on this front the hussars, coming up at a gallop, flung themselves. The lancers could not give ground; the hussars—light cavalry with their short swords — found themselves badly handicapped in the fight. Yet they hung desperately on to the front of the lancers, striving to reach their foes. The commanding officers of both the lancers and the hussars were slain, but nothing could shatter the impenetrable thicket of spear-points which formed the French front. The hussars were recalled, the lancers broke out of the town and came riding in loose order with triumphant shouts up the slope, and then Lord Uxbridge suddenly launched against them the 1st Life Guards.

Down the hill, a rush of big men on big horses, terrible in scarlet and steel, rode the Life Guards. The lancers saw the huge glittering squadrons riding at speed upon them; they hesitated, they went about; and, as their squadrons wheeled, the Life Guards crashed in upon them. Through them, and over them, swept the tall English horsemen. In a moment the road was strewn with fallen lancers, and back to Genappes, and through its narrow streets and out of its farther side, the stalwart Guardsmen drove their opponents. Kincaid, who saw the charge, describes the fierce straightforward fighting of the Guards as magnificent. They were young soldiers, but, he says, " the only young thing they showed was in every one who got a roll in the mud (and owing to the slipperiness of the ground, there were many), going off to the rear, according to their Hyde Park custom, as being no longer fit to appear on parade. I thought, at first, that they had been all wounded, but, on finding how the case stood, I could not help telling them that theirs was now the situation to verify the old proverb, ' the uglier, the better soldier ! ' "

A furious rain, of tropical volume and temperature, suddenly broke over the line of retreat. The soft fields became mere spongy wastes of mud, and whenever the troops left the paved road the horses were knee-deep, sometimes girth-deep, in the soft soil. This checked the eagerness of the pursuit, and, late in the evening, the French halted near La Belle Alliance, while Wellington's tired squadrons floundered up the soft slope of Mont St. Jean, to the ridge above where, to-morrow, the great battle was to be fought.

The Prussian retreat, meanwhile, had been conducted with great skill and energy. A strong rearguard posted at Bry formed a screen to the retiring columns; and late in the evening of the 17th, three Prussian corps were in communication at Wavre. Thielemann halted for some hours at Gembloux, and then moved slowly on toward Wavre, covering Blücher's rear from any attack. By nightfall of the 17th, in a word, Blücher held at Wavre a force of 90,000 men and 269 guns; he was less than ten miles from Waterloo, where Wellington now stood with 61,000 men, and 156 guns, a detachment of 18,000 men being held at Hal, twelve miles to the west.

Napoleon at noon of that day had despatched Grouchy with 33,000 men and ninety-six guns to pursue Blücher. That general began his wandering and ill-fated march at two o'clock. His soldiers were tired. Rain fell heavily. It was far on in the night when Grouchy's straggling divisions reached Gembloux. Here he found no Prussians, and practically no news of them. What news he had seemed to show that the retreating Prussians had divided, at least one column moving towards Wavre. With much mental disquiet Grouchy at last resolved to

move on Wavre himself, and he advised Napoleon
of his resolve. But he moved late on the next
morning, and moved too slowly to reach the field
of action in time.

The situation on the night of the 17th may be
described almost in a sentence. Grouchy was at
Gembloux, Napoleon at La Belle Alliance, parted
by twenty-two miles of wet and almost impassable
plains from each other. Communications along the
paved road running to Quatre Bras were possible;
but they stretched across a distance of nearly forty
miles. Wellington and Blücher, on the other hand,
thanks to the historic flank march of the Prussian
army, lay within less than ten miles of each other.
Napoleon's strategy thus was inverted and turned
against himself. He aimed to separate Blücher and
Wellington, and, keeping his own army concentrated, to fight and destroy them each in detail.
As a matter of fact, Blücher and Wellington were
united; 90,000 Prussians at Wavre were within
hand-grasp of Wellington's army of 61,000 at
Waterloo, and betwixt them was the link of a
definite and loyal strategy. It was Napoleon's army
that was fatally separated. He was in front of
Wellington with 72,000 men, while his left wing,
under Grouchy, 33,000 strong, was a dislocated and
wandering fragment, practically thirty miles distant!

Judged thus by the distribution of the armies
as night fell on the 17th, the Allies, and not

Napoleon, had won in the great game of generalship.
Napoleon had planned to fall with his whole force
on Blücher and Wellington separately; but Blücher
and Wellington next day were to fall upon him, at
the moment when one-third of his forces was beyond
his reach. And the noteworthy thing is that Napoleon was in almost absolute ignorance of the combination which was closing around him. He believed
that Grouchy was betwixt him and Blücher, or, at
all events, would come up as soon as the Prussians,
and in greater strength. On the morning of Waterloo, Napoleon was wandering in a mere fool's paradise. Blücher and Wellington had already beaten
him in strategy, as in the struggle of the next day
they were to beat him in tactics.

The night of the 17th was black with falling rain
and rough with winds. Two great armies were
encamped within a thousand yards of each other.
For some curious reason no fires were lit amongst
the French. Blackness lay unrelieved on the muddy
ridge where more than 70,000 soldiers, unsheltered
from the furious gusts of rain, waited for morning
—and for defeat! On the British ridge, however, a
thousand fires flamed. In the shallow valley below,
the British vedettes and pickets, almost within
speaking distance of the French outposts, kept their
watch in the darkness and the fast-falling rain.
Every few minutes deep reverberations of thunder
shook the night skies above, and the lightning, with

its white flame, lit the whole scene. From the British ridge the far-stretching fires sent a ruddy glow up into the sky, and, like some far-seen and crimson signal of war, that long stretch of pulsating colour burned in the midnight heavens.

About midnight Napoleon, who could not sleep, went out on foot with General Bertrand, and walked in the darkness and rain along the line of his out-posts as far as the wood of Hougoumont. Again and again he stopped, with bent head, to listen to the sounds that stole down from the British lines, or he stood, unconscious of the rain, staring into the darkness up the hill-slope, where to-morrow Ney's gallant horsemen were to make their last ride. Napoleon feared the British, behind the screen of their camp-fires, would silently vanish through the forest of Soignies. So he paused again, and yet again, and tried to interpret each sound that floated through the darkness and the rain from the camp of his enemies.

These restless midnight wanderings along the front of the English position, while waiting for the dawn of the day of Waterloo, have a weird sugges-tiveness. Did Napoleon's imagination paint on the screen of the darkness any picture of the wild conflict of the coming day, and of the mad ruin which was to crown it, with the solitudes of St. Helena beyond ? Did he realise that the last hour of Fate, for him, was about to strike ? While Napoleon, like a restless disquieted spirit, thus wandered, unrecognised, in the rain and darkness amongst his outposts, Wellington sat in a room in the village of Waterloo at his desk, with busy secretaries about him, and a constant flow of orderlies, who splashed in dripping with rain from the wet night, and splashed out again with their hurrying messages. The English general was busy framing in minutest detail the battle-plan of Waterloo.

CHAPTER XVI

THE FIELD AT WATERLOO

"Waterloo! What horrible recollections are associated with that name!"—NAPOLEON AT ST. HELENA.

"IL a jeté les dés; et ils sont pour nous." "He has flung the dice and we win!" That was Napoleon's summary of the chances of Waterloo at eight o'clock on that world-famous Sunday morning, June 18, 1815. He had not seen the face of an Englishman in battle since Toulon in 1793, and he did not understand the fighting quality of the British soldier. He expected the allied generals to shrink from his stroke. "The old fox will not come out," he had said two days before when he stood in front of Blücher's position at Ligny; and he could hardly believe that Wellington would stand in the open at Waterloo to meet him. But on that rainy June morning, with sodden soil beneath and wet skies above, the British army was standing steadfastly on the ridge in front of Mont St. Jean. Wellington, in Napoleon's phrase, had "flung the dice," and Napoleon, who was just then wandering through a fool's paradise of hope, told his generals "ils sont pour nous."

The battlefield of Waterloo—the board on which Wellington had flung the iron dice of battle—is easily described. It is a shallow valley lying betwixt a double ridge of low and curving hills, a little over two miles in length, running east and west, and crossing the main road from Brussels to Charleroi at right angles. The road from Wavre, a mere country lane, in places worn deep into the rich soil, runs —or rather at that time ran—along the low crest of the northern—or English—ridge, at right angles to the Brussels road, and fell into the Nivelles road at its western extremity. The Nivelles road from that point runs back at an acute angle into the Brussels road, and the angle formed by these two roads defined Wellington's right. The crest ebbs back in a gentle curve where the Brussels road crosses it, and Wellington's front stretched for a little over a mile on either side of that road.

Southward, looking towards the French position, the ridge sinks like some low, regular glacis into the shallow valley. On the reverse, or northern side, the dip is somewhat sharper. On the southern front the ridge had two outworks. The farmhouse of Hougoumont stood about 350 yards in advance on the western extremity of the line, about 1000 yards from the Brussels road, its north-western angle coming within 300 yards of the Nivelles road, with

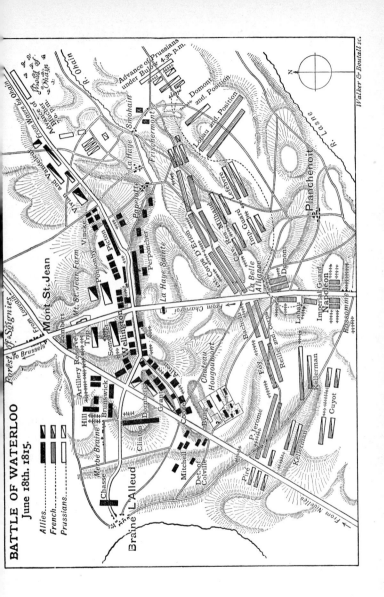

BATTLE OF WATERLOO
June 18th. 1815.

Allies..........
French..........
Prussians.......

Walker & Boutall sc.

which it was connected by a lane. Hougoumont was a solid cluster of brick buildings, set in a frame of orchards, with a patch of forest on two faces. With its small doors and windows, its outer shield of brick wall, and its screen of trees, Hougoumont was a

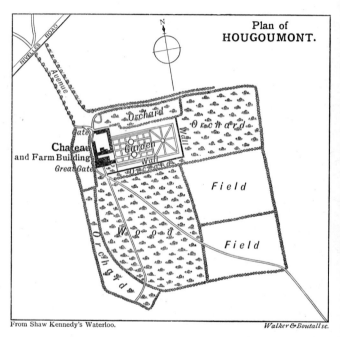

From Shaw Kennedy's Waterloo.   Walker & Boutall sc.

strong post against anything except artillery. It was a field-fortress, about a quarter of a mile on each face, covered with a living mask of foliage; and curiously enough, the French made no serious artillery attack upon it.

Some 300 yards in advance of the British centre, on the Brussels-Charleroi road itself, stood the farmhouse of La Haye Sainte, scarcely inferior in strength to Hougoumont, and capable of being stub-

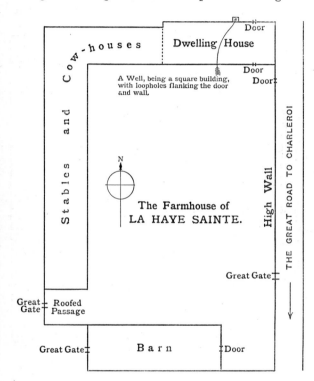

bornly held. On the opposite side of the road to the farm-house, and a little nearer the ridge, was an old gravel pit.

La Haye Sainte was the one point in his battle-line

which Wellington lost; and yet it was the one which he might, with the greatest security, have held. The buildings, very solid in character, formed three sides of a quadrangle, the fourth side—that parallel with the edge of the Charleroi road—consisting of a high wall. South of the buildings was an orchard; on the north was a garden. All the buildings were of good masonry and strongly roofed. The popular belief is that the front of La Haye Sainte, which looked towards the British line, had no doorway, and so ammunition could not be sent in to the troops holding the position. Wellington himself believed this, as did most of his staff. Yet the doorway existed, as is shown on the plan given herewith, taken from Shaw Kennedy's valuable work.

The truth is, the defence of La Haye Sainte was a detail left to the Prince of Orange, and quite forgotten, or neglected, by that very inexperienced general. No adequate preparations for the defence of the buildings were made during the night; the tools and workmen that should have been employed on that task were taken to Hougoumont and employed there. Scarcely anything was done in the way of loopholing the walls, building up gates and doors, &c. In fact, the troops were allowed to burn one of the great gates for firewood during the night. The building was large enough to hold a garrison of 1000 men, but only a light battalion of the King's German Legion, 400 strong, was detailed to hold it,

PRINCE OF ORANGE, 1816

From an engraving after a painting by JOSEPH ODERAERE

and by some crowning blunder no adequate supply
of ammunition was provided. Wellington said
afterwards, and quite truly, "It was the fault of the
Prince of Orange that La Haye Sainte was lost. But
no!" he added generously; "I ought to have looked
into it myself." When, during the night of the 17th,
the suggestion was made to the headquarters staff to
send in an additional battalion to strengthen the
defence of La Haye Sainte, the proposal was rejected
with something like contempt. Nevertheless, for the
neglect to adequately defend La Haye Sainte, the
British next day had to pay a tragical price in blood
and suffering.

The defence of Hougoumont was prepared with
great energy. On the evening of the 17th Wellington gave instructions that it was to be defended to
the uttermost. The workmen and tools from La
Haye Sainte, as we have seen, were carried to it. All
night long the business of piercing the walls, preparing platforms, &c., was pushed on with the
greatest energy. Abundant stores of ammunition
were placed in it. Its garrison consisted of Wellington's best troops, under an officer in whom he reposed
special confidence. As a result, Hougoumont was
triumphantly held through the whole day; a result
which might have been secured as certainly for La
Haye Sainte had the same means been employed.

Waterloo was not a strong position, and was held
mainly because it covered the junction of the

Charleroi and Nivelles roads. "I have just ridden along the whole line," said Picton, half-an-hour before the battle began, "and I never saw a worse position." It had been proposed a month earlier to strengthen it by earthworks. "No, no," said Wellington; "that would tell them where we mean to fight." So the only artificial defence was an abattis on the Brussels road above La Haye Sainte. But Waterloo suited Wellington's battle methods sufficiently well. He could keep his infantry on the reverse slope, unseen and sheltered till the moment came for action. The road traversing the ridge defined his battle front; it served in some places as a ditch, and made communication from end to end of the position easy. On either extremity the ridge curved forward with a well-defined shoulder, and so made the flanks strong; while Hougoumont and La Haye Sainte, thrust out like two horns in front, would break or divide the strength of a direct attack.

Looking southward across the shallow valley, at a distance of about 1200 yards, could be seen the ridge which was held by Napoleon. It suited his battle methods admirably. Napoleon understood the office of the imagination in war, and he loved to impress and terrify the imagination of his enemies by the spectacle of far-stretching infantry columns, glittering squadrons of cavalry, and long lines of frowning guns. His position at Waterloo lent itself perfectly to spectacular effects of this sort. It had, however, this disadvantage, that on the long sloping flank of La Belle Alliance his battle plan lay open like a game of chess. Wellington could note every movement in his enemy's lines, could see where the columns gathered for their onfall, judge on what point of his line the tempest was about to burst, and make, unseen, the necessary combination to meet it.

The whole scene of the fight, looked at from the British ridge, offered a strange picture of fertility and peace. On the undulating plain and the low swelling hills the ripening crops stood thick; sprinkled over the landscape were farmhouses nested in leafy orchards, and tiny villages with church steeples showing sharp above the poplars. It was Sunday morning, the rain had fallen all night, and was still falling softly. The air was heavy with mist. The rain-drops lay thick on the bearded grain; pools of water gathered in every hollow. The landscape, grey above, dark green below, and fading on all sides into the indistinctness of mist, was curiously sombre. And presently under the dripping skies and through the damp air the church bells were calling faintly to each other. They called the rustic worshippers to matins. But the brazen trumpet of war was about to rend the air with sterner notes. Within an area of about three miles by one, more than 130,000 armed men were preparing to join in the most famous battle of modern times. On the narrow

British ridge, as the grey dawn kindled in the east, more than 60,000 men awoke, and the stir of their waking, the call of so many human voices, the stamping of horses, made up a softened volume of sound which, says one who stood that morning on the ridge, "resembled the wash of surf on the sea-shore."

Wellington had at his disposal for the coming fight 67,000 men; 12,000 being cavalry, with 156 guns. Napoleon had a total of nearly 72,000 men, nearly 15,000 being cavalry, with 246 guns. It will be seen that Wellington was inferior to Napoleon in infantry and cavalry, and greatly inferior to him in artillery. But the difference in figures very inadequately represents the difference in strength of the two armies. Of Wellington's whole forces less than 24,000 were British. If to these be added the fine regiments of the King's German Legion, it still left less than 30,000 thoroughly reliable soldiers; and of Wellington's British three out of four were mere recruits. Not more than 6000, as we have seen, had ever heard a shot fired in actual battle. With many of the Nassauers and Dutch-Belgians courage was a doubtful quality, and loyalty one still more doubtful. The Nassauers had served under the French eagles, their arms, uniforms, and drill were still French, and during the battle his aide-de-camp only once persuaded Wellington to draw his bridle. It was when he was about to pass in front of a square of Nassauers. There was real fear that they might fire upon him instead of upon the French! At Hal, while the battle was raging at Waterloo, Clinton's division actually expected to have to fire on their Belgian allies.

The great Brussels road, which bisected Wellington's battle-line, may be taken as the starting-point in a description of the English position. The British front stretched for a little over a mile on either side of the Brussels road. Next that road, towards the right—or westward—stood Alten's division. It consisted of a brigade of the German Legion, one of Hanoverians, and Halkett's brigade, about 8000 men in all, and covering a front of about 800 yards. Farther to the right still stood the two brigades of the Guards (Maitland's and Byng's), 4000 strong; Byng's brigade holding Hougoumont and the ridge behind it. The extremity of the right was held by one of Colville's brigades—the 51st, the 23rd, and a battalion of the 14th—1800 men in all. Next to the Brussels road, eastward—to the left, that is —stood Picton's division, 7000 men, made up of Kempt's and Pack's brigades, and a brigade of Hanoverians ; two brigades of Cole's division—Lambert's and Best's, 5000 strong—came next. Beyond, were Vivian's and Vandeleur's light cavalry brigades.

In the second line, at the centre, on either side of the Brussels road, and 400 yards behind the infantry brigades, stood the two heavy cavalry brigades —the Household brigade, under Lord Edward Somerset, the Union brigade, under Ponsonby; and 300 yards to the rear of these was a body of Belgian horse. Perponcher's Dutch-Belgian division, 7500 men, held Papelotte in advance of the left wing, a brigade (Bylandt's) being on the slope in front of Picton's division. Wellington's reserves stood on his right in the triangle formed by the Nivelles and Brussels roads, with the cross-country road as a base—three brigades of Clinton's division and some Brunswickers, with Grant's and Dornberg's cavalry brigades. The front was thus a long chequer of red and blue infantry; with too little red and too much blue! The second line consisted of cavalry, the reserve of three powerful infantry brigades, and two of cavalry.

The Guards held the ridge above Hougoumont, the light companies of Maitland's brigade, under Macdonnell, holding the farm buildings and garden; those of Byng's brigade, under Lord Saltoun, holding the orchards and wood; a regiment of Nassauers was joined to these. Muffling believed Hougoumont was too lightly held, but Wellington curtly replied, " I have thrown Macdonnell into it," and in the fighting qualities of that tall Scotchman, and the steady valour of the Guards, Wellington, a keen judge of men and of troops, reposed the utmost confidence.

Wellington's hope of success rested on his own matchless skill in defence, and on the dogged fighting quality of his British troops. There was, of course, plenty of courage, of a sporadic sort, amongst the Belgians. Thus, in his account of the battle, Picton's "Staff officer" says that "a fine old brave Belgian colonel, having a cocked hat like the sails of a windmill," rode into one of their squares, followed by a cluster of his officers. His own regiment had dissolved in mere flight, but this brave soldier added himself and a few of his officers to a British square, and manœuvred and fought with them all through the wild day.

But the Nassauers early showed the doubtful strain in their soldiership. Thus when the battalions holding the wood of Hougoumont heard the shrill cries of "Vive l'Empereur," which presently came in waves of clamour from the French ridge, they grew uneasy ; they visibly trembled on the edge of mere flight. Wellington in person rode up to them, and showed how strongly they were supported by the British Guards. "It would not do," he said, telling the story afterwards, "and so bewildered were they that they sent a few shots after me as I rode off!" Wellington had to distribute his foreign and doubtful troops amongst his more steadfast battalions, so as to minimise the peril of their giving way.

Napoleon had organised his army in three corps, with the Imperial Guard and the cavalry of Kellerman and Milhaud and Pajol as a reserve. The two corps of D'Erlon and of Reille formed his front, the infantry being ranged in two lines, with an interval

of thirty-five yards betwixt them. D'Erlon's corps
formed the right wing, that of Reille the left. Milhaud's cuirassiers were in D'Erlon's rear, Kellerman's
cuirassiers and dragoons, with the heavy cavalry of
the Guard, in the rear of Reille. The Young Guard,
under Lobau, was in the centre of the second line
west of the Brussels road. As a reserve stood, in
black deep columns, with artillery on both flanks, the
Imperial Guard itself.

Napoleon spent two hours of the morning in a
great spectacular display. Over the low hill his
army came in eleven columns, their guns, battery
after battery, moving on the flanks of the columns,
while at a stately trot, with a sound of clashing
steel that rang far over the valley, came the cavalry,
mailed cuirassiers, lancers with their forest of glittering spear-points, dragoons with sword and plume.
The drums beat harshly; a hundred bands poured
their kindling music on the air. To give realistic
effect to the scene a fringe of skirmishers ran out
along the whole French line, and filled the slope
below with the white smoke and the sharp crackle
of their musketry. The whole army, as thus displayed, had, to quote Thiers, "somewhat the form
of a great fan, gleaming as the bayonets, sabres, and
cuirasses of the men flashed back the sunlight, which
just then had broken through the clouds." Suddenly
along the outer fringe of the "fan," so to speak, shot
at speed a group of horsemen, gay with plumes,

glittering with gold and steel and scarlet. It was Napoleon and his staff! A tempest of shrill cheering rose on the air. It flowed round that dazzling group, pursued it, ran before it, and the clamour deepened until it swept across the valley to the British line. Then it died away, and in silence the two great hosts faced each other.

Napoleon spent two hours of precious time in that great effort of what we may call parade soldiership. It was meant to kindle the imagination of his own men and to chill that of the enemy. Long afterwards, Napoleon, referring to the sight, declared "the earth seemed proud to bear so many brave men." As for any effect on the imagination of Wellington's soldiers, however, the scene was wasted. The British private is singularly unsusceptible to histrionic terrors. On the ridge opposite, such of the British soldiers as watched the sight leaned coolly on their muskets, and exchanged rough jests on the subject of "Nap" and his men in front of them. That ride along the front of his gallant army at Waterloo, it may be added, was Napoleon's last review—his last hour of military pride.

The movement which threw Napoleon's great army into battle-line was skilful in the highest degree, and, says Shaw Kennedy, "may be looked upon as a model." "Never," Napoleon himself said afterwards at St. Helena, "never have such masses moved with such celerity."

Napoleon's description of the battle-formation of his army is worth quoting. "It was arranged," he says, "in six lines forming six double W's. The first and second lines were formed of infantry flanked by light cavalry; the third and fourth lines of cuirassiers; the fifth and sixth lines of cavalry of the Guard, with six lines of infantry of the Guard perpendicularly placed at the point of those six W's."

At half-past ten o'clock the whole movement was completed. A profound silence lay on the battle-field. It was a moment's breathing-space; the two great hosts gazed across the narrow valley on each other.

Shaw Kennedy gives some interesting details as to the measurements of the field of Waterloo. The front of battle for either army extended for little over two miles; and as 3000 infantry drawn up in single rank occupy a mile of front, it is clear that Waterloo was a battle marked, on the part of both armies, by great concentration of force. The distance between Hougoumont and La Haye Sainte is 1000 yards, and through this gap the great French cavalry charges were made. As the interval was narrowed still further by the zone of fire from each building, it is clear that the French cavalry lines never had a front of more than 500 men. The great French battery took up its position not more than 250 yards from La Haye Sainte.

GENERAL ANTOINE DROUOT
COMMANDING THE IMPERIAL GUARD AT WATERLOO

From a lithograph after a drawing by MAURIR

The landscape of the battle has yet to be completed. Nearly ten miles to Wellington's right stood 17,000 men under Prince Frederick of Orange and Colville; a wasted force, a proof of the obstinacy with which Wellington clung to the idea that Napoleon would still strive to turn his right.   Seven or eight miles to Wellington's left, hidden by a screen of low wooded hills, was Blücher with 70,000 men, floundering with obstinate toil along the muddy cross-roads, to fall on Napoleon's flank.   It was in dependence on the arrival of Blücher that Wellington, with an army so much inferior, was standing to meet Napoleon in the shock of battle at Waterloo.   And the most remarkable feature in the story of the day is the fact that Napoleon at this stage had absolutely no knowledge of the tempest of battle about to break on his right flank.   Had he known it, he would scarcely have wasted those hours in mere spectacular parade.

Napoleon waited, on the advice of Drouot, his chief of artillery, till the sodden ground had grown dry; but at half-past eleven the guns on the French left opened fire upon the British right across the roofs of Hougoumont.   A cloud of skirmishers ran out, dark masses moved down the French slope, and broke with rolling volleys and a tumultuous clamour of voices into the wood that acted as a screen to the farmhouse.   The white whirling smoke, the angry bellow, the darting flames of cannon-fire, ran along the whole French front.   The great battle had begun!

CHAPTER XVII

THE STORY OF THE GREAT FIGHT: THE
FRENCH INFANTRY-ATTACKS

THE scale of the approaching battle was amply
realised by the leaders on both sides. "Were
you ever in a battle before?" said Wellington himself to a youthful aide-de-camp of foreign blood
whom he found amongst his staff. "No, sir," was
the reply. "Then you are a lucky man," responded
the Duke, "for you will never see such another!"
On both sides there was—perhaps with the exception of Wellington himself—the most cheerful confidence of victory. What was Napoleon's mood we
have already seen. Hill may, perhaps, be taken as
the type of British feeling. He rode that morning,
a composed and farmer-like figure, along the ridge
in front of his divisions, and no doubt as to the
result of the battle clouded his cheerful courage.
"You will see a great battle to-day," he said to an
English visitor, Lord Apsley, who happened to ride
up; "and," he added, "I think the French will get
such a thrashing as they have seldom had!"

The battle lasted a little over eight hours. The

first gun was fired a little before twelve o'clock, and
by eight o'clock at night the French were in wild and
hopeless retreat.   During those long hours, of course,
the batteries roared almost incessantly from the
French ridge, and the splutter of skirmishing fire
never ceased along the British slope.   But the battle
itself is marked by five great stages :—(1) The attack
of Reille's corps on Hougoumont.   It began a little
before twelve o'clock, and was designed as a feint
rather than a serious attack.   But it took a fury and
a scale beyond what was intended, and though the
passion of the struggle rose and sank, the contest
round Hougoumont practically was maintained till
night.   (2) A great infantry attack by D'Erlon's
corps on Wellington's left centre, which was launched
about two o'clock.   (3) The assaults of the French
cavalry on Wellington's centre, which raged from
four till six o'clock.   (4) A second infantry attack,
under Ney, on Wellington's centre, which began
during the later stages of the cavalry charges and
lasted till a little after seven.   (5) The attack of the
Old Guard about 7.30 P.M., and the general advance
of the British line which followed its defeat.

Napoleon's general plan was to fix Wellington's
attention on Hougoumont by a furious attack; then
to seize La Haye Sainte, break through the British
left, drive it across the Brussels road, and roll
Wellington's whole army in wreck and defeat on to
the Nivelles road.

Reille accordingly began the battle by sending Jerome's division against Hougoumont. The French came on gallantly. They broke through the wood, they swept along the lane to the west of the farm-house; the Nassauers and Hanoverians were driven like chaff before them. They believed they had carried the position. But suddenly the black trunks of the trees gave place to a long stretch of red brick wall, a wall that, in a moment, along its whole front, gleamed with the flames of deadly musketry volleys from which Jerome's infantry recoiled. A British battery on the ridge above rained shells on the struggling French in the wood. The Guards dashed out, and with one resolute charge pushed fiercely home, drove them clean to the southern edge of the enclosure. Again and yet again the French came on. Foy's division was flung into the struggle; the farmhouse was attacked on two faces at once. The barricaded gate was broken through, and the French actually penetrated the enclosure. But Mac-donnell himself, with four officers and a sergeant, slew the foremost French, drove back the others, and re-shut the gate in their faces. The French, in the passion of their attack, eddied round on to the north side of the enclosure—that on which the British ridge looked down—and Wellington, keenly watch-ing the struggle, sent down Colonel Woodford with four companies of the Coldstreams to drive them off.

Woodford took his men forward with great fire,

COUNT MAXIMILIEN-SÉBASTIEN FOY

From an engraving

drove back the French, and, entering the farmyard, strengthened its garrison. All day, to summarise the struggle at this point, the battle raged round Hougoumont. The Nassauers and Hanoverians in that fierce wrestle proved unreliable, and were withdrawn, and in all six companies of the Guards were sent as reinforcements to the handful of gallant men holding the post. Later in the day the French opened a heavy gun-fire on Hougoumont; the building broke into flames; the French attacked once more with extraordinary ardour and persistency. But the Guards were invincible. More than 12,000 of Napoleon's troops were drawn into the vortex of the fight round Hougoumont; and that Napoleon allowed nearly one-fifth of his entire force to be involved in what might almost be described as an irrelevant detail of the battle, is a reproach to his generalship.

But in that struggle of the many against the few, the few won! When, at nightfall, from out the shot-torn and blood-splashed wreck of Hougoumont the scanty survivors of the Guards defiled, with blackened faces and torn uniforms, they had played not the least heroic part in that day of heroes. Wellington, riding in the rapture of the final advance against the French, shouted to Muffling with a touch of exultation unusual to him, "Well, you see Macdonnell has held Hougoumont!"

Next came the second stage of the battle, the great infantry attack on the British left centre. For an hour and a half 74 guns, at a distance of little more than 600 yards, poured their fire on the crest of the ridge to the left of the Brussels road, where stood the brigades of Picton's division. At half-past one D'Erlon's corps, in four huge and close-massed columns, moved down the French slope. The French columns had a narrow front of about 150 men; but their depth was great, and the intervals between the battalions so narrow that there was barely room for the officers. The columns advanced in echelon at a distance of 100 yards from each other. Ney in person led the left column, Donzolet, Marcognet, and Durutte—all famous captains—the other columns. The brazen drums beating the *pas de charge* filled the air with their harsh vibrations. The French, as they came on with brandished arms and a tempest of shouts, their officers leading, seemed as if they must prove irresistible. Napoleon himself, with his glittering staff, took post on the side of the road, and the columns, as they filed past him, rent the air with continuous shouts of "Vive l'Empereur;" and to their shouts was added the incessant roll of the drums, the blare of a hundred trumpets, while over all the great battery of 74 guns poured its thunder. All this tumult was in strange contrast to the stern silence in the ranks of the waiting British, where orders were given in gestures, almost in whispers.

The great battery on the French ridge macadamised with its shot, so to speak, the path along which D'Erlon's columns were moving. On their left rode glittering squadrons of cuirassiers. Steadily through the swaying corn came the black masses. The left column was in advance. Its head swung to the right smitten by a fire from the gravel pit above La Haye Sainte, which was held by the 95th; the rear of the column was entangled in a furious attack on La Haye Sainte itself. Bylandt's brigade of Dutch-Belgians stood in the path of the innermost French columns. It fell out of shape as the massive French battalions drew near, and poured, a tumult of fugitives, over the crest of the ridge, through the intervals of the British line, and the French files, in all the rapture of imagined victory, pushed eagerly up to what seemed the vacant crest. As the head of the advancing columns, deep-massed and black, crowned the summit, the great French battery that had been firing over their heads died into silence. With a tumult of shouts the leading files reached the hedge that defined the Wavre road.

Picton, a keen soldier, held Kempt's brigade in line a few yards distant, with Pack's Scotch brigade in support, and just at this moment he led Kempt's brigade forward. "To form a just estimate of Picton's nerve, judgment, and decision on that memorable occasion," says a staff officer in the *United Service Magazine*, "we must remember that to meet the attack of three divisions, numbering fully 13,000 bayonets, he had no more than 3000 British infantry,

being all that remained of the 4600 with whom he
had borne the brunt of the severe action at Quatre
Bras; that a Dutch brigade, posted in front of the
British, fled to the rear almost before the French
came within musket-shot; and, lastly, that he had no
infantry whatever behind him as a reserve in case
of disaster.   The maintenance of our entire position
depended, in fact, on the ability of 3000 men, formed
only two deep in line, to defeat four massive columns
of attack, each of which exceeded the strength of
Picton's division."

But Picton's attack, delivered with so much fire
and energy, was a splendid stroke of soldiership.
Rolling volleys from the far-stretching English front
smote the French as they tried to deploy; then
through the hedge came Kempt's line, somewhat
broken in order, indeed, as it crossed the road, but
eager to close with the French.   It was a combat
of 3000 men against 13,000.   Picton, riding on its
flank, was shot through the head and fell dead, but
the rush of Kempt's bayonets was too much for the
French column immediately attacked.   Its leading
files fell into confusion.   The whole mass seemed to
pause, and it began to ebb in disorder down the
slope.

It is a matter of dispute whether or not Picton's
lines had flung back the leading French column, or
was itself broken at the point where the thin line of
scarlet actually crashed on the narrow and solid front

of the French column. It is certain that Picton's last words to his aide-de-camp as he fell from his horse were, "Rally the Highlanders." The next French column by this time had reached the hedge, the column still next in order coming up a little later. Suddenly a deep sound—the sound of a myriad galloping horse-hoofs—came over the ridge. What a moment before had seemed empty space was filled with a long line of tossing horse-heads, of crested helmets, and gleaming swords. The Union Brigade —the Royals, the Greys, the Inniskillings—a tempest of fiery horsemen, breaking out of the smoke at a distance of less than a hundred yards, were riding on the helpless French columns!

It is worth noting here how diversely the two commanders appealed to the imagination of their opponents. Napoleon loved display; Wellington, concealment and surprise. Napoleon spread on the hill-slope of La Belle Alliance all the magnificent pageantry of his army. Wellington offered, say, to D'Erlon's columns as they came on, a ridge naked of defence, the guns standing out in relief and without supports. That naked ridge had a weird look! Then suddenly it gleamed from end to end with the faces and bayonets of advancing infantry, or it was filled with a front of swiftly-moving and sworded horsemen, who seemed to leap out of the mist of battle-smoke! How nerve-shattering that sudden apparition was may easily be guessed.

Lord Uxbridge, who commanded Wellington's cavalry, had watched D'Erlon's huge columns moving on the British centre ; he saw the cuirassiers on their left flank break and sabre the brigade of German infantry on the slope ; and he rode at speed to the spot.   On the western side of the Charleroi road stood the Household Brigade, consisting of the 1st and 2nd Life Guards, the Oxford Blues, and the 1st Dragoon Guards.   Scarcely drawing bridle, Lord Uxbridge ordered it to form in line in preparation for the charge ; then he crossed the road to Ponsonby's brigade—the Royals, the Greys, and the Inniskillings—and ordered it to wheel into line and charge simultaneously with the Household Brigade. He then returned and led the Guards himself to the charge.

Both brigades went forward at the trot, which quickened into a gallop as they reached the crest and saw the crowded slope, and, within less than a hundred yards of their swords, the columns and squadrons of their foes.   The opportunity was one to set what may be called the cavalry imagination on flame.   The Guards and the Blues to the right saw before them a smooth green incline across which two brigades of French cuirassiers were moving, disordered by their pursuit of the German battalions they had just broken.   The Union Brigade on the left saw through the smoke four great columns of French infantry, dense and narrow and far-stretching. Their shape made it impossible for them to form square; they had not the front of fire which a line formation would have given.

Seven regiments of the finest cavalry in the world, in a word, went racing down upon their unprepared foes on either side of the Brussels road. Two armies watched their charge. The blood of the galloping horsemen was kindled to fire, and in the rush and rapture of the charge generalship was forgotten. Lord Uxbridge himself rode like a trooper in the first line. The eager impulse to reach and strike their foes overbore all formal tactics. The Blues were to be "in support" of the Household Brigade, the Greys of the Union Brigade. But the Blues quickly found their way into the front line, the Greys, edging past the flank of the Inniskillings, saw through the smoke Marcognet's column a little on their left shoulder, and, wheeling slightly, rode straight for it.

On the right of the Brussels road the cuirassiers met the Life Guards gallantly enough, and the two fronts of charging horsemen met with a crash like two living walls. But the Guards, big men on big horses, coming down the slope at speed, literally smashed through their opponents and rode over them. The cuirassiers were rent into fragments by the shock, and in scattered groups, but still fighting desperately, were driven by the victorious British horsemen down the slope and across the Brussels road. Then, bringing up their right shoulder, the Life Guards swept across the road in pursuit, and plunged into the great infantry mêlée which was raging on the slope beyond.

On the left side of the road the Royals caught Donzelot's column in the rapture of an imagined victory, when there broke upon the startled French this apparition of helmeted regiments of British cavalry riding upon them at speed. A splutter of alarmed musketry broke from the column, but, without drawing bridle, the Royals crashed in upon the helpless infantry, and the wildest scene followed. An English officer, recalling the spectacle, says, " I remember a dreadful confusion, thick smoke, horses and men tumbling headlong; soldiers receiving their death-wounds, springing up and falling down dead! The ground was so covered with dead and dying, that we could not avoid treading on them." A French officer describes the sensation of the moment from another standpoint: " As I was pushing one of our men into his proper place in the ranks," he says, " he suddenly sank under a sword-cut; turning briskly round, I saw the English dragoons riding into our column in every direction, cutting our men down right and left. In vain did our poor fellows try to defend themselves with their bayonets; they had not a chance against these dragoons, mounted as they were on powerful horses. The few shots this hapless and bewildered crowd

could fire proved as dangerous to our own men as
to the cavalry. We were totally defenceless before
these terrible dragoons."

Here and there a solitary French private, or
some gallant officer, broke loose from the mass,
and stood, single and desperate, in the rush of the
charging horse, until trampled out of shape by the
thundering hoofs. But the column itself was practically destroyed in those few wild moments. The
Inniskillings were riding, drunk with the fury of
battle, through the French column next in order.
The Greys, to reach Marcognet's column, had to pass
through the intervals of the 92nd. This was a
Highland regiment, still on fire with the passion of
its own charge, and the bonneted men of the 92nd,
as they saw the well-known grey horses of their
cavalry kinsfolk sweep past them, kindled to a new
excitement. The men, as an officer who was present
records, "simply went mad." Wild greetings in Gaelic
flew betwixt horsemen and footmen; many privates
of the 92nd caught the stirrups of the Greys, and
raced forward with them in their charge. The whole
Union Brigade counted less than 1000 sabres, each
regiment numbering about 320 men; but their rush
on D'Erlon's unhappy columns was like the passage
of a cluster of aërolites. Unbroken battalions of the
bewildered French flung down their arms as they
stood, in token of surrender, and the next day the
muskets still lay, spread out in long and orderly

lines, showing where the battalions, at the mere spectacle of the oncoming of those fierce horsemen, had surrendered.

"I never saw such a scene in all my life," says Kincaid. "Hundreds of French infantry threw themselves down and pretended to be dead while the cavalry galloped over them, and then got up and ran away." "The solid mass I had seen twenty minutes before," says another English officer, "was there no more, and had now become a defenceless crowd. French officers were brought up from the hollow in great numbers, delivering up their swords. One of our privates brought up two, pushing them before him with his bayonet. They were hatless, and had a flushed and vexed kind of look. They came and delivered their swords to our colonel, and were then sent to the rear."

But the British cavalry regiments were now completely out of hand. The Blues still held together in a fashion, but the other regiments, in irregular clusters of eager horsemen, were charging everything within their reach. They caught two field-batteries in the valley, slew riders, gunners, and horses, and left fifteen guns useless. Still pressing onward, they mounted the French ridge. The Greys galloped over the great battery, leaving it half destroyed, then wheeled to the left and rode eastward, slaying at will. Some men from other regiments, pressing on, reached the second French line, broke in upon some artillery waggons, the drivers, mere boys, sitting and weeping helplessly on their horses. The colonel of the Greys and the colonel of the King's Dragoon Guards were both slain on the very crown of the French ridge. Those who from the British crest watched the scene, saw far away, deep in the masses of the French, on the slope of La Belle Alliance, tiny patches of white moving fiercely to and fro, and spreading confusion everywhere. They were scattered groups of the Greys in the midst of their enemies!

The British cavalry leaders by this time had begun to remember that they were not mere troopers, with no other business than the joy of fighting. Lord Uxbridge afterwards wrote ruefully, " I committed a great mistake in having myself led the attack." He ought to have led the second line, and kept it in hand to support the first line when it fell back. But all niceties of order had vanished. Colonel and general had jostled shoulders with the galloping privates, as eager as they for the combat. Sir William Ponsonby, the leader of the Union Brigade, rode his horse to a standstill in the soft deep soil of the French slope, was there caught by the French lancers, and pierced with a score of thrusts. When the British cavalry leaders had, however, recovered their heads, the rally was sounded and an attempt made to re-form the squadrons. "But," says Lord Uxbridge, "neither voice nor trumpet availed." Two regiments of Milhaud's cuirassiers were flung by Napoleon him-

self on the broken English regiments, while a brigade
of lancers rode in on their flank.

With blown horses and broken order, the British
cavalry were in turn driven down the French slope,
and would have been literally destroyed had help not
come.   Two fine brigades of British cavalry—those of
Vivian and of Vandeleur—were drawn up on Wellington's left, and Muffling urged them to move to the
support of the broken squadrons now being driven
down the French slope; but both Vivian and Vandeleur
refused, urging they dare not move without orders.
Wellington's ideas of discipline were stern, and long
afterwards, discussing the story with Muffling, Wellington said he would have brought both of these
generals to court-martial if they had moved, even if
they had been successful.

As a matter of fact, Vandeleur at last did move,
and without instructions.   His brigade consisted of
the 11th, 12th, and 16th Light Dragoons.   Moving
on the reverse slope of the ridge some distance,
Vandeleur brought up the right shoulder of his
brigade, and came over the crest, the 12th Light
Dragoons leading.   The tail end of one of D'Erlon's
columns yet maintained its order, and was falling
steadily back.   Beyond the column was the spectacle
of the French lancers slaying the disordered fragments
of the Union and Household Brigades.   The 12th
rode furiously on the French infantry column, broke
clean through it, and spurring forward caught the

lancers beyond it, in turn, on their flank.   The 16th, riding clear of the infantry, struck the lancers with still more wrathful impact, and in a moment they were being whirled across the valley.   Vandeleur kept his lines coolly in hand, but individual soldiers broke loose, and, in the madness of the fight, rode up to the French crest and were slain there.

The broken regiments of the two brigades, covered by Vandeleur's Light Dragoons, had now reached the British crest again.   They were breathless, disordered ; they had left half their numbers in the valley or on the French slope beyond.   Of one squadron of the 1st Dragoon Guards only two men returned.   " The squadron," says Tomkinson in his " Diary of a Cavalry Officer," " rode completely into the enemy's reserve and were killed."   But they had performed a marvellous feat.   They had practically destroyed an infantry corps, with its artillery, and two brigades of cuirassiers; they had captured 3000 prisoners and two eagles.   " When I was returning to our position," says Lord Uxbridge, " I met the Duke of Wellington surrounded by his staff, who had from the high ground witnessed the whole affair. . . . I never saw so joyous a group. . . . They thought the battle was over."

Wellington certainly did not think the battle was over, but even his cool impassive nature was stirred by that great cavalry exploit.   The moral effect of the charge was greater than even its immediate practi-

cal results.   D'Erlon's infantry were out of the fight
for the rest of the day ; "and," says Lord Uxbridge,
"although cuirassiers frequently attempted afterwards
to break into our lines, they always did it *mollement*,
and as if they expected something more behind the
curtain." Sir Evelyn Wood sums up the story of
this great charge by describing it as "one of the
most brilliant successes ever achieved by horsemen
over infantry."

Cold arithmetic dissolves into mere obscuring
vapour in the passion of Thiers' rhetoric when
describing this stage of the battle. Thus he turns
the entire Union Brigade—Royals, Inniskillings, and
Scots Greys—bodily into "Scotchmen," and at the end
of that magnificent charge, which wrecked D'Erlon's
massive columns, says, "The Scots, in doleful plight,
fell back, leaving dead or wounded 700 or 800
of the 1200 that originally composed their brigade."
The great charge, in a word, was, according to Thiers,
a melancholy defeat for the British ! As a matter of
fact, the Scots Greys in the long day of Waterloo
had only 102 killed and 97 wounded ; the total
losses of the Union Brigade in the whole battle
were only 526 ; and the entire Union Brigade—
Royals, Inniskillings, and Greys—counted slightly
less than 1000 swords.

The story of a great battle is always strangely confused and entangled, but from the account of the
fight given by an officer in Picton's division, pub-

MARQUIS OF ANGLESEY (LORD UXBRIDGE)

lished in the *United Service Magazine* for 1841, it would seem that, when the great bulk of D'Erlon's columns had been swept in ruin down the slope, one fragment of a column kept its order, passed unobserved by the charging horsemen, and coming up slowly, reached the front of Kempt's infantry line. "This second column of attack," says the writer, " composed of fine, fresh-looking men, approached us with great steadiness and regularity, with a drummer at the flank of each company.   It was evidently the intention that they should deploy, open fire, get up supports, and so penetrate our line; but, to our great amazement, they stood stock-still, looking like people bewildered.   I imagine their commander must have been killed in coming through the hollow, as there was apparently no one at their head to give them the order to deploy: also the officer of the grenadiers, leading the head of the column on the point flank, was killed just as he gained the eminence.   His decoration of the Legion of Honour was my only *spolia opima* of that day.   I am of opinion, however, that they would have deployed of their own accord, but some British officer called out ' Charge ! charge !' (he was directly knocked over with the word in his mouth), on which the head of the French column got confused, threw down its arms, accoutrements, and knapsacks, and surrendered, those in the rear following their example. . . . I observed next morning, on my visit to the field, that their track up

the slope and near the crest of it was marked distinctly by their packs and accoutrements, which still
lay on the ground as thrown off in a long line, and I
counted about forty brass drums, mostly all of which
were on the reverse flank of the column.   Therefore
I presume there were four regiments at least."

The charge of D'Erlon's columns had, however,
produced one curious effect; it had altered the
physiognomy of the British battle-line.   The red
battalions along its front were steady; the blue had
in some instances vanished; in others they had fallen
back a little, and had lost their sharp formation.
The pressure of Napoleon's battle was thus already
making evident the unequal quality of Wellington's
army.

But at this stage of the battle the Prussian advance
was also visibly affecting Napoleon's tactics.   While
D'Erlon's columns were forming for their attack,
Napoleon himself saw on the heights of St. Lambert,
far to his right, what seemed a moving shadow, but
what was quickly discovered to be a body of troops,
and he despatched two divisions of light cavalry
to ascertain what these troops were.   If they were
Prussians they were to be held in check; if they
were, as Napoleon, in defiance of reason, believed, the
heads of Grouchy's columns, instructions were to be
given them as to the places they were to occupy.
Before his cavalry could report, a Prussian hussar
was brought in as prisoner who bore a letter from

Bülow to Wellington. "The whole Prussian army," the letter ran, "was moving from Wavre to Waterloo." Napoleon thereupon sent urgent instructions to Grouchy to move in the direction of Planchenoit. But that unfortunate general, at that very moment, was listening in a garden at Sart-lez-Walhain, twenty-two miles distant, to the faintly-heard roll of the guns at Waterloo, and disputing with his generals as to whether he should march on that sound. Lobau, with the Young Guard, was to have taken part in D'Erlon's attack, but he was held back in readiness to move against the Prussians if necessary, and, later in the afternoon, with his division (10,000 strong), he was despatched to resist the Prussian advance, taking up a position in the wood of Paris, and at right angles to the French line of battle in front of Wellington.

CHAPTER XVIII

THE STORY OF THE GREAT FIGHT : THE
CAVALRY ONFALL

NAPOLEON had now failed in two great infantry attacks. The battle next fell to the cavalry, and from four o'clock till six o'clock, through the 1000 yards interval betwixt La Haye Sainte and Hougoumont, the magnificent cavalry of Napoleon's army—cuirassiers, lancers, dragoons, and mounted chasseurs of the Guard—was poured in successive charges. No less than twelve times, indeed, Ney led his glittering columns of squadrons up that slope on to the British centre ; and twelve times, broken, breathless, defeated, but still full of the fury of battle, the flood of horsemen eddied back down the slope. This, indeed, makes the most dazzling and picturesque feature in the whole physiognomy of the great fight.

This great cavalry onfall had been foreseen and prepared for by the British leaders ; but no one on the British side imagined that it would be made upon a portion of the line as yet unshaken by any infantry attack. Napoleon denied that he ordered this great cavalry effort; "it was," he said, "premature," and due entirely to the rashness of Ney and the warlike contagion which seized the whole French cavalry. As Napoleon, with his staff about him, watched his cavalry waste themselves on the English crest, he exclaimed, "He has begun an hour too soon." "This man," added Soult, speaking of Ney, "is always the same. He will compromise everything, as he did at Jena and Eylau." "Ney," said Napoleon afterwards, "behaved like a madman! he got my cavalry massacred for me." In his bulletin written after the battle Napoleon says, "Our two divisions of cuirassiers being engaged, all our cavalry ran at the same moment to support their comrades."

But if all this was true, it constituted the gravest reproach on Napoleon's own generalship. As Ney afterwards said, "This movement was executed under the eyes of the Emperor. He might have stopped it; he did not do so." What, indeed, is the position of a general who complains that for two hours his cavalry, 12,000 strong, were wasted under his very eyes in mistaken efforts, and he never stopped them?

The chief fury of the great French cavalry attack was expended on the 3rd Division, and Shaw Kennedy, who was the deputy-assistant quartermaster-general of that division, has left an interesting account of the formation which enabled the British squares to withstand an assault so furious. That Napoleon would use his overwhelming cavalry strength was clear; it was clear, too, from the formation of the ground, that the cavalry attack would fall on the ground held by the 3rd Division; and on the morning of the battle the Prince of Orange and General Alten debated how the division should be placed in view of the great cavalry assault sure to be directed against it. Wellington rode up while the debate was in progress, and being referred to, answered briefly, "Form in the usual way," and rode on. This scarcely settled the matter; and finally Shaw Kennedy asked to be allowed to form the division.

Shaw Kennedy had seen the fury and strength with which the French cavalry had fallen on the 3rd Division at Quatre Bras; in the fight now approaching it was certain that these attacks would be repeated with immensely augmented power. From the manner in which the French guns were placed, it was clear, too, that the division would be under a heavy artillery fire. It was necessary to choose a formation which would enable the division to fall into square or extend into line with the utmost possible rapidity; and that the squares should be so placed as to support each other. Shaw Kennedy reproduces the sketch made by him on the morning after the battle showing the formation adopted. The 3rd Division consisted of about 6000 men. The battalions were placed so that, when it was necessary to meet cavalry, they fell into ob-

longs rather than squares, the front and rear of the
oblongs consisting of four companies each, the sides
of one company. The front line consisted of five

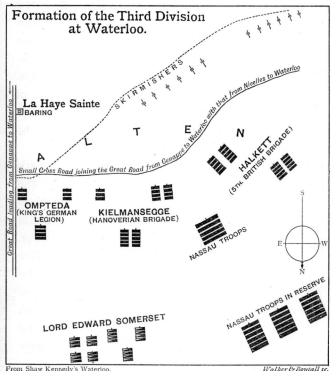

Formation of the Third Division at Waterloo.

From Shaw Kennedy's Waterloo.   *Walker & Boutall sc.*

of these oblongs, the second line of four, placed
chequerwise; the oblongs of the second line covering the openings in the first line. This arrangement
gave a great front of fire on the advancing cavalry;

and when the charging horsemen poured through the intervals in the first line, they were still riding on the fire-darting front of the oblongs of the second line. As they struggled, broken and shaken, through this, they were instantly charged by the British cavalry in the rear.

The British centre, on which the strength of the French cavalry was about to be hurled, was first swept by a heavy fire of artillery, nearly 100 guns scourging it with grape, constituting such a concentrated fury of artillery-fire as a battle-field has not often witnessed. Then Ney himself led to the attack Milhaud's cuirassiers and the light cavalry of the Guard, forty squadrons in all. This portion of the British line was held, as we have seen, by the 3rd British division, 6000 strong; and on this scanty cluster of regiments 12,000 splendid horsemen, first and last, were hurled. The British regiments were lying down a little back from the ridge. The ridge itself on their front seemed to be empty and abandoned. A few batteries occupied it, but the guns were without supports.

The whole space between La Haye Sainte and Hougoumont at that moment appeared one oncoming glittering mass, an undulating sea of crested helmets, gleaming spear-points and sword-blades, tossing heads of horses, with red expanded nostrils and flowing manes. That huge mass of men and horses, glittering with steel and gay with colour, undulating with each curve of the ground over which it passed, and filling the air with the tumult and clang of its approach, formed a moving target upon which the British guns played with deadly effect. But, with a front of from four to eight squadrons, the mass came steadily on. Macready, who served in the 30th, gives a vivid description of the French cavalry as they came near. "As soon as they quickened their trot into a gallop," he says, "the cuirassiers bent their heads so that the peaks of their helmets looked like vizors, and they seemed cased in armour from the head to the saddle."

The gallant French horsemen thus rode with bent heads and swords pointed forward, the officers on their flanks. They mounted the crest : the British gunners, firing their last charge point-blank into the mass when at a few yards distant, abandoned their guns, and ran to fling themselves for shelter beneath the bayonets of the nearest squares. Then the French cavalry saw spread before them the barrier in their path—nine steadfast squares, five in the first line, four in the second, covering the intervals. These red oblongs, steel-edged and steadfast, were suddenly edged with smoke and flame,—the darting pointed flame of musketry volleys,—as the galloping French came near. The flame ran round three faces of each square as the charging squadrons broke in two, and swept past their flanks upon the second line. Here a zigzag of fire ran round the faces of a new line of squares, and through the lanes between the squares, scourged thus with deadly musketry fire, the French cavalry broke, to be instantly charged by the British horsemen in the open ground beyond, and driven back through the tangle of squares again, smitten with incessant volleys, till they eddied backward in disorder over the crest.

On that mass of moving and glittering steel the storm of English bullets played with terrible effect. "Through the smoke could be seen helmets falling, steeds rearing in agony and terror, the riders falling prone." Some of the leading files tried to back their horses on to the square, as they would not face the bayonet points. But these gallant horsemen were quickly shot down. When at last the disordered mass had disappeared over the crest, then the British gunners ran out, and poured on the recoiling squadrons a tempest of grape-shot. Down in the valley the officers, with uplifted swords and shrill outcries, rallied their broken squadrons, dressed their lines again, and led them once more to the charge. Twelve times over that wild scene was repeated, and with each charge new masses of cavalry joined in the fight.

When that first long wave of battle, crested with steel and moving in thunder, burst upon the ridge, who can doubt but that amongst Wellington's raw militia lads, at least, a strange thrill of startled feeling ran. Here was such a cavalry attack being

launched upon them as perhaps no earthly battlefield had ever yet beheld! But the stubborn English
kept their dogged lines, and poured their musketry
fire with unfaltering diligence into that great wave
of rushing horsemen. Presently, indeed, the English
squares began to realise their power. They met each
new storm of cavalry attack with a coolness not
unflavoured with contempt. The difficulty of the
officers, in some cases at least, was to keep the
impatient ranks steady, so as to allow the French
squadrons to come near enough before they fired.

On the French side Thiers shows clearly the process by which, without order, or even against orders,
one body of the French cavalry after another was
drawn into the madness and rapture of the ride on
the English centre. Napoleon, he says, gave Ney
Milhaud's cuirassiers for the purpose of piercing the
shaken British line above La Haye Sainte. The
advance of that mass of glittering horsemen fixed the
attention of the whole French army. As it passed
before the light cavalry of the Guard, drawn up in
squadrons, Milhaud himself grasped the hand of
Lefebvre-Desnouttes, and cried, "I am going to
charge; support me." Lefebvre-Desnouttes caught
fire, or perhaps took Milhaud's words as an order,
and at once put his squadrons in movement in support of Milhaud. When the first and second charges
had been repulsed, and cuirassiers and lancers in
broken order were recoiling down the slope of the

British ridge, Ney, his coat and hat torn by balls, and wild with the excitement of the charge, looked round and saw on the French ridge yet another body of cuirassiers, and 2000 mounted grenadiers of the Guard, watching the fight with breathless excitement.   Almost with a gesture Ney drew them into the combat, and led them in a mad ride through the chequer of the English squares.

Kellerman was next sent into the fray, according to one account, by Napoleon's direct orders, and this time seventy squadrons, in one furious charge, were launched on the tormented British centre.   "At this stage," says Thiers, "the heavy cavalry of the Guard hastened forward, though nobody knew why."   Some of its officers had ridden far to the front watching the fight; they saw the abandoned English guns on the ridge, and the squadrons of French horse beyond riding to and fro amongst the English squares as though they owned them.   They flourished their swords and cried "Victory."   "On this," says Thiers, "the nearest squadron, regarding this as a signal to charge, advanced at a trot.   The entire mass followed, yielding to a species of mechanical impulse;" and another mass 2000 strong of dragoons and lancers was thus poured on the tormented plateau, and led by Ney himself against "the brazen wall of the British squares."   In this way, apparently without plan, by the mere contagion of the fight, or by the fiery and reckless ardour of Ney, the whole strength

GENERAL KELLERMAN, 1814

From an engraving

of the French cavalry was poured in twelve con-
secutive charges on the British position.

During the early stages of these charges the fighting had one uniform characteristic. The charge
was delivered in mass at a slow trot up the slope;
the pace was quickened into a gallop when the crest
was reached. In the scene that followed, the double
line of oblongs resembled little red islets, fringed with
gleaming steel, with jets of red flame and clouds of
drifting smoke, and set in a sea of rushing horsemen
and waving swords and glittering accoutrements. In
the centre of each British square were two or three
mounted officers coolly watching the scene. Nothing
could surpass the dogged courage of these little
human islets, on which so fierce a surge of battle
was breaking. Once or twice, indeed, a wounded
horse, staggering forward as it fell, struck the front
of a square, and for the moment disordered it; but
instantly the front was dressed again.

The Hanoverian squares by no means reached the
iron coolness of the British regiments. Thus a staff
officer, describing the scene, says: "I repeatedly
noticed unsteadiness amongst them, and men running
from them to the rear. It was amusing at times;
several would start from an angle of a square, and
immediately one or two staff officers would gallop
off to intercept them in their flight, and always
succeeded in driving them back to their colours.
I assisted in this duty more than once, and was

surprised at the readiness with which the foreigners returned as soon as we got into their rear." Describing the manner in which the horsemen came on, the staff officer says: "The squadrons thundered on for a brief space, then opened out and edged away from every volley. Sometimes they even halted and turned before they had been fired at—sometimes after receiving the fire of the standing ranks only. Some halted, shouted, and flourished their sabres; individuals and small parties here and there rode close up to the ranks. At some points they actually cut at the bayonets with their swords, and fired their pistols at the officers. Sometimes the whole mass would halt and gaze at the formidable triple row of bayonets; then two or three individuals might be seen to leave their places in the ranks, striving by force and gesture to urge them forward. Placing their helmets on their swords, they waved them aloft, a bootless display of gallantry; for the fine fellows addressed remained immovable, knowing that certain death would be the consequence of any nearer approach."

It is curious to note how the cool, unshaken valour of the British infantry impressed even the French. A French officer of cuirassiers long afterwards told the mess of the 51st, that when his regiment was re-forming for a new attack just near the British position, he observed that the men of the 51st had ordered their arms and were standing at ease. "See how coolly those fellows take it," he said to his major. "That must be one of the old Peninsula regiments, and we shall make no impression on it."

It is impossible for a body of men—least of all Frenchmen—to keep for two hours in a fiery effervescence of excitement, especially when the excitement has not been fanned by success. In their later charges the horsemen came on as bravely as ever, but much more slowly and coolly. Having expended all their pistol-cartridges, shouted themselves hoarse, and ridden their horses almost to a stand-still, they resorted to what may be called facial warfare. "The troopers," says an actor in the scene, "would encompass us with fierce gesticulations and angry scowls, in which a display of incisors became very apparent to all. These peculiarities of manner, of looks, and gesticulations, amongst the French became so remarkable towards the end of the day, consequent upon a repetition of failures, and the attacks being sustained by our side with such coolness, and even good-humour, that when the colonel issued the command to prepare for cavalry, his officers would thunder out the exhortation to the men—having a tincture of sarcasm in it—'Now, men, make faces!'"

The charge of the wearied French cavalry, in a word, cooled down to an exhausted walk; mail-clad cuirassiers, spear-armed lancers, dragoons with naked swords, rode to and fro on the ridge, to use Wellington's phrase, "as though they owned it." "I had the infantry," he said, "for some time in squares, and the French cavalry walking about us as if it had been their own." The English squares and the French squadrons, said Lord Uxbridge, "seemed almost, for a short time, hardly taking any notice of each other."

"The French cavalry," wrote another officer, "were riding about amongst our squares in a manner never before seen; when, all firing having ceased, they might have been mistaken by any one unacquainted with the uniforms for our own. While large bodies occupied spaces between the squares of infantry on the crest of the allied position, smaller parties might be seen riding round them, and even menacing those of the second line." The French cavalry, in a word, had exhausted its attacking power. The squares were inexpugnable. Yet the proud Frenchmen, though they could not conquer, scarcely knew how to yield.

Napoleon was accustomed to say afterwards that if Murat had led his cavalry at Waterloo he would have broken the English squares. Some one asked Wellington if he thought Murat would have done this. "No," he answered, "he would not! Nor ten Murats!"

Thiers' rhetoric, it will be noticed, achieves for Ney's cavalry a much more shining degree of success than was attained by their own swords. "In their first charge," he says, "they galloped upon Alten's division, broke the squares, and commenced a furious slaughter. Our cuirassiers glutted their rage by a merciless massacre of the English." The light cavalry of the Guard next joined in the mêlée, and "broke some more squares." Kellerman's squadrons next appeared on the scene. They "broke the first line of the British entirely," "cut to pieces" Alten's unfortunate division once more, and "broke several squares." Next came the heavy cavalry of the Guard, and they "did wonders in breaking the squares." Kellerman's carabineers in reserve next rode furiously on to the ridge, "broke several squares, cut the men in pieces, and destroyed three-fourths of their second human wall." After so many squares had been "broken," it is a marvel that anything was left standing! As a matter of fact, there were only nine oblongs on the ridge when the helmets of Ney's cuirassiers first came over the crest, and there were exactly nine —somewhat shrunken in size, it is true, but quite unshaken in form and order—when the last French horseman had vanished in retreat. Thiers must be left to the occupation of breaking—with the help of his ink-bottle—entirely imaginary squares—a literary feat which has much consoled French imagination. But, as a matter of sober history, 12,000 French cavalry rode for two hours round those nine dogged oblongs, and not one was wrecked.

The squares suffered most, as a matter of fact, during the intervals when the French squadrons had

ebbed from the ridge, and, with much clamour, were
re-forming in the valley below.   Then the French
guns had their chance, and smote with great slaughter
the solid masses of British infantry.   A single cannon
ball is said to have slain seventeen men in the ranks
of the 71st.   "There was," says an officer of the
52nd, "one incessant roar of round shot and shells
passing over us or through our ranks."   Some of
the French light batteries were brought up to the
British ridge itself, and fired at point-blank distance on the squares.   By a single blast of grape
one side of a German square was literally blown
away.

The British gunners fought magnificently.   When
before, indeed, had English artillerymen, lying for a
moment of shelter beneath the friendly bayonets of
an English square, to watch their guns in possession of French cavalry, and to run out, as the
wave of hostile swordsmen flowed back over the
ridge, re-load their pieces, and keep up a frantic
fire until a new wave of helmeted and sworded foes
swept once more over the guns?   How magnificently, and with what deadly effect the British
batteries of horse-artillery fought that day can only
be realised by one who reads the thrilling tale of
Mercer's guns.

After their twelve charges on the British squares,
the exhausted horsemen owned themselves beaten.
But it was not till nearly two-thirds of their number

strewed the narrow plateau on which the English stood, or the slope that led to it. Nothing indeed in this wonderful duel betwixt 6000 British infantry and 12,000 splendid French cavalry is more wonderful than the completeness with which this great body of proud and gallant horsemen was destroyed. A hundred wrecked squadrons drew off in all stages of disintegration, but as an organised body Napoleon's whole cavalry was destroyed.

By six o'clock the French cavalry attack had exhausted itself, and Ney sent a message to Napoleon asking for infantry to support these cavalry rushes. This drew from the Emperor the angry exclamation, "Infantry! Where does he suppose I can get them? Does he expect me to make them?" On the other hand, Wellington, as he watched this third great effort to break his line fail, cried to Adam, in a very brisk and animated manner, "By G——, Adam, I think we shall beat them yet!" That "yet" is expressive; it reveals the strain on Wellington's mind, and the mood—stubborn but not sanguine—in which he was fighting Waterloo.

At some hour which it is difficult to fix, but during the later stages of the cavalry charges, the assault on La Haye Sainte was renewed, and this time with success. The Germans, under Baring, held that post gallantly. Even when the French had gained the orchard to the south, Baring's men stubbornly clung to the buildings nearest the British line. At last ammunition failed. The Germans were armed with rifles, and no supplies of the special cartridges they needed reached them. The triumphant French broke in; many climbed on the roof and shot down the defenders beneath them; and towards six o'clock Baring himself, with a handful of his gallant men, smoke-blackened and exhausted, escaped to the British ridge, and the French held the farmhouse, with the gravel-pit on the other side of the road above it.

They had now established themselves within sixty yards of the British crest, and it seemed as if the wasted lines of the British infantry might be easily broken. A massive infantry attack, supported by cavalry and with guns on its flanks, might well have broken through at that point. But Napoleon's infantry resources were by this time almost exhausted. Reille's corps was entangled in the bloody fight round Hougoumont; D'Erlon's columns had never recovered from the tempestuous rush of the Household and the Union Brigades. Ney's cavalry, too, had been practically wrecked in their two hours' wrestle with the indomitable British squares. But La Haye Sainte and the gravel-pit became the centre of a fierce and sustained skirmishing attack by the men of Donzolet's division, a skirmishing onslaught that grew ever more venomous and angry, till it shook the British line against which it was directed. How deadly was this infantry attack may be judged from the fate of the 27th. This fine regiment had marched from Ghent all through the night of the 17th; it reached Waterloo at 9 o'clock on the morning of the battle, the men falling into an exhausted slumber as soon as they had gained the post assigned to them. The thunder of the battle failed to awaken them; but, later in the afternoon, they were aroused and brought up to the line above La Haye Sainte. And in a space of time to be measured in minutes, literally every second man in the regiment was shot down!

Sometimes the British regiments charged forward, and for a moment drove back these galling and deadly skirmishers. The sharpest fighting took place just where, through a somewhat deep cutting, the Brussels road crossed the edge of the ridge. A staff officer of Picton's division describes a curious atmospheric effect which attended one of these charges. "The slanting rays of the setting sun," he says, " reaching us through the medium of the smoke from the guns, rendered the atmosphere a camera obscura on a grand scale. Our horizon was exactly on a level with the ground on which the contest between the two advances was going on, and we could see the figures, as on a camera obscura brought out in strong relief, and flitting backwards and forwards like shadows. Sometimes the French darted forward out of the ravine and fired one by one, others behind them advanced some steps and fired also, his neighbour again preceded him, and so on, till they came up to our advance (who had in like manner kept up a fire), and at last were almost muzzle to muzzle. Neither party would recede. The contest was terrible. The British recoil a few paces! All is lost, we thought, though we said nothing, though highly excited, and with beating hearts, as if we were watching a prize-fight. Again the British rally; they push the French back, step by step, by dint of musketry, and almost muzzle to muzzle, over the ravine, or small breastwork, in disorder."

This stage of the struggle — the fourth great stage of the battle—was attended with one tragedy. With boyish rashness, the Prince of Orange ordered Colonel Ompteda, who commanded a brigade of the German Legion, to take forward a battalion and drive back a column of French infantry. At that moment Ompteda had no cavalry to support him, and the helmets of some squadrons of French cuirassiers could be seen over the ridge. It was certain that an infantry line moving down the slope would be instantly charged and destroyed. The Prince of Orange would listen to no remonstrance, and repeated his order to attack in line with bayonet. Ompteda, a soldier of the finest type, calmly replied, "Well, I will," drew his sword, ordered his battalion to form line, said to his lieutenant-colonel, "Try and save my two nephews," and rode out in advance of his men.

The French, according to one account, "seemed

astonished at the extraordinary calm approach of the solitary horseman, whose white plume showed him to be an officer of high rank." Ompteda rode straight up to the French muskets, but before his men could reach him the cuirassiers were upon them, flank and rear, and out of the whole battalion only six officers and eighteen unwounded men found their way back to the British ridge. The Prince of Orange himself later in the day was wounded, a fortunate circumstance for his fame; it helped the world to forget that he had destroyed one regiment at Quatre Bras, and another at Waterloo, through pure incompetency and rashness.

The flags of the British regiments were convenient targets for the French guns, and a dreadful fire was concentrated upon them. The 40th had nearly twenty sergeants killed and wounded while carrying its flags; those of the 42nd were entirely shot away and nothing but the poles left. The 30th and the 73rd sent their flags out of action, so murderous was the fire they attracted. It is an odd proof of the jealous regard of the regiment for its colours, that later in the day, when the 72nd formed fours for the final advance, the officer in command rolled the colours round the body of a trustworthy sergeant. There were no officers left to carry them!

CHAPTER XIX

THE STORY OF THE GREAT FIGHT : THE
SCENE ON THE RIDGE

THE fight had now raged for nearly seven hours, and the very appearance of the heroic but wasted British lines showed how fierce the struggle had been. La Haye Sainte had fallen. Hougoumont was in flames. Along the British crest the batteries still fired, but the slain gunners lay thick about their pieces and many a gun was silenced. The British brigades had shrunk almost to regiments, the regiments to companies. The cavalry had suffered almost as much as the infantry. "Where is your brigade?" Vivian asked Lord Edward Somerset, who commanded the Household Brigade. "Here," said Lord Edward, pointing to two scanty squadrons, with many riderless and wounded horses. The two magnificent cavalry brigades, that rode with such power on D'Erlon's columns, had shrunk to a couple of squadrons at nightfall. Some of the squares had fallen back for shelter from the ridge, and the positions they had first occupied were still perfectly defined on the trodden and muddy soil by the

LORD EDWARD FITZROY SOMERSET

From a print in the possession of Mrs. Edward Somerset

dead that lay in ranks. Seen sometimes through the whirling smoke, the square of the dead looked more solid than the square of the living.

Long after the battle Wellington remarked of this period of the day, " I looked oftener at my watch than at anything else. I knew that if my troops could keep their position till night, I must be joined by Blücher before morning, and we should not have left Bonaparte an army next day. But I was glad as one hour of daylight slipped away after another, and our position was still maintained."

" The officer commanding the 27th regiment," says Picton's staff officer, " when there was a temporary cessation of fire from artillery, rode up to our major, and announced that he had barely an officer left to command each company. Major Browne offered to lend him some from the 40th. This, however, was at once imperatively declined. 'The sergeants of the regiment liked to command the companies,' he said, 'and he would be loth to deprive them of the honour.'" At one stage a couple of sergeants of the 73rd came up to Major Kelly and told him they had no one to command them, their officers being all killed or wounded. Kelly was on the staff of his division, but he told the sergeants he would come and command the regiment himself. The men of the 73rd cheered as Kelly came up to be their leader, and the cheer had an unexpected effect. It was caught up by the regiments on either side and ran far, and the wave of exultant sound instantly stiffened the sorely shaken line.

With La Haye Sainte in French hands the centre of Wellington's army lay uncovered, and from a distance of scarcely sixty yards the French, pushing forward infantry and guns, were able to pour a most destructive fire on Alten's left and Kempt's right. Ompteda's brigade was practically destroyed, and Shaw Kennedy galloped direct to Wellington and reported that his line of battle immediately behind La Haye Sainte was practically broken; the whole space between Halkett's and Kempt's brigade was empty. At that moment, in Shaw Kennedy's judgment, and at that point, the whole issue of the battle was in peril. Napoleon, however, failed to push his attack at the vital point with overmastering energy, while Wellington showed the utmost coolness and resource. He bade Kennedy "get all the German troops of the division on the spot you can, and all the guns you can find;" while he in person brought up some Brunswick troops. "In no other part of the action," says Kennedy, "was the Duke of Wellington exposed to so much personal risk as on this occasion, as he was necessarily under a close and most destructive infantry fire at a very short distance, and at no other period of the day were his great qualities as a commander so strongly brought out."

But the French, too, were shaken by the long strain

of the fight. "The attacks," says Mitchell, "no longer bore the appearance of being made by disciplined and well-organised troops, but resembled rather the fierce and irregular onsets made by the soldiers of the Middle Ages, who rushed forward in large or small bands, as accident or the influence of favourite leaders prompted, in order to try their individual courage against whatever adversaries some similar impulse might throw in their way."

For two hours there was a sort of procession of these unrelated, wrathful, and desperate attacks on the British line at this point, attacks which represented not any effort of generalship on the part of the French, but the fury of individual combatants. Two or three squadrons of cuirassiers, with half a battalion of infantry, apparently under some self-elected leader, would suddenly emerge from the smoke, dash in on the slender British line, persist in the attack till most were shot down, then the survivors stalked sullenly back into the smoke again. More than once a single French cavalry officer rode alone at the English line, like a Malay running amuck, and perished there.

The spot above La Haye Sainte became a sort of "duelling-post" betwixt the two armies. A hundred successive combats were waged on it. The French infantry attack grew deadlier. "For two or three hours," says Kincaid, "there was no variety with us, but one continued blaze of musketry. The smoke hung so thick about that, though not more than eighty yards apart, we could only distinguish each other by the flashes of the pieces. Our division, which had stood upwards of 5000 men at the beginning of the battle, had dwindled down into a solitary line of skirmishers. The 27th were literally lying dead in square a few yards behind us. I had never yet heard of a battle in which everybody was killed; but this seemed likely to be an exception, as we were all going by turns."

The atmosphere of the battle at this stage is graphically described by Mercer, whose battery of artillery, forming part of the reserve, was suddenly called to the front by Sir Augustus Frazer in person. The battery went forward at the gallop. "I rode with Frazer," says Mercer, "whose face was as black as a chimney-sweep's from the smoke, and the jacket-sleeve of his right arm torn open by a musket-ball or case-shot, which had merely grazed his flesh. As we went along, he told me that the enemy had assembled an enormous mass of heavy cavalry in front of the point to which he was leading us, and that in all probability we should immediately be charged on gaining our position. 'The Duke's orders, however, are positive,' he added, 'that in the event of their persevering and charging home, you do not expose your men, but retire with them into the adjacent squares of infantry.'"

"As he spoke, we were ascending the reverse slope of the main position. We breathed a new atmosphere; the air was suffocatingly hot, resembling that issuing from an oven. We were enveloped in thick smoke, and, malgre the incessant roar of cannon and musketry, could distinctly hear around us a mysterious humming noise, like that which one hears of a summer's evening proceeding from myriads of black beetles; cannon-shot, too, ploughed the ground in all directions, and so thick was the hail of balls and bullets that it seemed dangerous to extend the arm lest it should be torn off. In spite of the serious situation in which we were, I could not help being somewhat amused at the astonishment expressed by our surgeon (Hitchins), who heard for the first time this sort of music. He was close to me as we ascended the slope, and, hearing this infernal carillon about his ears, began staring round in the wildest and most comic manner imaginable, twisting himself from side to side, exclaiming, 'My God, Mercer, what is that? What is all this noise? How curious! How very curious!' And then, when a cannon-shot rushed hissing past, 'There! there! What is it all?'"

The scene to the rear of the British army was as remarkable, if not as tragical, as that on its front. In an army of such mixed nationalities and uncertain degrees of loyalty, the drift of stragglers to the rear was more than ordinarily great. "The roads," says Mitchell, "were crowded with broken carriages, wounded men, dismounted dragoons, and an innumerable train of followers and attendants,

whose very existence had hardly before been suspected. The soldiers of some of the foreign corps
attended a wounded comrade in whole bands: one
man carried the sufferer's cap, another his musket,
a third his knapsack; and the bleeding invalid himself was often supported by as many friends as could
possibly assist him: most of these compassionate
persons forgot to return to the field." "Whole companies of certain regiments," says an eye-witness,
"seemed to have marched off, for I saw arms piled
with some regularity, fires blazing, and cooking
kettles suspended over them, while men were lying
about, smoking, sleeping, or engaged in culinary
operations, as coolly as if no enemy was within a
day's march of them. That such should have been
the scene within half a mile of the battlefield is, I
imagine, without a parallel in the annals of warfare,
but really ought not to surprise us when we consider
how many thousands had no stomach for the fight."

All this makes intelligible Muffling's story, how
that, when the leading files of Ziethen's Prussians
caught their first glimpse of the battlefield from the
nearest height, they suddenly turned round and
marched briskly back. Muffling rode at speed to
learn the secret of this extraordinary movement, and
found that the Prussians believed that what they
saw was the spectacle of the whole British left wing
in full retreat; and only on Muffling explaining that
these were mere swarms of stragglers and deserters,

and that the British line remained unbroken, did Ziethen consent to advance.

The forest tracks behind Waterloo, however, showed other and nobler scenes than these. Carey, an officer in the commissariat department, after describing the tide of fugitives flowing towards Brussels—Belgians in whole companies, both horse and foot, wounded soldiers, prisoners, camp-followers, &c.—describes how a detachment of Scots Greys and Inniskilling Dragoons came riding proudly through this ignoble multitude. They were some twenty-five in number; every man bore some bloody wound. Some had lost their helmets and had handkerchiefs bound round their heads, from under which the blood ran thick over their faces. Their uniforms were torn; the horses they rode were, in many instances, gashed with sword-cuts; but the men rode with a proud and fierce air. They were convoying two French eagles captured in the great charge which had destroyed D'Erlon's massive columns. One captured eagle was carried high in air, the other had been broken from its pole in the struggle to capture it.

Equally striking was the spectacle of a detachment of British artillery, with ammunition, pushing their way—silent, grim, and resolute—through the stream of fugitives towards the battle raging in the front, a picture of disciplined valour. The cluster of Greys and Inniskillings, bloody with sword-wounds, but carrying their captured eagle high amid the disorderly rout fleeing from the battle, offers the more picturesque spectacle perhaps; but that tiny detachment of British artillery, pushing resolutely on with trained and silent courage to the front, where their countrymen were dying, while the tide of rabble flowed past them towards Brussels, is a fine picture of loyal and disciplined valour.

CHAPTER XX

THE STORY OF THE GREAT FIGHT : THE DEFEAT
OF THE OLD GUARD

BUT Blücher's battle was now telling with great effect on Napoleon's right wing. Few things in the history of war are more impressive than the story of the loyalty and energy with which Blücher struggled over the cross-roads from Wavre to join his English ally at Waterloo. The march was of extraordinary difficulty. " The rivulets had become torrents ; every hollow was filled with water ; some of the forest roads actually resembled watercourses, through which the men had to wade for hundreds of yards together ; deep pools of water, that constantly forced the troops to break their files, had been formed in every direction. The columns extended at times over miles of ground. If the cavalry and infantry were retarded by such obstacles, the case was far worse with the artillery. The guns frequently sank axle-deep into the loamy soil, and had to be worked out by the tired and exhausted soldiers." When the tired soldiers seemed about to give up, Blücher appealed to them as his "children" not to make him break faith with Wellington.

Late in the afternoon news came that Thielemann, who covered Blücher's rear-guard, was being attacked at Wavre. The belated Grouchy had at last reached that town, and was falling upon the Prussians he found in possession of it. But nothing shook or changed the purpose of the indomitable Blücher. "Tell him to do his best," was the Marshal's reply to Thielemann's demand for reinforcements; "the campaign of Belgium must be decided at Mont St. Jean, and not at Wavre."

The real time of the arrival of the Prussians is one of the most clearly defined facts of the whole history of the battle. All the witnesses agree upon it. Gourgand says that "at half-past four General Domont observed a division of 8000 to 10,000 Prussians debouching from the woods of Frischenois." The Prussian official account says: "It was half-past four o'clock. The difficulties of the road had retarded the march of the Prussian columns, so that only two brigades had arrived at the covered position which was assigned them. The generals resolved to begin the attack with the troops which they had at hand." Siborne says that at half-past four o'clock the Prussian force which had come up amounted to 16,000 men.

Wellington, indeed, long afterwards declared, "I saw the Prussians, within four miles of us, filing over a stream at ten o'clock in the morning; but the impediments were so great that they did not reach us till seven in the evening." But Wellington was plainly mistaken. He did not see the Prussians so soon, nor did they arrive so late, as he imagined. A little later than half-past four Bülow's attack on Napoleon's right was in progress. Napoleon, as we have seen, had sent Lobau with 10,000 of the Young Guard to keep back the Prussian advance. Planchenoit was, for the French, a very strong position. The village church is surrounded by a low stone wall, curving like a horse-shoe, and commanding the exit of both the lanes which run through the village. The French held the village and the curving wall in great strength. The Prussians advanced in solid column up the lanes, and were shot down in whole battalions. The murderous slaughter round the churchyard held by the French in Planchenoit explains the great loss sustained by Blücher's forces on June 18. In spite, however, of the most gallant resistance, Lobau was steadily pushed back, and Napoleon had to send a division of the Old Guard to his support. About the same time Ziethen came into touch with Wellington's left wing, though their first contribution to the fight was very disastrous to the British. A battery of Prussian guns mistook an English battery for an enemy, opened a cruel flank fire upon it, and almost completely wrecked it.

But the pressure of Blücher's advance had already

drawn at least 16,000 good troops from Napoleon's reserve, while Ziethen's advance had made Wellington's left safe. Napoleon was now fighting on two fronts at once. He had reckoned on defeating Blücher and Wellington separately, but Blücher and Wellington were now closing in resistless strength upon him. Napoleon's hand, in a word, was caught betwixt the hammer and the anvil.

Napoleon now delivered his last stroke on the stubborn British front. He flung his famed and invincible Guard into the fight. Napoleon in person formed the Old Guard for its assault. The attacking column consisted of ten battalions, with two battalions held as a reserve; it was a force 6000 or 7000 strong, the very flower of Napoleon's army. It is still a matter of vehement dispute whether the Guard was formed in two columns or one. The balance of evidence seems to show that it was intended to form a single column; but, as it moved, it parted into two fragments, and each fragment moved on a slightly different course from the other, the general point of attack being towards the British right centre. Napoleon himself, with a fierce gesture, pointed out to the battalions of the Guard the path they were to take, and told them he must sleep in Brussels that night, and they must make a way for him. The advance of the Guard was well known to be the crowning and decisive stroke in Napoleon's battles, and, as the great bearskin caps of the Guard became

visible, moving down the French front, the whole
battle seemed to deepen in fury. The French guns
flamed anew along the whole ridge; the deadly
skirmishing fire far up the British slope, and especially above La Haye Sainte, grew fiercer. It was
the crisis of the day's fight.

Napoleon's fourth attack, as we have seen, had
gained a real amount of success; but, curiously
enough, Napoleon failed to see, or failed to use, the
success he had won. In his fifth attack—that of
the Imperial Guard—he completely ignored the
advantage which the capture of La Haye Sainte
gave him. Had the Guard attacked from La Haye
Sainte, its advance would have been covered to
within sixty yards of the British line; it would have
struck that line at its weakest point, and would have
had the highest chance of success. Napoleon, however, launched his Guard on that part of the line
held by Maitland's brigade of the British Guards.
This was the only one of Napoleon's five attacks
which was of a combined and general character.
Along the whole battle-front the strife re-awoke.

Wellington, with cool skill, strengthened the point
on which it was clear the assault of the Old Guard
would break. He brought up his last reserves—
many of them, unfortunately, Nassauers, on whom
little reliance was to be placed. His sole remaining
cavalry, the brigades of Vivian and Vandeleur, were
summoned from the left wing. Maitland's Guards

held that point in the line on which the French
Guard was moving, but they were kept back below
the ridge and out of sight.   The English Guards had
marched out two days before 1997 strong.   On the
evening of Waterloo, they numbered only 1627;
when they swung into line to meet the attack of the
Imperial Guard, they had not 1200.   To the right
of Maitland were the scanty remains of the 95th and
of the 71st, and the far-famed 52nd, a formidable
regiment nearly 1000 strong, under one of the best
soldiers that fought at Waterloo, Sir John Colborne,
and destined to play a remarkable part in the
struggle that followed.   Adam's whole brigade had
numbered when the campaign began 2621; it was
now less than 2000.

Just at this stage of the fight, the sound of
heavy guns far to the French right grew deeper and
louder.   That sound marked the Prussian advance;
but Napoleon sent an aide-de-camp to gallop along
his whole front with the tidings that the sound
they heard was from Grouchy's guns, and the battle
was practically won!   Having disseminated what
Thiers calls "this useful falsehood," the Guard was
sent forward.

Each of its ten battalions was commanded by a
famous general.   Ney rode at the head of the
column, and when his horse was shot, struggling
clear from the falling beast, he still led, sword in
hand, the veterans of the Old Guard.   Napier's

battery, drawn like a bar of flame across the path of the great column, smote it cruelly with grape. Friant fell, and Michel, and many a well-known leader. Presently through the smoke the great bearskin caps of the Guard were visible from the British position. The French, on their part, saw before them what seemed an empty ridge. They could distinguish dimly through the smoke, says Siborne, only "the cocked hats of a few mounted officers;" one of those cocked hats, as it happened, covering the head of Wellington himself.

Steadily the French moved on. Suddenly Welington called up the Guards, who were lying down in rank. In a moment what had been a wall of grey smoke became a long red line of British Guardsmen, with muskets falling to the level. Wellington denied that he used the classic phrase "Up, Guards, and at 'em!" "What I may have said, and possibly did say," he told Croker, "was 'Stand up, Guards,' and then gave the order to attack." That sudden apparition of a menacing red line drawn across their path for a moment made even the Old Guard hesitate. For one breathless instant the two bodies confronted each other. "With their high bearskin caps," as one who took part in the fight describes it, "the French appeared to the British through the smoky haze like a corps of giants bearing down upon us. Arrived within about eighty paces of us (on the following morning I

measured the distance which separated their dead
from ours), they halted, and, for a moment, stood
as if amazed at our effrontery in offering opposition
to their onward movement. Then, saluting us, they
commenced that work of death so often narrated,
and our thinned ranks told but too well with what
precision their fire was given."

The fire of the French column, it is true, was deadly ;
but the fire from the wide front of the English Guards
was overwhelming.   Again, and yet again, the dancing
flames of their volleys ran from end to end of the
English line.   The French column seemed to suffer a
convulsive shock, and to shrivel as that blast of lead
smote it.   Its outer ranks became a mere frieze of
falling bodies.   The 33rd and 69th, on the right of
the English Guards, poured their fire on the shoulder
of the column.   The Old Guard endeavoured to
deploy, its officers, with waving swords and frantic
gestures, trying to complete the movement.   " Now
is the time, boys !" cried Colborne, and the English
Guards, with levelled bayonets, instantly charged.
The French column broke, it spread out like water
escaping from a dam.   Packs and weapons were flung
down ; muskets were fired in the air from the centre
of the column, and the whole shaken mass reeled in
confusion down the slope.   The English Guards
followed fiercely, but, getting out of order, Maitland tried to steady his men.   In the confusion
a shout arose of " Form square," and in some con-

fusion the Guards fell back to the ridge, where they instantly fell into line again.

It is a matter still debated whether the body thus driven back by the English Guards was really the first of the two so-called columns of the French Guard, or merely a great mass of skirmishers thrown out in advance of the column itself. Mr. Leake, who carried the colours of the 52nd that day, has written two solid volumes on things in general, and on the defeat of the Old Guard in particular, in which, with great strength of evidence, he undertakes to show that the force which Maitland and his men overthrew consisted merely of the skirmishers which covered the approach of the column of the Old Guard; and the 52nd alone—to use Mr. Leake's words—"defeated single-handed that portion of the Imperial Guard of France, about 10,000 in number, which advanced to make the last attack on the British position."

Without undertaking to decide this much-vexed question, it is certain that the 52nd, under Colborne, by a most daring movement, wrecked utterly that part of the Old Guard which Maitland's men had not touched, and pushed its own victorious advance so far that it practically decided the great fight. The 52nd were nearly 1200 strong; and having been in reserve all the day, were, as they themselves said, "as fresh as larks." There was nothing of the airy gaiety of larks, however, in their temper. They had listened for hours to the thunder of battle in their front; had watched the tide of wounded men ebbing past them to the rear, and were consumed with that stern eagerness to join in the fight which brave men feel who watch for hours their comrades contending and falling. The second segment—or, as it is sometimes called, the left column—of the Old Guard moved coolly and swiftly up the slope, undisturbed by the defeat of the battalions in advance of it. Colborne saw his opportunity. The massive column offered its shoulder to the 52nd, and a quick and daring movement would serve to bring that regiment down upon the far-stretching and unsheltered flank of the Old Guard. Colborne was without orders; if he took his regiment into the open, and in line, he was liable himself to be broken by a charge of French cavalry.

But Colborne faced all risks. He took the 52nd in quick time directly forward, until his own left was in a line with the leading company of the French Guard. The left company of the 52nd then "marked time." Colborne gave the order. "Right shoulders forward," and the long line of the 52nd wheeled round till it was parallel with the flank of the French column. Just then Adam, his brigadier, rode up and asked Colborne what he was about to do. "To make that column feel our fire," was the answer. The group of generals on the ridge saw the advance of the 52nd, and Hill afterwards described it as "one of the most beautiful advances" he had ever seen.

One who stood near Wellington, and watched his
face, said that the only time he wore an anxious
look was when the Old Guard was moving up with
such grim resolution on his centre, and that look
of anxiety melted into one of relief as he saw the
magnificent advance of the 52nd.

The outer files of the French column now halted,
faced the advancing 52nd, and opened a hurried but
deadly fire upon it. No less than 140 men of the
52nd fell in less than five minutes. But the mounted
officers of the regiment were in its front, together
with Adam, who commanded the brigade. Chalmers,
the major of the 52nd, put his cap on the point of
his sword, and, standing up in his stirrups, cheered
on the regiment. Officers and men realised the
greatness of the moment. They had caught the far-
famed Imperial Guard at a disadvantage. It out-
numbered them by three or four to one, and yet
they felt sure they could destroy it. Directly the
wheeling movement was complete, and the long
front of the 52nd was parallel with the flank of the
French column, the British regiment poured in a
wasting and cruel volley, and then charged with the
bayonet. The solid mass of the Old Guard seemed
to stagger and disintegrate. Its head broke into
flight, its rear, still keeping some order, fell hastily
back. But the mass of the column still was under
the bayonets of the 52nd; and that gallant regiment
swept onward, pushing the broken column before it

in a line parallel with the British ridge. As the
great mass, rent with musketry volleys and torn with
bayonets, drifted, so to speak, eastward, the spectacle
of the broken Old Guard, driven athwart the British
front by a line of British bayonets, had a magical
effect on the French skirmishers that clustered thick
along the whole British ridge. They fell back in
haste. The far-famed Imperial Guard was destroyed,
and two armies saw that portent! Once, indeed,
there arose in the smoke to the right of the triumphant 52nd a tumult of galloping cavalry. Its right
company wheeled instantly round, and fired a volley
into the approaching mass. As a matter of fact,
the approaching horsemen consisted of some British
light dragoons, with French cuirassiers in pursuit.

The wrecked column of the Old Guard was thrust
in the fashion we have described clean across the
Brussels road. Here Colborne, a cool soldier, halted
to re-form. The regimental colour and the covering
sergeants were ordered out, and the line was being
dressed, when Wellington rode up. "Well done,
Colborne," he said, "well done! Go on; don't give
them time to rally." And the 52nd moved on again,
crossed the road, brought up its left shoulder sharply,
and proceeded to push the shattered battalions of
the Old Guard back towards the French slope.

Colborne, in a word, tumbled that great column of
French veterans for half a mile athwart the British
front, and was now driving it, hopelessly disorganised,

SIR JOHN COLBORNE, AFTERWARDS LORD SEATON

From an engraving

back on La Belle Alliance! But, though broken and
defeated, the French Guard still maintained a sort
of wrathful courage. "I shall never forget," says an
English officer, "some of the French Guards turning
to look at their redoubtable enemies; some lingering
rays of the sun falling on their faces through the
smoke, now nearly cleared away, threw a lurid kind
of glare upon their countenances, and gave them a
fierce look, particularly when the gleam from the
musketry assisted." Hooper describes this remarkable movement, the course of the 52nd across the
trampled and corpse-strewn slope, as "a bright beam
of red light streaking the sombre and misty field."

Wellington, with the keen vision and lightning-
like resolve of a great general, seized that moment to
hurl his yet remaining cavalry on the French reserves. An eye-witness thus described the scene at
the time: "The Duke, who had been attentively ob-
serving what was passing in the French and Prussian
armies, suddenly shut up his telescope and exclaimed
to the officers near him, 'Now every man must
advance!'"

Up to that moment the battle still looked black
for the British army; one-third of its guns lay
silent, its wasted regiments could cover with little
more than a screen of skirmishers the ridge they
held. The Belgian and Nassau troops were with
difficulty held from mere flight. Vivian, indeed, at
one point kept some Nassau battalions from quitting

the field by using his cavalry as a living and un-
yielding fence, beyond which the broken battalions
were not suffered to pass. The Nassauers fell, or
rather drifted, back *en masse* against the horses'
heads of the 10th Hussars, who roughly closed their
files, and, with oaths and menaces, and sometimes
with threatening sword-blades, prevented further
retreat. The French batteries were still firing furiously from beyond the valley. It was possible that
the Old Guard might rally, and D'Erlon's columns,
or those of Reille, move afresh to the attack.

But Wellington knew how the overthrow of the
Old Guard, under the eyes of the whole French
army, would affect its imagination. He had still
the brigades of Vivian and Vandeleur in effective
strength, and he at once launched Vivian's brigade,
followed by that of Vandeleur, on the disordered
French.

Vivian was ordered not to attack any infantry
squares, unless they were visibly shaken, but he
was to destroy all the French cavalry he met.
Vivian took his squadrons down the slope, the smoke
eddying thickly about him, with fugitives on every
side. The 10th Hussars led, the 18th and the 1st
Hussars of the German Legion in support. Maitland's
Guards cheered the Hussars as they rode past their
front. Vivian, with his first line, broke in succession
a regiment of lancers, one of carabineers, and some
squadrons of cuirassiers. Then, leaving the 10th to

re-form, he rode back, and brought up the 18th, galloped over a battery of artillery, and swept on towards the French summit. Vandeleur's brigade, riding on a line farther to the west, broke some bodies of formed infantry, while the 11th Dragoons captured a battery—the last of the French guns in position. "We were riding in all directions," says one of Vivian's staff, " at parties who were attempting to make their escape, and in many instances had to cut down men who had taken up their arms after having in the first instance laid them down. From the appearance of the enemy lying together for safety, they were a mass some feet in height, calling out, from the injury of one pressing upon another, and from the horses stamping upon them."

Now came the thrilling and sublime climax of the great struggle. Wellington ordered the advance of his whole line, and he himself, accompanied by only a couple of officers, rode in the van. The strain of the long fight was over, Blücher was pressing fiercely in on the French right, its centre was rolling back in confusion. In the drifting mass of wrecked regiments and flying squadrons, some squares of infantry, moving in stern order, were visible, and a squadron of the 10th, led by Major Howard, rode gallantly upon one of these, Howard and his leading files dying on the very bayonets. But the stubborn square remained unbroken.

Yet another square, however, was charged, and

destroyed.   It was commanded by Cambronne, who, as a matter of fact, did not utter the famous saying about "the Guard dies, but never surrenders."   Neil Campbell describes Cambronne, whom he met at Elba, as a desperate, uneducated ruffian, who had been a drummer with Napoleon in Egypt, and still kept the manners of a drummer.   Cambronne's sense of honour was on a level with his manners.   When the square he commanded was attacked it dissolved, and Cambronne himself surrendered with praise-worthy meekness to Halkett in person.   Halkett was conducting his prisoner to his battalion, when his horse was shot, and the heroic Cambronne took to his heels to escape.   He was overtaken, however, by Halkett, captured afresh, and marched off to the rear in charge of a sergeant.

Napoleon had watched the advance of his famous Guard with anxious gaze.   He sat moveless on his horse, his eyes fixed on the long black column growing fainter in the smoke; his fate hung on its success!   He saw its head crushed by Maitland's brigade; he beheld the yet more fatal apparition of the 52nd breaking in on its flank.   Those who stood near and watched his face saw it darken.   "Ils sont mêles ensemble," he whispered.   Then came the spectacle of the British advance.   The long-tormented lines, sadly wasted indeed, but mad with the joy of being at last allowed to strike back, were moving at every point down the British slope.   Vivian's horsemen were riding and slaying in the French centre, Vandeleur's on the French left. Louder and sterner and nearer sounded the Prussian guns to the right. Napoleon looked over the landscape of the battle. It was his last battlefield, and everywhere the scene was one of wreck and flight. "Tout est perdu," he said, and turned his horse to fly. According to Lamartine, "as he contemplated the disastrous scene, he turned pale, stammered, and shed some tears, the first he had ever shed on a field of battle." At three o'clock he had despatched a courier to Paris announcing that victory was certain; six hours later he had no longer an army.

He took refuge at first in a square of the Guard, but Soult put his hands on the Emperor's reins and persuaded him to ride on. Kellerman declares that "Napoleon had so completely lost his senses at the end of the battle as neither to know the persons by whom he was surrounded nor to understand what was said to him, and that he had to be led out of the fray in a state of total helplessness." We catch a more heroic glimpse, indeed, of Ney than of Napoleon at this stage of the fight. On horseback, with bared head, and dress torn with shot and stained with mud, fierce with excitement and waving a broken sword, Ney strove to rally the fugitives, exclaiming, "Come with me, and I will show you how a marshal of France can die upon the field of battle."

How Wellington's long-tormented and wasted battalions, who for so many hours had stood to be shot at, received the order to advance may be imagined. The signal for the entire British line to advance changed, in an instant, the whole physiognomy of the battle. It is difficult to realise the almost utter blackness, the narrow area of vision, hedged with strangling smoke, in which for hours the British battalions above La Haye Sainte had fought. Kincaid tells how he could see nothing before him but a wall of smoke, out of which darted incessantly the red flames of French muskets, and nothing on either side but the bodies of slain men and horses. After hours of that fierce combat in smoke and darkness, suddenly, far to the right, was heard the sound of a cheer. It grew nearer, louder. The much-enduring battalions caught it up eagerly. Some warlike instinct told the men it was the signal to advance. The line closed in; its front was "dressed," and at the quick-step it went forward, driving the French before it. A few steps took it out of the obscuring smoke, and the whole landscape of the battle broke on the gaze of the men. "It was a fine summer's evening, just before sunset. The French were flying in one confused mass. The British lines were seen in close pursuit, and in admirable order, as far as the eye could reach to the right, while the plain to the left was filled with Prussians."

The Prussians, indeed, were now coming up fast, full of admiration for the part the British had played, and on fire with zeal to pursue the French. Leake tells an amusing story of how a column of Prussians, at the quick-step, passed the 52nd as it halted at Rosomme. The column fell into slow step as it caught sight of the British regiment, its band played the National Anthem, its general, riding up, asked to see the English colours. The flag was shown him; he let go his reins, grasped the shot-torn and glorious fragment to his breast, and solemnly kissed it, crying, "Braves Anglais!" Blücher and Wellington met at some point which is in dispute, and the old "hussar general," with the spectacle of Napoleon's whole army in flight before him, embraced and kissed the somewhat disconcerted Wellington, with a rapture almost too great for words. Such words as he did use were an odd compound of German and French: "Mein lieber Kamerad!" he exclaimed, and then "quelle affair"; "which," says Wellington, "was pretty much all the French he knew!" The Prussians took up the pursuit, and keenly did they urge it. All night long the tumult of the great flight rolled southwards. Earth has seldom witnessed such a spectacle of wreck and panic and hurrying flight. When the Prussian infantry columns could no longer hang on the rear of the flying French, their cavalry still urged the pursuit, and when these, in turn, were outfled, drummer-boys were mounted on horses, and sent forward to cling to the rear of the distracted fugitives. Nine times that night, it is said, when the wreck of the French army tried to rest, it was roused to new flight by the mere roll of the Prussian drums.

Wellington, meanwhile, turning his back on Prussians and French, rode slowly back to his quarters. Darkness had fallen. The air was bitter with the acrid odour of smoke and the scent of the trampled crops. More than 30,000 dead or dying lay scattered over an area of a few square roods. "During the ride back, which was performed at a walk, and may have occupied about half-an-hour, he spoke," wrote one of his staff afterwards, "to no one of his suite, and was evidently sombre and dejected. Well might he be so in the midst of his triumph, for death had been busy that day amongst his old and well-tried followers. The few individuals who attended him were scarcely less silent than their leader, wearing, too, rather the appearance of a little funeral train than of victors in one of the greatest battles ever fought. But, in truth, we were a set of mourners, since all had left friends or associates, more or less valued, stretched upon that bloody field—how many we as yet knew not."

WELLINGTON

From a mezzotint after the painting by ROBERT HOME

CHAPTER XXI

AFTER WATERLOO

" I NEVER fought such a battle before, and I hope
I shall never fight such another;" that is Wellington's summary of Waterloo. And, in the scale
of its slaughter, the fierceness of its passions, and the
decisiveness of its results, Waterloo deserves Byron's
description of the "first and last of fights."

The night which followed the great struggle was
almost more terrible to the French, at least, than the
battle itself. All through the night, as we have seen,
the tumult of distracted flight, and of fierce, unpitying pursuit, rolled southwards. Under the smoke-
filled skies, made darker still with gathering night,
the "grand army"—infantry, cavalry, artillery—dissolved into one vast host of fugitives, with all order
lost and all distinctions forgotten. They struggled
together and trampled on each other along the
narrow paved road, or in the muddy fields on either
side; while on their rear the pursuing Prussians rode,
and slew with unpitying swords.

The final stand was made at Genappes, where the
last French gun was captured and 800 men slain. At

five o'clock the next morning Napoleon was trying, and trying in vain, to rally the fugitives at Charleroi; within forty-eight hours masses of the flying French had reached Laon, nearly a hundred miles from the field of battle. The speed of the flight from Waterloo, says Mitchell, "stands altogether without parallel in history." Out of the 75,000 men who took part in the magnificent parade on the slopes of La Belle Alliance on the morning of Waterloo, not 15,000 ever again assembled under the eagles. And the wreckage of the flight was, perhaps, more astounding than even its speed. "The roads," Gneisenau wrote to his wife, "resembled a sea-shore strewn with cannons, limbers, muskets, ammunition waggons, and wreckage of all sorts."

Delafosse, in his Memoirs, gives a curious account of the French generals in the flight. A cluster of them rallied some broken infantry just outside the Hougoumont wood. There were Reille, Foy, D'Erlon, Bachelu, and others; "all were gloomy and sorrowful, like vanquished men. Their words were, 'Here is all that is left of my corps, my division, my brigade —I, myself!'" "We were humiliated; we were hopeless; we marched like a troop of mourners." That band of unhappy generals, without followers or staff, struggled forward all night long, with many rough experiences amongst the flying troops, till, at six in the morning, they crossed the Sambre. They reached Marchiennes, where they found Ney, who had outridden them, and was sound asleep. Describing the general flight, Delafosse says that "the rushing and entangled stream of a torrent in flood-time is a feeble image of that heap of men, of horses, of equipages, rushing one upon another; and when arrested by some obstacle, breaking over it, and about it, with fury."

The field of Waterloo itself, the morning after the battle, was a sight more tragical than even the long southward running road strewn with the débris of the great flight. The rich green crops that, on the morning of the 18th, stood thick and tall on the slopes and in the valley where two armies were about to contend, had been trampled out of existence. The eye wandered over what seemed a vast fallow, strewn with the ruin, not of one army, but of three. It seemed, says Kincaid, as if the world had tumbled to pieces, and three-fourths of everything had been destroyed in the wreck.

The story of the great fight was scribbled visibly in bloody characters on the now silent battlefield. Where the fiercest attacks had been delivered, there the dead lay thickest. The slaughter round Hougoumont was great, and its scale is brought out in a curious way. Describing the battle afterwards, Wellington himself said, "I remember seeing a large French column entering the wood behind Hougoumont, and another, about as large, going out on the other side. I said, 'This is the oddest manœuvre I ever saw;' but, on looking closely, I found that the second column consisted of the wounded. There were thousands limping off the field!" The face of the hill near La Haye Sainte, and from thence to Hougoumont, had more the appearance of a breach carried by assault than an ordinary and extended field of battle. Where the British squares had stood was clearly marked by a thick and ordered tracery of dead bodies. Where the columns of the Old Guard had halted, smitten in front by Maitland's fire, or torn by the terrible flank fire of the 52nd, could easily be distinguished. The long lines of the slain, looking grim in death still, with their bristling moustaches and tall bearskin caps, traced in dreadful outline a sort of human map of the wrecked column. The lines of the fallen Guard stretched almost to the crest of the British position, showing how gallantly Ney had led his battalions, and how nearly they had won. The plunderers had been busy over the whole field of the battle; the dead, and even the wounded, in most cases were stripped. But a sort of awe fenced, even in death, the veterans of the Old Guard from indignity. "Their arms, knapsacks, drums," says a British officer who describes the scene, "everything, in short, was untouched; no night-plunderers having been, as yet, bold enough to molest these fallen and defeated veterans."

No one understands Waterloo who does not keep in vivid remembrance the strangely composite character of Wellington's army, and the unreliable quality of at

least one half of it. A curious incident, illustrative of
the temper of the Nassauers and Belgians, who formed,
it will be remembered, nearly one-third of Wellington's
forces, is reported by Maurice. One of Colville's
aides-de-camp was asked why his division was left
unused at Hal, when Wellington's army was so sorely
pressed at Waterloo. He replied, "All I can say is,
that we were expecting all day long to have to fire on
the Belgians who were with us." Colville had not
only to guard Wellington's right, but to keep in check
a mass of doubtful allies! And one-third of Wellington's battle-line at Waterloo was held by troops of
this quality and temper. Shaw Kennedy, a perfectly
competent judge, says that, having regard to the
mixed quality of Wellington's army, its fighting
power as compared with that of the French was as
four to seven.

But Wellington had relied, and with justice, on
the stubborn valour of his British regiments. They
were young troops; they could not, perhaps, manœuvre; they had not the resourcefulness of veterans.
But they could stand to be shot at through patient
hours, or hold their places in the steadfast squares
while unceasing swarms of cavalry rode down on
them, with a cool and cheerful valour unsurpassed
in the records of war. Napoleon himself quite mis-
read the quality of the troops he was about to assail.
"I had no idea," he said long afterwards, "that the
British had such fine troops."

Reille himself, instructed by sad experience in the Peninsula as to the unconquerable stubbornness of the British soldier, warned Napoleon on the morning of Waterloo of the task he had before him. "The English," he told the Emperor, "were very inferior in attack, but were superior to any other European forces when acting on the defensive." Foy, another Peninsular veteran, told the Emperor, "Sire, these English fight like the devil." Soult told him later in the day that "it was vain to try to break English squares with cavalry." "You believe Wellington is a great man because he always beat you!" was Napoleon's angry reply. The Emperor was advised not to attempt a direct assault, but to manœuvre. "I know," said Napoleon in reply, "it is difficult to beat the English when in position, but I intend to manœuvre." Yet this is exactly what he did not do; or at least he did it very badly. "We were manœuvred," records Marbot, "like so many pumpkins." Wellington himself said Napoleon "did not manœuvre at all. He just moved forward in the old style in column, and was driven off in the old style!"

Muffling is a witness to the merits of the British soldier quite without bias, or, if he had a bias, it was of an unfriendly sort. But in a letter written within six days of the battle, and only published in 1891, he first dwells on the stern fury of the struggle itself. "I have never yet seen," he writes, "such a furious and bloody battle as this one was." At one stage of the battle, he says, " the French cuirassiers were assailing Wellington's third line, while masses of French infantry were falling upon his battalions at the front." Then Muffling passes on to declare of the British soldiers, that " for coolness, bravery, and interior discipline, there is nothing like them in all Europe." He adds grudgingly, "They have little manœuvring power," and makes the odd suggestion that "if we could but add Prussian *élan* to British stubbornness we should be invincible." Yet, as a matter of fact, the British soldier is both quicker-footed and quicker-witted, and more ready to attack than his Prussian rival.

Muffling grows enthusiastic over the part that Hougoumont played in the great fight. " Before we arrived there"—at the site chosen for the battle —" I said to the Duke, ' If only there were an apparently weak point in the right flank of your position, so that Bonaparte might assail it furiously, and neglect his own right wing '—on which Blücher would fall—'to such an extent that he should fail to discover the march of the Prussians.' And see ! when we arrived, there lay the advanced post of Hougoumont, upon which he (Bonaparte) indeed fell." Hougoumont, in Muffling's view, was invented by Heaven in order to tempt Napoleon to attack in the wrong place ! It was, he piously reflects, as if Heaven had guided everything so as to effect Bonaparte's downfall !

It is difficult to over-praise Wellington's personal contribution to Waterloo. It may be argued, with some justice, that he had failed in generalship in the early hours of the campaign. He concentrated too late. He failed to penetrate Napoleon's strategy. He was caught at Quatre Bras at what might easily have become a fatal disadvantage. But in the later stages of the four days' campaign he recovered himself magnificently. The cool retreat to Waterloo; his tactics during the whole of the great day's battle; the hawk-like vision with which he detected each coming attack; the swift, unfailing resource with which he met it; the unshaken courage with which he maintained the fight against such odds and through so many hours; the flash of lightning-like resolve—a true inspiration of soldierly genius—which made him, at the moment the Old Guard was wrecked, assume the offensive, and launch his wasted and heroic battalions in one fiery assault on the French—there is nothing finer than all this in the history of war.

Lord Ellesmere, writing, it is understood, on behalf of Wellington, declares that the Duke was "from first to last satisfied of his ability to maintain the post until his allies should arrive to his support. . . . Even had the whole of Napoleon's force been at his disposal the Duke had nothing to fear pending Blücher's arrival." But that was written in 1842; it may be suspected that it does not quite accurately represent what the Duke felt on the morning of June 18, 1815. In twenty-seven years many things had grown faint, even to the Duke himself. If Grouchy had been present with 32,000 men, and Lobau had not been withdrawn with 10,000, this would have made a difference of 42,000 good troops in Napoleon's battle-line. It is impossible to believe that even Wellington's stubborn squares could have held the ridge against such overwhelming forces. They might have died to a man, but they could hardly have stayed the French advance. To discuss, however, what might have happened if Napoleon had not divided his army is a very idle performance.

A picture of how Wellington bore himself during those long hours of battle is given by Picton's staff-officer: "His look and demeanour were always perfectly calm and composed, and he rarely spoke to any one unless to send a message or give an order; indeed, he generally rode quite alone—that is, no one was at his side—appearing unconscious even of the presence of his troops, while his eye kept scanning intently those of his opponent. Occasionally he would stop and peer for a few seconds through a large field telescope, which he carried in his right-hand; and this the docile Copenhagen permitted without testifying a symptom of impatience. Thus he would promenade in front of the troops along the crest of the position, watching the enemy's preparation for their attacks."

As he rode to and fro amongst his wasted and shot-tormented battalions, his presence everywhere seemed to stiffen their ranks. As his well-known cocked hat and hooked nose were recognised through the smoke, the word would run round the lines of some much-enduring square : "Silence! Stand to your front. Here's the Duke!" Wellington himself was coolness incarnate, unhurried, undisturbed, his voice keeping its natural key, his eyes their cheerful and steadfast look. He drew up beside a square on which a French battery was firing with deadly effect. "Hard pounding this, gentlemen," he said; "we will see who can pound the longest." "Stand firm, my lads," was his address to another sorely buffeted square; "what will they say of this in England?" Again and again the men in the ranks asked to be let loose at the French. "Wait a little longer, my lads," was Wellington's steady answer, "and you shall have your wish."

How constantly Wellington was under fire is told by the fact that of his staff no less than twelve were killed and forty-six wounded ; indeed, every member of his staff save one was wounded or slain. Wellington himself explained the circumstance that he rode unharmed amid the thronged and flying deaths of Waterloo for so many hours by saying, "The finger of Providence was upon me." The only sign of personal exultation Wellington showed was at supper, after the battle was over. "Repeatedly," says Sherer, "he leaned back in his chair, and, rubbing his hands convulsively, exclaimed, 'Thank God! I have met him.'"

But behind Wellington's steady features and air of iron composure there was plenty of natural human feeling. Dr. Hume has recorded how he woke the Duke early on the morning succeeding the battle. His unwashed face was still black with smoke and dust. Hume took the Duke's hand and commenced to recite the list of the slain amongst his own staff, and, as he ran over name after name, he felt dropping on his hand the hot tears that ran from the great soldier's eyes as he realised how much Waterloo had cost him. When, two days afterwards, he met Lady Mornington at Brussels, the "Iron Duke" broke once more into tears, and said, with shaking voice, "The next greatest misfortune to losing a battle is to gain such a victory as this."

Blücher is a figure in the landscape of the great battle as noble and lofty as Wellington himself. The march on Wavre from Ligny was a stroke of profound and resolute strategy; yet it may be doubted whether Blücher adopted it for strategic reasons, or even understood all its strategic possibilities. It was the fighting impulse in his blood, and the dogged, unshakable loyalty to his brother general, which made Blücher abandon his own communications, and march northward through the night towards Wavre after the struggle and defeat at Ligny. A great fight was raging, or was about to rage, and he must be in it! There were technical blunders, no doubt, in Blücher's generalship on the 18th. He reached Waterloo hours after the time agreed upon. Bülow's corps had taken no part in the fight at Ligny, its ranks were unshaken by defeat, its ammunition supply unwasted; so it was to lead in the march on Napoleon's flank. But, by a curious blunder, it was left on the night of the 17th on the farther side of Wavre from the scene of action at Waterloo. Precious hours on the morning of the 18th were wasted while Bülow's columns crossed the Dyle and defiled through Wavre. A fire broke out in that village, and detained Bülow's centre and rear for yet other hours.

But minor tactical blunders may well be over-looked. All that the world remembers is the fine loyalty with which Blücher kept his pledge to Wellington, the passionate energy with which he urged his columns over the muddy cross-roads betwixt Wavre and Waterloo, and the fire of his pursuit of the broken French all through the night of the 18th. In the panorama of the great fight there is no more wonderful feature than—to use Chesney's words—the spectacle of "the long columns toiling through deep, muddy lanes on the French flank, the sturdy legions of North Germans with clenched teeth and straining limbs forcing their guns through mire and over obstructions; the fierce old chieftain seen wherever his encouragement is needed, and everywhere greeted as their 'father' by those he urges on."

Napoleon's figure scarcely shows on a heroic scale amid the smoke and confusion of this brief and hurrying campaign. That he gained great advantages in the early part of the campaign is undeniable. He took both Blücher and Wellington by surprise. He was inferior in numbers to the allied forces, taken together, by over 60,000 men; yet he was equal in numbers to Blücher at Ligny, and at Quatre Bras he was greatly superior to Wellington. But for the strange blunder that left D'Erlon's corps wandering aimlessly between the two battlefields on the 16th, he must have destroyed Blücher or driven back Wellington in wreck. He gained these advantages by the subtlety of his combinations, the secrecy and speed of his movements.

But the catalogue of his blunders outstretches even the list of his successes. It was not Ney's failure to attack at Quatre Bras, or Grouchy's loitering march towards Gembloux, which ruined Napoleon's fortunes in the campaign. Napoleon destroyed himself by want of decision, by mysterious and helpless delays, by failure to grasp obvious facts, and by tactical failure in the last great struggle of the campaign, Waterloo itself. Napoleon failed at Quatre Bras because he did not give definite orders to Ney. He failed at Ligny by delaying his attack too long, and by neglecting to make use of D'Erlon when that general

wandered to the edge of his battlefield. He failed
still more signally on the 17th by not moving earlier
in the day on Wellington's flank, by losing his grasp
of the beaten Prussians, and commencing his pursuit
of them too late and in a wrong direction. When
he ought to have employed every bayonet and sabre
at his command in an overwhelming attack on
Wellington, he detached 32,000 men in a planless
and loitering pursuit of Blücher. He failed on the
morning of the 18th, again, by mere waste of time,
by his ignorance—fatal to his fame as a general—of
the presence of Blücher within striking distance of
his right wing. The failure of his strategy, indeed,
may be judged from the plain fact that, on the
morning of the 18th, with nearly one-third of his
army under Grouchy fourteen miles off, he was
about to fight Wellington assisted by three Prussian
army corps under Blücher; and he was in entire
ignorance of this latter surprising circumstance!

Napoleon's great blunder of the campaign can be
condensed into a sentence. He divided his own army
just as Wellington and Blücher were uniting their
armies: he despatched Grouchy with 30,000 men
to check or destroy a hostile force of 90,000, and
he despatched this force in the wrong direction,
and with totally mistaken instructions. If Blücher
was, as Napoleon believed, thoroughly demoralised
and routed, 30,000 men were too many to pursue
him; if he was not, they were too few. On all

orthodox military rules, no doubt, Blücher ought to have retreated on his own reserves—on Bülow, that is, at Gembloux; but Blücher was hardly a leader to be fettered by the pedantries of generalship. And Napoleon made the fatal mistake of assuming he would adopt a tame and selfish strategy, and did not take the trouble to despatch a squadron of cavalry to ascertain whether the Prussian general might not have taken the more ominous course of retreating in the direction of his ally—Wellington.

That Napoleon blundered in the actual tactics of Waterloo is admitted. What was meant to be a mere demonstration against Hougoumont was allowed to become a vehement struggle, which absorbed an entire army corps. D'Erlon's attack was that of infantry without adequate cavalry support; Ney's attack, later in the afternoon, was of cavalry without infantry support; and by the time the Old Guard advanced, Napoleon had used up—or had permitted his generals to use up—his reserves so completely, that he could not adequately support that attack with either cavalry or artillery.

Napoleon failed, it would seem, from simple lack of energy. His will-force seems to have exhausted itself. When he had brought his columns within striking distance of his enemy, he then lacked energy to strike. Through most of the tempestuous hours of Waterloo he sat at a table in the open air, with a bundle of straw under his feet, and repeatedly his head sank, overpowered with drowsiness, on the table. While the battle, on which hung his fate, raged on the slopes before him, and its thunder was shaking the very skies, Napoleon—almost incredible as it may seem—slept! When he rode from the battle amid his flying army, he seemed like a man in a stupor. He had become, to quote Professor Sloane, "an object of pity;" his eyes set, his frame collapsed, his great head rolling in a drowsy stupor. Montholon and Bertrand rode on either side of him, holding him in his saddle, else he would have fallen. Waterloo, in a word, left Napoleon, if it did not find him, mentally and physically bankrupt.

Marmont points out the fact that Napoleon's military experience had one curious gap. He stepped without an interval from being a simple officer of artillery to the command of armies. He never personally had command of a regiment, a brigade, a division, or a corps d'armée. So he lacked experience in the details of tactics, and he left more of the actual business of fighting to his divisional commanders than a general usually does. This circumstance perhaps helps to explain why in the actual tactics of Waterloo, Ney and D'Erlon and Kellerman and Jerome enjoyed such a measure of what seemed to be independent action.

According to one story, Count Flahault asked Napoleon, as they rode in the darkness and tumult from the field of Waterloo, "Is not your Majesty surprised?" "No," was Napoleon's reply; "it has been the same since Creçy." That reply is probably an English invention. Napoleon, even in the hour which followed Waterloo, would never have paid such a compliment to English soldiership. But he was willing to excuse his own failure at the expense of his soldiers. "Waterloo was lost," he said, "because no one would do his duty."

French vanity must have a scapegoat, whose miraculous blunders, or yet more miraculous treachery, explain the otherwise inconceivable circumstance of a French defeat. Grouchy plays this part in all French accounts of the battle of Waterloo. The battle was lost, and France was ruined, equally by what Grouchy did and by what he did not do. He pursued the Prussians too late, and he pursued them in the wrong direction. He failed to march on the sound of the guns at Waterloo when he heard them, or to obey Napoleon's orders to march when he received them. And when he did turn the heads of his columns towards Wavre and the Prussians, he failed to push on at speed. Grouchy's failure to appear on the scene of strife at Waterloo is the one sufficient explanation of Napoleon's defeat there which French literature knows.

Grouchy was a veteran singularly familiar with war. He had served the Bourbons and the Revolution before he served Napoleon. He had been the friend and associate in turn of Hoche and Moreau;

he commanded the cavalry at Jena, won the grand
cordon of the Legion of Honour at Friedland, and
commanded the Sacred Squadron which formed the
body-guard of Napoleon in the retreat from Moscow.
No braver or more experienced soldier stood at the
side of Napoleon during the campaign of the Hundred
Days.

The story of his pursuit of Blücher is one long
catalogue of blunders; but they were chiefly of other
people. The pursuit began with a fatal delay, and
was governed by an equally fatal misconception.
Grouchy had to wait till twelve o'clock on the 17th,
before he could see Napoleon and receive his final
instructions. He had to pursue an army which had
fourteen hours' start of him with the two corps (of
Vandamme and Gérard), which had suffered most in
the bloody fight at Ligny, and were therefore least
ready to start. Grouchy for many years persisted in
the statement that he had verbal orders only from
Napoleon; as a matter of fact, he had written orders,
which he in the interests of his own fame suppressed,
and which were only published in 1842. These
written instructions bear date "June 17, 3 o'clock.'
"It is important," they ran, "to know what Blücher
and Wellington intend to do, and if they propose to
reunite their armies and save Brussels and Liège. . . .
Explore his march and instruct me as to its movement." The instructions show that at last, and
fatally late—after he had actually divided his forces

MARSHAL EMMANUEL, MARQUIS DE GROUCHY

From an engraving after the painting by JEAN-SÉBASTIEN ROUILLARD

—Napoleon began to suspect that Wellington and
Blücher might be joining theirs. This was exactly
what was happening, and Grouchy was marching
east while Blücher was moving north! At 10 P.M.
on the 17th, Grouchy writes the Emperor that "the
Prussians seem to have divided into two columns, and
that one may perhaps infer that one portion is going
to join Wellington. If the mass of Prussians are
retiring on Wavre, I shall follow them in that direction . . . so as to separate them from Wellington."
In his own published defence Grouchy tampered with
his letter; for the words, "so as to separate them
from Wellington," he substituted the phrase, "for
the purpose of attacking the Prussians as soon as I
shall overtake them." The literature of Waterloo is,
unhappily, thick with fraud. It bristles with documents which, in the interests of some imperilled
reputation or other, have been ingeniously doctored,
or even boldly forged. And the lies are equally thick
on all sides. Gourgand, for example, who wrote in
Napoleon's interests, declares that Napoleon sent two
despatches to Grouchy on the night of the 17th, and
gives these alleged despatches in full. But they are
mere *ex post facto* forgeries, designed to show that
Napoleon actually gave the orders he ought to have
given, but did not.

As a matter of fact, no orders were sent to Grouchy
until 10 o'clock on the morning of the 18th. At
2 A.M. on that day Grouchy had discovered that the

main body of the Prussians had retreated towards
Brussels. He notifies this to Napoleon, and reports
that he himself will march on Wavre; but Grouchy
was still under a delusion. He believed that Blücher,
if he joined Wellington at all, would join him in front
of Brussels. He did not know that Wellington was
standing at Waterloo; and what is more notable,
Napoleon did not tell him of that circumstance. Not
that Grouchy guessed wrongly, but that Napoleon
left his own right wing without either information
or instructions, is the fact that explains Waterloo.

Grouchy did not leave Gembloux till 8 A.M. At
11 A.M. he writes again to Napoleon. " Three Prussian
corps," he says, " are marching Brussel-wards. This
evening I shall be massed at Wavre, and shall thus
find myself between Wellington, whom I presume to
be in retreat before your Majesty, and the Prussian
army." Grouchy had not even yet guessed that
Blücher would leave one of his corps standing in his
path, and march with the others to join Wellington
in crushing Napoleon. Grouchy had scarcely sent
off his 11 o'clock despatch to Napoleon when, from
the west, the faint deep sound of far-off guns caught
the attention of his staff. A great battle was in progress ! Gérard, taking fire at the sound, urged they
should march direct upon it; and many believe if
that had been done Waterloo might have had a
different ending.

But Grouchy held by his instructions. That Napo-

leon was closing in battle on Wellington created
no new situation. This was exactly what Napoleon
intended to do, and Grouchy's movement was part of
his strategy. Why should the distant echoes of a
battle which was known to be part of Napoleon's
plans cancel Napoleon's instructions? So Grouchy
pressed stolidly on towards Wavre, and took the
outer roads, so to speak, by Sart-a-Walhain, not by
the Dyle. He described a curve, that is, *from*
Napoleon, a step explained by the fact that he still
believed Blücher's objective to be Brussels, and not
Waterloo. But if Gérard, and not Grouchy, had
been in command, and had marched direct on
Waterloo, this could not have changed the course
of events. Planchenoit could have been reached by
Grouchy's columns only after struggling across some
fourteen miles of rain-soaked plains; the Prussians,
90,000 strong, stood in their path. They could not
have reached Waterloo, marching at speed, before
6 P.M., and their march would have been across the
front of a Prussian army three times as numerous as
themselves. Would Blücher have arrested the march
of 90,000 men because a French army of 30,000 had
appeared on his flank? But, as a matter of fact, at
10 o'clock Napoleon himself had despatched a letter
to Grouchy announcing that he was about to attack
the English, and directing him to continue his march
on Wavre. "You see I was right!" said Grouchy,
when this letter reached him.

Grouchy is blamed for not having marched straight on Waterloo when, at noon on the 18th, he caught the sound of the cannonade raging there. But if Grouchy, guessing from the sound of the far-off cannonade that a great fight was in progress, ought to have marched on it, Napoleon, who knew hours before that the great battle would take place at Waterloo, ought to have ordered Grouchy to march on that field. If Grouchy failed in not answering the faint and far-off summons of the guns, Napoleon failed in a yet higher degree by not sending express orders to Grouchy long before the guns opened their fire!

Thus, to sum up the story, it is demonstrable that Napoleon, not Grouchy, is responsible for the belated pursuit of the defeated Prussians after Ligny, and for the wrong direction in which that pursuit was urged. It is equally capable of proof that by no energy of marching could Grouchy, when at last Napoleon's orders to march on Mont St. Jean reached him, have arrived on the battlefield there in time to influence its course. It is equally demonstrable that if Grouchy, guessing what Napoleon himself had failed to guess—Blücher's real strategy—had pushed straight on to Wavre at dawn of the 18th, he could not have prevented Blücher falling with fatal effect on Napoleon's flank. He had only 32,000 men; he could not have stayed the march of 90,000.

As a matter of fact, Blücher left Thielemann, with

a single corps that had suffered great slaughter at
Ligny, to hold Grouchy back while he marched on
Waterloo; and Thielemann performed that task with
entire success. Gembloux was fourteen miles from
Wavre. Had Grouchy started at dawn on the 18th,
yet the process of struggling through fourteen miles
of muddy country roads would have left him, with
exhausted columns, in front of an enemy nearly thrice
as strong as himself. As it was, he reached Wavre at
4 P.M., and spent the rest of the day in angry duel
with Thielemann. It was Napoleon's own blunder
that permitted his right wing to wander off into
space, and to be out of the sphere of action, when
he himself was fighting for existence with the
combined armies of Wellington and Blücher at
Waterloo.

The slaughter of Waterloo was great. Wellington's killed and wounded reached 15,000. Blücher's
losses were nearly 7000. No accurate return of the
slaughter in the French army exists, but its loss in
killed, wounded, and prisoners was probably not less
than 30,000. Chesney quotes, as a proof of the
share taken by the Prussians in Waterloo, the fact
that their losses were equal to those of the purely
British regiments themselves; but his arithmetic is
misleading. The purely British regiments lost 6036;
but this was out of less than 24,000. The Prussians
lost 6998; but this was out of a total force of nearly
90,000! Taken proportionately to the numbers en-

gaged, the strictly British loss was, roughly, four times that of the Prussians.

The French at Waterloo, it may be added, fought with magnificent courage, and instances of individual daring, unsurpassed in fire and recklessness, could be given by the score. Thus the records of the 44th tell how, in one of Ney's cavalry charges, a French officer lingered behind his squadron. He threw off his helmet, wrapped his cloak round his cuirass so as to disguise his nationality, then rode straight down to the rear centre of the 44th. One of the sergeants called out, "Here is a staff officer; open out." A few British files fell back, and through the gap thus made this solitary Frenchman, suddenly spurring his horse, rode at a gallop, charging straight at the regimental colours. His trick was discovered, and he was slain by the thrust of a dozen bayonets; but what instance of more absolutely reckless valour can be so much as imagined! Napoleon himself has offered many explanations of Waterloo, but one is marked by a quite singular ingratitude. "The battle was lost," he once said, "because nobody did his duty in it!" That is a stupendously ungrateful slander on the thousands of gallant men who died for Napoleon at Waterloo.

CHAPTER XXII

A LOST THRONE

NAPOLEON brought the news of his own defeat to Paris. Great events, indeed, in some silent and mysterious fashion, report themselves over vast distances of space with a speed that outruns all messengers; and in this way some whisper of the tragedy of Waterloo had reached Paris in advance of Napoleon. Quinet tells how, on the night of the 20th, a card-party had assembled at the house of Carnot. The friend who was playing with Carnot happened to look up, and saw the stern visage of the Minister furrowed and inundated with tears. The cards were flung down, the group rose. "The battle is lost," cried Carnot, with broken voice.

At four o'clock on the morning of the 21st, Napoleon himself reached Paris, and alighted at the Elysée Bourbon. He had consulted with his generals on the road as to the course he ought to adopt; whether to stay with his broken army, or hurry on to Paris. His generals knew that Paris was the danger-spot, and they urged him to hasten thither. "Well," he said, "I'll go to Paris; but you make me

to commit a folly. My true place is here." So on
the morning of the 21st Paris learned that Napoleon
bringing the news of a ruinous calamity, had reached
the capital.

Ugly memories awoke with those tidings. It
was remembered that twice before Napoleon had
suddenly returned to Paris—from Moscow and from
Leipsic—and each time alone, without an army!
Only six days before he had led a proud and gallant
army across the French frontier to battle; and the
third time he had returned to Paris leaving a great
host, slain or scattered, behind him. Napoleon explained Waterloo to Caulaincourt by saying, "A
sudden panic seized the army, and all's been lost."
But even at this early stage he had invented a
scapegoat. "Ney," he said, "conducted himself like
a madman; he caused my cavalry to be massacred."

Lavalette has left on record the story of his meeting
with Napoleon on that sad morning. "He came to
meet me," he says, "with a frightful epileptic laugh.
'Oh, my God,' he said, raising his eyes to heaven
and walking hurriedly up and down the room. He
demanded 'two hours of sleep and a warm bath,'
before he would consult his Ministers. When he
met them he broke out, 'I have no longer an army;
they are but a set of fugitives. I may find men, but
how shall I arm them? I have no muskets.'" This
illustrates the wild alternations of mood through
which Napoleon passed. He had written from

Philippeville to his brother Joseph on the 19th—the very day after Waterloo, that is—"All is not lost," and he had gone into calculations, showing that by raking his barracks and depleting the National Guard he could still raise 300,000 men. "I will horse my artillery," he wrote, "with carriage-horses. I will raise 100,000 conscripts. I will arm them with muskets taken from the Royalists. . . . I will raise the whole of Dauphiné, the Lyonnais, Burgundy. I will overwhelm the enemy. . . . Write me," he adds, "what effect this horrible piece of bad luck (Waterloo) has produced in the Chamber. I believe the Deputies will feel convinced that their duty in this crowning moment is to rally round me and save France."

But now this mood of hope had vanished. He could see no gleam of light anywhere. He had neither men nor arms. He took counsel with the inner circle of his Ministers, his brothers Joseph and Lucien, Caulaincourt, Carnot, and Fouché, and urged that he should be made Dictator. He might seize the Dictatorship, he explained, "but it would be more useful were the Chambers to give it me." But this was the very last act the Chambers contemplated. They were already prepared to jettison Napoleon in order to make peace with the Allies. Why should they take any further risks for a defeated monarch and a falling throne?

The Chamber declared its sessions permanent, and every attempt to dissolve it was decreed in advance

to be an " act of high treason." " Why," it was asked
—at first in whispers, but soon in louder tones—
" Why should not Napoleon abdicate?"   Lucien
accused Lafayette, who took the lead in the debates,
of " ingratitude " to Napoleon.   Lafayette's reply was
overwhelming.   " During more than ten years," he
said, " three millions of Frenchmen have perished for
a man who wishes still to struggle against all Europe.
We have done enough for him; our duty now is to
save the country."   In the House of Peers Carnot
argued that Blücher had been defeated at Ligny and
Wellington crippled at Waterloo, and France could
easily hold out against her enemies.   Ney, who was
present at the sittings, broke out furiously, " It is
false!   You are deceiving the Chamber!   Wellington
is advancing.   Blücher is not defeated.   There is
nothing left but the corps of Grouchy.   In a week
the enemy will be at the gates of Paris."

All this was true.   On June 23 Blücher and Wellington met at Chatillon, and agreed on the next step
in the campaign.   Grouchy, who, with real soldierly
ability, had escaped from the forces converging upon
him and had reached Soissons, was to be ignored, as
also was Soult, who, at Philippeville, was rallying the
wrecks of Waterloo.   Blücher and Wellington resolved
to march straight on Paris, and every day brought
news of the progress of their threatening columns.
The Chambers, growing more confident, summoned
the Ministers to its sittings to give an account of

affairs. They appointed a commission to negotiate with the Allies. They demanded the abdication of the Emperor. "If abdication is delayed," said Lafayette, "I will propose deposition." "Let us wait an hour," cried Lucien. The word was caught up, and, by a formal vote, one hour was given to Napoleon to choose betwixt abdicating or being deposed; so far and so low had he fallen!

Napoleon himself, during these stormy hours, wandered moody, restless, abstracted, from room to room. He was broken in spirit. His brain seemed to have lost its energy; his will its capacity to resolve. When some one spoke to him, he appeared like a man waking for a moment from a dream and quickly relapsing into a dream. Regnault broke in upon him with the news of the terms offered him by the Chambers. "They have given you an hour's grace. Do you hear? Only an hour!" Then Napoleon summoned up his resolution. He would abdicate. "I offer myself," he wrote, "as a sacrifice to the hatred of the foes of France. . . . My political life is ended. I proclaim my son, under the title of Napoleon II., Emperor of the French." But the proclamation of another Napoleon satisfied neither the French Chambers nor the allied sovereigns, whose columns were steadily marching on Paris. The Chambers declined to appoint a regency; instead they nominated an executive, charged with all the functions of government.

On June 23 Napoleon took up his abode at Malmaison, the house that had been the residence of
Josephine, and so was full of bitter memories for the
fallen Emperor.   Here he spent some restless, agitated
days, in a sort of waking dream—a dream haunted
by anguished recollections and perplexed by frantic
schemes.   Events moved on without him; he had
no party and no friends.   "Fifteen years of his reign
as Consul and Emperor," says Hooper, "had demoralised the whole realm."   Every man mistrusted his
neighbour.   Patriotism was almost extinct.   French
politics under Napoleon had known only one principle, the worship of force.   And in the hour of his
defeat Napoleon, on his own principles, was justly
abandoned.   He represented failure, and for failure,
in the Napoleonic ethics, there was neither pity nor
loyalty.   When the Allies actually entered Paris, an
officer of Picton's division reports encountering an
agitated Parisian who cried "Vive le plus fort;" and,
ready for every emergency, wore a two-faced cockade,
white on one side and tricolour on the other.   This
was the type of Frenchman Napoleon himself had
evolved!

The new executive was busy negotiating with the
allied generals.   Fouché was working for the restoration of the Bourbons.   Napoleon was, if not forgotten,
yet looked upon as an inconvenient and useless
figure, to be got out of the way as quickly as possible.
The allied generals, on their part, refused to treat

for a suspension of arms except on condition that
the French army retired beyond the Loire, and the
National Guard agreed to hold Paris subject to the
orders of Louis XVIII. Wellington was convinced
that a permanent peace with France was not possible
except under a Bourbon ruler, and he really saved
the French throne for the Bourbons. Whether that
was any contribution to the happiness of mankind
at large may well be doubted. But he knew that
the allied sovereigns had neither respect nor affection
for Louis XVIII., and that monarch's one chance of
reconquering the crown lay in grasping it before the
allied sovereigns could reach Paris, and deflect the
negotiations in progress. Wellington, for this reason,
persuaded Louis XVIII. to make use of the services
of Fouché; and this ex-regicide, who had served and
betrayed all parties in turn, and whose very name
stank with the foulest deeds of the Revolution,
became the agent and the Minister of Police of the
restored Bourbons.

On July 2 commissioners met at St. Cloud to
settle the terms on which Paris was to capitulate.
The French army was to march beyond the Loire,
private property was to be respected, there was to
be an amnesty for everything done in the Hundred
Days. The French commissioners desired to keep
the works of art French armies had plundered from
so many cities; but Blücher said bluntly, "I shall
take back everything Prussian." On July 7 the

Allies entered Paris, "where," to quote Alison, "an English drum had not been heard for nearly 400 years." Wellington, with characteristic moderation, marched into Paris only a single brigade; Blücher poured three army corps into the city. The Executive Government practically vanished. The door of the Chamber of Deputies was locked against its members. On July 8 Louis XVIII. reached Paris, the white flag flew above the Tuileries. The Hundred Days had ended!

But, for the madness of the Hundred Days, France paid a terrible price. The first Treaty of Paris had been moderate, nay, even generous, in its terms. It imposed no indemnity on France; it exacted the return of no plundered works of art; it gave to France even more than the boundaries of 1792. But the second Treaty of Paris imposed harsher conditions. Serious plans for the dismemberment of France were considered by the Allies, and only rejected under the influence of the calmer wisdom of Wellington. It is curious to note that Hardenberg, the Prussian Minister, proposed that Alsace and Lorraine should be rent from France. Wellington declared that if the Bourbons represented to France lost provinces, their tenure of the throne would be of the very briefest, and the plan of dismemberment was rejected; but Hardenberg only antedated history by some fifty-five years. Sedan had to be fought and lost before Alsace and Lorraine ceased to be French!

Napoleon's brief royalty of a hundred days, in a word, cost France not merely the slaughter of Ligny, of Quatre Bras, and of Waterloo; it was followed by a war indemnity of forty millions, and the occupation by the Allies of its northern provinces for years. The Allied Powers enforced the restoration of the plundered works of art to their original owners from French museums and art galleries. Blücher, indeed, would fain have written his revenge in black characters on the very face of Paris. He wanted to pull down the pillar of Austerlitz and blow up the bridge of Jena; and, according to a story, which is sometimes doubted, but which is perfectly true, Wellington only prevented this latter stroke of Prussian revenge by the device of planting a British sentinel on the bridge. "We posted an English sentry on it," Wellington said afterwards. "Blücher nevertheless attempted to blow it up even with an English sentry on it; but," added Wellington, "the Prussians had no experience in blowing up bridges. We could have done it in five minutes; our experiences in the Peninsula had taught us. The Prussians made a hole in one of the pillars, but their powder blew out and hurt some of their own people."

The restoration of the plundered works of art to their original owners was a difficult task. The French had emptied more than half the cities of Europe of their artistic treasures. The list of statues,

pictures, gems, &c., taken from Prussian palaces and
art galleries alone filled fifty-three closely-printed
pages.   The total articles reclaimed by Blücher
numbered 2000; and from this may be guessed the
total volume of French booty.

The return of the Bourbons was marked by some
bloody acts of personal vengeance.   Many who had
taken an active part for Napoleon were banished,
and three of the chief offenders were sentenced
to death.   Ney was the most conspicuous of the
military traitors; Labédoyère was earlier in treason
than even Ney; Lavalette had set the civil branches
of the administration the example of abandoning
the Bourbons.   All three were condemned to death.
Lavalette escaped, but both Ney and Labédoyère
were shot.

Ney's fate has curiously impressed the imagination of the world.   He might have escaped; he had
reached the French frontier, indeed, disguised and
under an assumed name.   But his soldierly pride
revolted at the ignominy of flight, and he returned,
flinging all disguises aside.   He was arrested, but a
difficulty was found in constituting a court to try
him.   No court-martial would consent to sit on him.
He was at last tried by the Chamber of Peers, and
sentenced to death by a vote of 139 to 17.   Under
the capitulation of Paris an amnesty was assured
to every one within its walls for all political acts
during the Hundred Days.   It was argued that this

did not apply to Ney, as he happened not to be in Paris at the time; and further, Louis XVIII. did not ratify the capitulation. But the Bourbon had profited by it. He owed his throne to it. Yet he refused to allow it to shelter his enemies! Wellington was known to be strongly opposed to the execution of Ney, but his sense of soldierly duty restrained him from interfering strongly in a judicial process.

On the morning of December 6, Ney was set against a wall in the gardens of the Luxembourg. He stood erect, his hat in his left hand, his right hand on his heart, facing the firing party. "My comrades," he cried, "fire on me," and he fell, pierced with ten bullets. But they were French bullets, fired from French muskets and by French hands; and if there be "dishonour" in the deed, it lies on France. Murat, two months earlier, had been shot at the castle of Pizzo. He refused to allow his eyes to be bandaged, and himself gave the fatal word, crying— with a touch of characteristic and inextinguishable vanity—"Spare the face, straight to the heart!" Evil days had fallen upon the marshals of Napoleon.

Napoleon himself lingered at Malmaison with what may be called a gambler's hope that some strange turn in events would yet give him back his crown. He dictated a farewell to his army, but the Executive refused to allow it to appear in the *Moniteur.* He had asked to be allowed to take command of the French forces defending Paris as "the first general of the Republic;" but this, too, was refused him. He hoped that Paris would call him to her help, or the army summon him with clamours to its head, or the Chambers discover that they needed his help. But he was a man forgotten. And Blücher was approaching Paris, and was fiercely eager to have Napoleon in his power. The surrender of Napoleon was the invariable condition on which he insisted in his conferences with the French commissioners, and his hope was to shoot him on the very spot where the Duc d'Enghien was executed.

Professor Sloane says that if Napoleon had fallen into the hands of either Blücher or Wellington, he would have been instantly shot; but that statement is a libel upon Wellington, at least. Muffling gives the correspondence which took place on this subject. Blücher writes that the summary execution of Napoleon is "what eternal justice demands." Wellington declared that "such an act would hand down our name to history stained by a crime;" and Blücher then writes, "out of deference to the Duke's wishes he will abstain from this measure." Gneisenau adds a memorandum declaring that "in this matter Wellington thinks and acts as a Briton. Great Britain is under weightier obligations to no mortal man," he continues, "more than to this very villain (Napoleon); for, by the occurrences whereof he is the author, her greatness, prosperity, and wealth have attained their present elevation." But the Prussians, Gneisenau goes on to argue, were in a very different position, and they would incur the reproaches of all Europe if they "left undone the duty" of shooting Napoleon! He adds that they agreed to leave Napoleon unshot "from esteem to the Duke—and weakness!" It is plainly because Professor Sloane has not read with sufficient care the literature of the subject that he accuses Wellington of a desire to shoot Napoleon.

Napoleon at last, and only just in time to escape the Prussian cavalry, fled from Malmaison and reached Rochefort. Here he lingered five days. Maitland, in the *Bellerophon*, guarded the roadstead, and to put to sea was to ensure capture. Yet to stay in Rochefort was impossible. The messengers of the Bourbons were already on their way to arrest him. Wild schemes were framed for putting to sea in a half-decked boat, of escaping hidden in a cask in an American merchant ship. At last Napoleon determined to surrender himself to the *Bellerophon*. Here, at least, he was sure of fair treatment. He tried, indeed, to make terms in advance with Maitland. He would take up his abode, he urged, as a private citizen, under an assumed name, in England.

Maitland could promise nothing. Then, on July 15, when he knew he was in imminent peril of arrest, Napoleon went on board the *Bellerophon*. "I come like Themistocles," he wrote, "to seat myself at the hearth of the British people." He proposed, thus, to transform himself by the magic of an adroit phrase from a prisoner of war to the trusting and honoured "guest" of Great Britain! "I put myself," he declared, "under the protection of its laws." As a matter of fact, Napoleon went on board the *Bellerophon* to escape the clutches of the officers sent by Louis XVIII, to arrest him. Yet he had the most absurd notion of the reception he might expect in England. One of Napoleon's suite asked Maitland on the voyage to England if he thought the Prince Regent would confer the Order of the Garter on Napoleon!

The *Bellerophon* sailed for England, and anchored on July 24 at Torbay, and then proceeded to Plymouth. Napoleon was not allowed to land, and for six days the *Bellerophon* lay in Plymouth while English statesmen held debate over the fate of the fallen Emperor. Hundreds of boats hung round the ship, and all day long curious sight-seers stared at the massive black hull in which, a prisoner, lay the man by whom the imagination of the world had been so long hag-ridden. The English Cabinet was greatly perplexed as to what to do with its captive. His dangerous plausibility alarmed them almost as much as his ambition. "D—— the fellow," said Lord Keith after an interview with Napoleon on the *Bellerophon;* "if he could obtain an interview with the Prince Regent, in half-an-hour they would have been the best friends in England!" Lord Liverpool bluntly expressed his regret that Napoleon had not been captured by the Bourbons and summarily shot. This would have greatly simplified the political situation! The allied sovereigns took part in the debate as to Napoleon's fate. No one would undertake the responsibility of becoming his gaoler. Yet it was felt he must be kept under restraint as a mere menace to the peace of the world.

Finally, it was decided that St. Helena should be his prison. It was a lonely rock, set in the desolate wastes of the Atlantic Ocean, the point most remote from all civilised lands, and about which the sea-power of England could draw a zone of sleepless watch and ward which would make escape impossible. On August 2 the allied sovereigns declared Napoleon to be their common prisoner. The English Parliament passed an Act which placed St. Helena under a special government, broke it off from all communication with the outside world, "for the better detaining in custody of Napoleon Bonaparte." Napoleon received the news of his fate with loud-spoken protests. "I will not go to St. Helena," he cried. He would prefer being delivered up to the Bourbons or being sent to Botany Bay! He drew up a solemn "protest, before God and man," against the "injustice" offered to him in the violation of "his most sacred rights." He appealed to history. He had come voluntarily in his misfortune, he said, to seek an asylum under English laws. What return had

England made for that "magnanimous" act? It
had "sacrificed" him!

Napoleon's famous protest against being sent to
St. Helena is, of course, a bundle of lies. He had
surrendered himself to the *Bellerophon* to escape
being shot by the Bourbons. He had been received
as a prisoner of war, and it scarcely lay with a man
who had trampled so ruthlessly on the "rights" of
others, who had plundered whole nations of their
liberty, who had shot the Turkish prisoners at Jaffa,
and stolen the crown of Spain, and sent to death
thousands of his enemies, to talk about "the violation
of my most sacred rights in disposing by force of my
person and my liberty." If he had been dealt with
on his own principles, he might have been shot as
he had shot the Duc d'Enghien, or Palm, or Hofer.

Napoleon appealed to history, and that appeal has
been heard and judgment given. But it is not in
favour of Napoleon. "He who had declared," says
Fyffe, "that the lives of a million men were nothing
to him, trusted to the folly or the impotence of the
English nation to provide him with some agreeable
asylum until he could again break forth and deluge
Europe with blood." No fortified walls could have
hidden Napoleon. No monarch in Europe would
undertake the perilous task of being his warder. It
only remained to find some far-off and lonely isle, set
in the deep wastes of the estranging sea, where British
ships could girdle him with their ceaseless watch.

CHAPTER XXIII

ST. HELENA

AN ingenious attempt was made—or was about to be made—to employ the authority of the English law-courts for the purpose of enabling the fallen Emperor to land in England. A writ of habeas corpus was to be moved for, or Napoleon was to be subpœnaed to give evidence in some suit got up as part of the legal plot. Whether writ or subpœna would run on the quarter-deck of a man-of-war, and override the authority by which a prisoner of war was held, may be doubted. But the British Admiralty were not anxious for a duel with the law-courts, so Lord Keith sailed with his squadron hastily from Plymouth, and was instructed to transfer Napoleon to the *Northumberland* out at sea.

In reply to Napoleon's angry protests, Lord Keith suggested that there were worse possibilities than being sent even to St. Helena. Would he prefer to be sent to Russia? "Russia!" exclaimed Napoleon hastily, "God forbid!" He raged against his English custodians; but, after all, he knew he was safer with them than with any other. He kept up, however,

the form of despairing and injured protest.   He
would not, he declared, quit the *Bellerophon* alive.
His followers announced they would perish resisting
the whole British navy rather than be carried to
St. Helena.   Sir G. Cockburn took these heroics with
entire composure, and merely inquired what hour
his boats were to be in attendance next day to
tranship Napoleon and his staff.   When his boats
came at the hour appointed, Napoleon, with his
followers, stepped into them with almost Christian
resignation.

And so the long voyage to the lonely islet, which
was to be both his prison and his grave, began.   The
cliffs of Cape La Hogue faded on the horizon, and
Napoleon, from the quarter-deck of the *Northumberland,* gazed moodily at the dim coast-line as it
vanished.   Behind those hazy cliffs, growing faint
against the evening sky, lay the stage on which, for
an hour so brief, he had played a part so amazing.
It was Napoleon's last vision of France!

On October 16, 1815, Napoleon, with his suite,
landed on St. Helena.   On May 6, 1821, he died.
And those five and a half wrangling, shrewish
years form the most ignoble, if the most harmless,
period of Napoleon's life.   The purple robe of the
Emperor had fallen from him; the sword of the
soldier had slipped out of his hand.   There remained
a shrieking, passionate egotist, without dignity or
restraint, or truth, or fortitude.   If Napoleon could

face great perils with haughty courage, he did not
know how to bear small troubles with patience. St.
Helena, it may be admitted, was very unlike the
Tuileries or St. Cloud. It was a cluster of splintered
crags, the shattered peak of an ancient volcano,

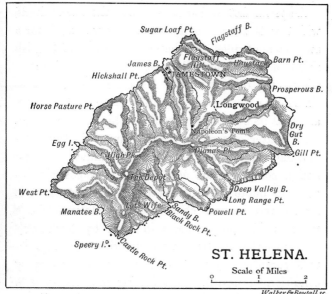

Sugar Loaf Pt.
Flagstaff B.
Flagstaff Hill
Haystack
Barn Pt.
James B.
Hickshall Pt.
JAMESTOWN
Prosperous B.
Horse Pasture Pt.
Longwood
Napoleon's Tomb
Dry Gut B.
Egg I.
Diana's Pk.
Gill Pt.
High Pk.
The Depot
West Pt.
Deep Valley B.
Long Range Pt.
Lot's Wife
Sandy B.
Powell Pt.
Manatee B.
Black Rock Pt.
Speery I.
Castle Rock Pt.

ST. HELENA.

Scale of Miles

0   1   2

Walker & Boutall sc.

rising like a broken spear-point out of the desolate
wastes of the Atlantic. It is almost equidistant
from Africa and South America, and has a total
area of only 45 square miles. It is, in fact, a mere
cone of rock set in the immeasurable solitudes of
the grey and melancholy sea. But St. Helena was

a prison, a cage in which to hold fast the fierce and restless spirit whose ruthless ambition had, for nearly a generation, wrecked the peace of the world, and still menaced it. And it is hardly the business of a prison to be spacious, or picturesque, or elegant.

A special Act of Parliament put the island itself, with a wide stretch of its encircling waters, under a stern code of rules, and the vigilant patrol of English ships of war practically made the island inaccessible to the outside world. Napoleon protested that St. Helena was worse than Tamerlaine's iron cage, and that its evil climate would be his death-warrant. As a matter of fact, St. Helena, lapped in the ever-blowing trade-winds, has a cool climate, and its health conditions are admirable. It is possible, indeed, to quote a French testimony to the climatic merits and natural charms of St. Helena. In a report published in Paris in 1804 by Napoleon's own authority, St. Helena was described as "a terrestrial paradise," with pure air, soft skies, and every condition of health. But St. Helena then was a possession which Napoleon hoped to seize. When it became his prison he naturally took another view of its qualities as a residence.

At St. Helena Napoleon had a suite of thirty persons, with twelve personal attendants. He had an allowance of £12,000 per annum for his household expenses, and an area of twelve miles round his dwelling within which he might ride and walk at pleasure. Outside those limits he must be accompanied by a British officer. Napoleon regarded himself under these conditions as a sort of early Christian martyr, a pensive sufferer, hated for his virtues by a wicked world; and he filled the ears of mankind with his laments and protests. He employed the most audacious rhetoric to describe his "sufferings." He told Lady Malcolm, "I have worn the imperial crown of France, the iron crown of Italy. England has now given me a greater and more glorious than either of them; for it is that worn by the Saviour of the world—the crown of thorns!" "Even the poor sentinels of the 53rd," according to Napoleon, "wept at his unworthy treatment!" But Napoleon was, in fact, a prisoner of war who had once already broken his parole, with a result in bloodshed to be measured by Ligny and Quatre Bras and Waterloo. All the Great Powers still regarded him as an object of dread. If he escaped from his prison-island and landed on the shores of France, a yet more desperate Ligny, a more bloody Waterloo, might have to be fought, and Paris be again occupied by the combined forces of Europe. In the interests of the peace of mankind, and to prevent more seas of blood being spilt, Napoleon must be kept securely guarded.

So a chain of sentinels kept watch all day round the bounds assigned to Napoleon. At nightfall, the circle of armed soldiers was drawn closely round Longwood itself. Once every twenty-four hours a British officer was required to actually see Napoleon, so as to be sure he had not vanished from the island.

The possibility of Napoleon's escape haunted the imagination of the statesmen of Europe like a nightmare. No letters were allowed to reach him, or any member of his staff, without being first examined. Great Britain, too, with a touch of unwise rigidity, added one specially irritating condition. Napoleon was to be addressed as "General Bonaparte," and the title of "Emperor" was strictly denied to him. Lord Castlereagh, it will be remembered, refused to sign the first Treaty of Paris because it recognised Napoleon as "Emperor of Elba." As Great Britain had always recognised Louis XVIII. as "King of France," it could not logically regard Napoleon as Emperor of that country; and the title which had been denied to the victor of Austerlitz and of Jena was not to be granted to the prisoner of St. Helena. Moreover, if the imperial title and rank had been granted to Napoleon in St. Helena, he would have turned it into a weapon against his gaolers. He would have fenced himself behind imperial etiquette, and the task of keeping watch over him would have become doubly difficult. Yet, to quarrel over half-a-dozen purely ornamental syllables, and to deny to Napoleon the title by which he is best known in history, seems absurd.

It can hardly be said that these conditions, applied to a prisoner of war who had cost the world so much, and who had achieved one escape already, were unreasonably harsh. Yet under them was bred an amazing swarm of "grievances" and "wrongs" and "outrages"—crimes against the sacred person of Napoleon, which, when translated into literary terms, and recited with due shrillness, took captive the sympathies of half the world, and clothed "the prisoner of St. Helena" with the robes of a martyr. The truth is, that the deliberate policy of Napoleon was to make his imprisonment impossible, and to turn his guards into objects of detestation to the whole world by the invention of ever-fresh "wrongs." This was what was called by Napoleon's own followers "La politique de Longwood," a deliberate policy, carried out with infinite skill and patience; the end of which was to ruin the reputation of everybody who had anything to do with the detention of Napoleon on St. Helena, and to arouse the sympathy of the world in his favour. In a moment of indiscreet frankness, Las Cases, who perhaps did more than any one else to make Napoleon's histrionic shrieks audible in the ears of the world, wrote in his Journal, "The details of St. Helena are unimportant; to be there at all is the great grievance."

As a matter of fact, the "grievances" of Napoleon, when read at this distance of time, seem absurd. They constitute not so much a tragedy as a farce. The world is asked to weep over the manner in which his shirts were washed, or were not washed; the length of time he had to wear his old coats; the quantity of wine — only one wretched bottle per head per day—allowed to his servants; the style of the iron railings erected round Longwood, &c., &c. The manufacture of grievances became a fine art. Napoleon had his plate, or part of it, broken up, and the intelligence sent to Europe, to illustrate the "poverty" under which he suffered —with only £12,000 a year from the pockets of British taxpayers, as his allowance. He had some of his coats turned to give an idea of the straits to which his wardrobe was reduced. He accused the unfortunate Sir Hudson Lowe, who was now governor of St. Helena, of every crime, from stealing his milk to attempting his life. That the English governor tried to poison Napoleon, or to hire some one else to poison him, was a tale diligently circulated. "We don't believe it ourselves," Count Montholon said, indiscreetly, to a friend, "but it is always well to say so."

Napoleon's personal followers, it may be added, were admirably fitted to carry out that campaign of artificial grievances and loud-shrieking complaints which formed "La politique de Longwood." The change from the Boulevards of Paris or the tumult of camps to the grey seas, the solitary cliffs, the

SIR HUDSON LOWE

From an engraving

brooding silence of St. Helena, represented for them a mere descent into Purgatory. They were naturally in a mood to shriek. Then they had no will but that of Napoleon himself, and they had no embarrassing restraints of truth and honour. Years afterwards, Sir Harris Nicholas undertook to edit the correspondence betwixt poor Sir Hudson Lowe and the French artists in misrepresentation at Longwood. "By the time I have finished," he wrote, "I think I shall have been in the company of more liars than any living author!"

Sir Hudson Lowe was, it may be admitted, a somewhat unhappy choice as the custodian of Napoleon. He was a gallant soldier, with an honourable record. He had commanded the Corsican Rangers, served on the Russian staff, was Quartermaster-General to the army in the Low Countries, was knighted for carrying to London the news of Napoleon's first abdication. He brought to his post a sleepless vigilance, an anxious loyalty to duty, a high standard of personal honour. Lowe had at least some qualities which fitted him for his post. But he was an inarticulate man. He took his duties even too seriously. He had no sense of humour and no perspective. And it is impossible to read the literature of St. Helena without seeing that Lowe's unsmiling stolidity was a serious drawback to his fitness for dealing with the artists in quarrels and grievances at Longwood. The popular idea about Sir Hudson Lowe at St. Helena is that he was a very small man, who spent his time in tormenting a very great one. Napoleon under his care was a fettered Titan being diligently stung by a gadfly. But this is a mere burlesque of the situation. It represents an almost complete inversion of the facts. It was poor Sir Hudson Lowe who was daily stung by French gadflies.

As a matter of fact, he had, during all his years of office, only five interviews with Napoleon, and in nearly all of them Napoleon exhausted even his rich vocabulary of abusive epithets on the unhappy and inarticulate Lowe. He did not satisfy Napoleon's fastidious taste as to "manners"! "His manners are so displeasing to me," Napoleon said, "that if he were to come to tell me that a frigate was ready to take me to France, he could not give me pleasure!" He wanted to drive Lowe to some act or word which would be a real grievance, of size and quality visible to the whole world. His design, as described by even a French pen, that of Lamartine, was "to provoke insults by insult, and then to exhibit these insults as crimes, to the indignation of the Continent." The unfortunate Sir Hudson Lowe could only take refuge in silence, and escape from Napoleon's presence as promptly, and enter it as seldom, as possible. But Napoleon found a new offence in Sir Hudson Lowe's very silence. It was a grievance that, after being smitten by so many epithets, the English governor crept out of the room without even slamming the door!

Lowe, beyond doubt, took his instruction at some points too literally. He would receive no communication from Longwood in which Napoleon was referred to as "Emperor," and Napoleon accordingly thrust that title into every document, even into the grocer's bills and the washing lists, sent from Longwood. So a sort of epistolary deadlock arose. It was agreed betwixt the high contracting parties, at length, that the simple words "Napoleon Bonaparte" should be used in all correspondence; but Lowe went on hunting for the term "Emperor" and suppressing it, as a terrier might hunt for rats and suppress them. Napoleon, for example, presented Coxe's "Life of Marlborough" to the mess of the 20th Regiment. The imperial title was written on the fly-leaf of the volumes, and Lowe solemnly required them to be sent back! He feared, apparently, that a British regiment would be seduced from its allegiance if a book in its library described Napoleon as "Emperor." On Napoleon's coffin his followers wished to place the simple word "Napoleon," with certain dates; but Lowe insisted that the inscription should run "Napoleon Bonaparte," as per agreement; and in this unseemly squabble over Napoleon's coffin the inscription vanished altogether.

Lowe, in a word, was a precisian, with an uncomfortable conscience, and absolutely no sense of humour. An archangel entrusted with the business of keeping guard over Napoleon might well have

failed. He would certainly have failed to give satisfaction to Napoleon himself, and would have been
described as a fiend. And poor Sir Hudson Lowe,
with his simplicity, his straightforwardness, his smileless and somewhat owl-like gravity, fell an easy prey
to Napoleon. He was exhibited as a ridiculous and
hateful object to the whole world. His duties were
diligently made impossible to him. Napoleon, for
example, used as much art as he expended in any of
his great campaigns in the business of evading the
eyes of the unfortunate British officer who had to
report each day that he had actually seen him. The
unhappy officer had to prowl round Longwood like a
thief, trying to catch a glimpse of his prisoner, the
entire household being engaged in a conspiracy to
make that feat impossible. "Yesterday," the unfortunate officer writes, "I was on my feet ten hours,
walking about the Longwood garden—it was raining
all the time—trying to see Napoleon Bonaparte, but
failed."

Sometimes, after hanging about the house for
an entire day, the officer would catch a glimpse of
a cocked hat, which might, or might not, be that
of Napoleon. Lowe at last had to give orders that
the officer should enter the house, and knock at
every door in turn till he had caught a glimpse of
Napoleon. "It was necessary," as Las Cases wrote
in his journal, "to reduce to a system . . . even our
privations, in order that we might thereby excite

a lively interest in Europe and provoke the English Opposition to attack the Ministry." It was Napoleon's business to have complaints. So Lowe's communications were diligently misunderstood. Concessions which it was known he could not grant were insisted on as matters of life and death. Acts of courtesy were subtly twisted into elaborate insults. " If they really wanted anything," said the unhappy Lowe, "they carefully concealed the want, in order to proclaim it afterwards as a proof of our neglect."

The "Longwood politics" to a certain extent succeeded. The rock of St. Helena, according to Bodley, was the first cause of the revival of the Napoleonic legend. It put a glamour of pity and of wrongful suffering about Napoleon. It made it possible to describe him as "the Christ of the French Revolution wickedly nailed to the rock by the malice of kings." A nearer and more comfortable prison, another Elba, would have ruined Napoleon's memory.

When Napoleon was not tormenting Sir Hudson Lowe, he was employed in dictating those memoirs which partake more of the characteristics of fiction than of veracious history. His treatises on the art of war, on army organisation, &c., have real value. But on the St. Helena literature generally the judgment of even a French critic, Lamartine, may be quoted: "That monologue of six years," he says, "which Napoleon addressed to the world from the summit of his rock, and the most trivial words of which were registered by his courtiers to be transmitted to his myrmidons as the gospel of party, was nothing more than a long diplomatic note, void of good faith, addressed to his partisans, and speaking in turns the language of all the factions that he wished to nourish with his memory."

A friendly critic explains the many gross inventions in which the memoirs abound by saying that Napoleon honestly mistook his imagination for his memory. He described what he intended to have done, or now wished he had done, and thought he was recording what he actually had done. But Napoleon used his memoirs quite as much to take away the character of other people as to protect his own. Thus he describes his generals in syllables of gall. Berthier was "an idiot;" Ney, a mere bundle of rashness; Murat, a "glittering fool;" Massena succeeded by pure luck; Soult was only fit to be a major-general; Kleber was not even fit to be that. And Napoleon distilled gall as abundantly on his brothers as even on his generals.

Henry, in his "Events of a Military Life," gives a graphic pen-picture of Napoleon at St. Helena. "His stature was short and thick, his head sunk into his shoulders, his face fat, with large folds under the chin; the limbs appeared to be stout and well-proportioned, complexion olive, expression sinister, forbidding, and rather scowling. On the whole, his general look was more that of an obese

Spanish or Portuguese friar than the hero of modern times."

But the end was drawing nigh. At the close of 1819 Napoleon's health began to fail. No one, as yet, suspected the real nature of his disease—cancer of the stomach—but its effects were visible. A new physician, Antommarchi, with two priests, arrived at St. Helena, the one to care for the body, the others to minister to the spiritual needs, of the sick man. Napoleon himself asked for the presence and counsel of a priest, but he did it in a very pagan-like mood. "I am not yet brought to bay," he said, "in a state to require the succours of religion." "Still," he reflected, "I may be reduced to that plight. . . . Who knows! Voltaire himself asked for the consolations of religion before his death; and perhaps I also might find much comfort and relief in the society of an ecclesiastic capable of inspiring me with a taste for religious conversation." This is a somewhat inadequate conception of religion and its offices!

A religious teacher who was at once a sage and a saint might have found the spiritual ministration of Napoleon a task too great. But the priests sent—and they were chosen by his uncle, Cardinal Fesch—were of a very unsatisfactory type. One was an old Italian priest who had been the confessor of his mother, but who was no theologian; and the other, when he came to St. Helena, could neither read nor write. Napoleon's religious views were crude. His physician, Antommarchi, was an atheist; but Napoleon had too keen an intellect to make that creed of fools possible to him. "Physicians," he said, "have faith only in matter; they believe in nothing." "I," he declared, "am of the religion of my father. I believe in God. Everything proclaims His existence; and besides, the greatest minds have thought so." He was a fatalist. "All that is to happen," he said, "is written down." The heaven of which he dreamed, and to which he had no doubt he was going, resembled the Valhalla of Northern mythology rather than anything known to Christian faith. "I shall behold my comrades in arms," he said, "in the Elysian fields . . . Duroc, Ney, Massena. They will come to greet me. . . . We will discourse of our wars with the Scipios, Hannibal, Cæsar, and Frederic." A heaven in which the saints are Ney, Murat, and Frederic, and where the theme of eternal converse is the march of columns, the deploying of battalions, and mere conflict and slaughter, is, on the whole, less desirable than the paradise of the Koran.

Napoleon's health was now fast failing. He had long intervals of stupor, varied by hours of acute pain, and the pain left him curiously exhausted. He could retain little food. "What a delicious thing rest is," he said. "I would not exchange it for all the thrones in the world. Once I was Napoleon, now I am no longer anything. . . . I do not live; I merely exist." He aggravated his own sufferings by obstinately rejecting medicine and refusing medical help. He despised Antommarchi; he rejected English doctors for the sake of maintaining a grievance against Sir Hudson Lowe. He would lie for whole days in an unlit room. When at last an English physician, Dr. Arnott, was allowed to approach Bonaparte, it was in complete darkness. "I could not see him," Arnott records, "but I felt him, or some one else."

On March 17 Napoleon took his last drive. On April 15 he made his will, that curious bit of legal literature into which he crystallised the resentments and the illusions of his life. No word of repentance for the many lives his ambition had destroyed ever fell from his lips. No shadow from the swift-coming eternity seemed to chill his imagination. Extreme unction was administered to him on May 3, and he declared he "died in the Roman Catholic faith." But, as a matter of fact, he was without faith and without fear. He seriously appeared to regard himself as outside ordinary morality, or above it.

Steadily the world and its affairs grew faint to the dying man's faculties. He forgot everything, and recognised no one. As night fell on May 6, a furious tempest swept in on St. Helena from the mighty brooding spaces of the encompassing sea. The very island itself seemed to shake with the fury of the storm. Trees were uprooted, houses were wrecked. And so, amid the tumult of the raving sea and the shaking land and the tempest-torn skies, the fierce spirit of Napoleon passed away. In imagination he was playing his part in some great and bloody fight at the very moment of his death. The last words that fell from his lips, "tête d'armée," are syllables caught from the battlefield.

NAPOLEON

As laid out on his Austerlitz camp-bed; sketched by Captain Marryat, R.N., fourteen hours after his decease, at the request of Sir Hudson Lowe, Governor of St. Helena, and with the permission of Count Montholon and General Bertrand. (*From a contemporary lithograph.*)

CHAPTER XXIV

AT THE BAR OF HISTORY

A POST-MORTEM examination showed the true cause of Napoleon's death. The body was extremely fat, but the internal surface of the stomach, through nearly its whole extent, was a mass of cancerous disease, and at one spot an ulcer had eaten the coats of the stomach completely away, leaving a perforation. Death had sealed with its frosty calm the dead man's features, and a curious serenity seemed to lie on the finely sculptured brow and the deep-set eyelids.

On the morning of May 8 Napoleon's body was borne to its grave in a little valley, where, under some weeping willows, a fountain broke out. The place had been consecrated by the Anglican chaplain of one of the regiments, with the prayer, "O Lord, may it please Thee to consecrate this ground for the reception of the mortal remains of Napoleon Bonaparte." At one point in the slow journey to the grave the coffin had to be taken from the hearse, and borne along a narrow footpath on the shoulders of twelve grenadiers of the 20th, and, in turn, twelve

of the 66th. As the soldiers of the nation he had
hated so bitterly, and fought against so long, carried
the coffin along the hillside goat-track, the regimental
flags which were borne before and after it gleamed
with the words "Talavera," "Albuera," "The Pyrenees,"
"Orthes;" words that were for the dead soldier
symbols of defeat. Over the grave the English
soldiers fired three rolling, far-heard volleys, while
the hills shook to the deep roar of the answering
broadsides from the English line-of-battle ships in
the harbour far beneath. There was surely a touch
of the remorseless irony of history in the fact that
the man who had warred so long against England
was carried to his grave by English soldiers, and laid
to rest with the gleam of victorious English battle-
flags above him, and with the roll of English
musketry volleys for his requiem !

Twenty years afterwards, on October 15, 1840, that
grave was re-opened and the body of Napoleon was
surrendered to France, and borne to that stateliest
of all tombs, under the dome of the Invalides at
Paris. Yet the irony of history pursued the dust of
Napoleon even to that gilded sepulchre. The body
of Napoleon lies there in a sarcophagus of red
granite, hewn from Russian quarries, and the gift of
a Russian monarch. Thus the two nations that did
most to destroy the empire of Napoleon joined in
unconscious charity in giving him a grave. England
gave his dead body its first resting-place on that

lonely pile of rocks set in the lamenting solitudes of the sea at St. Helena; Russia gave the granite sarcophagus in which it now rests.

It is impossible to offer any estimate of Napoleon which will satisfy all judgments. His name is still a mere battle-flag, the symbol of strife, round which a hundred controversies rage. Time, that cools so many enmities and clarifies so many judgments, has lost its office as far as the career and character of Napoleon are concerned. But it is, at least, possible to come to a definite judgment about some features of his character and some results of his career. There are many mythical Napoleons, unquiet ghosts that have disquieted the imagination of the world and haunted the pages of history for more than a generation, which now, at last, may be laid to rest.

One myth, which is chiefly responsible for the evil power of the Napoleonic legend in modern France, represents the dead Emperor as a champion of freedom against slavery, of democratic ideas as against aristocratic tyranny, of the national honour of France against a wicked conspiracy of foreign despots. But this theory becomes credible only when two-thirds of Napoleon's career are diligently forgotten. He was the sword of France against the first Coalition in 1796–97. He was the champion of France against the Holy Alliance in 1814–15. But what was he betwixt those periods, when he ruled France with absolute authority, and entered

one European capital after another at the head of
his legions ?

At home he was a despot, as absolute as one
of the later Cæsars: abroad he was a conqueror
as ruthless as Attila.   In France itself he suppressed the press, he abolished free institutions.
He gathered all power into his own hand; he thrust
his espionage into every household.   "His spy
system," says Morris, on the whole a very friendly
critic, "his organised informers, his repression of
thought, remind us of the Rome of the later Cæsars."
Abroad he plundered and partitioned almost every
European State in turn.   "By looking only at the
beginning and at the end of Napoleon's career, and
by disregarding all the intermediate period," says
Seeley, "an imaginary Napoleon has been obtained,
who is a republican, not a despot; a lover of liberty,
not an authoritarian; a champion of the Revolution, not the destroyer of the Revolution; a hero
of independence, not a conqueror; a friend of the
people, not a contemner of the people; a man of
heart and virtue, not a ruthless militarist, cynic,
and Machiavellian."

But the Napoleon thus created is only a myth.
Napoleon's politics were in truth a mere kaleido-
scope, a dance of changing colours.   He was everything in turn—a Terrorist with Robespierre, an
Anti-Jacobin against the Directory, a liberty-hating
despot on his own account when he became First

Consul and Emperor. In Paris, he was fiercely anti-clerical; in Egypt, he was willing to use his sword for Mohammedanism against Christianity. Yet, after making the Pope his captive, he established the Concordat, and issued a catechism teaching all little French boys and girls that he was God's minister, that to obey him was the sum of all piety, and to resist him the most damnable of heresies. "Were we then to believe," asked Madame de Staël, "that Bonaparte could award hell in the next world, because he gave the idea of it in this?"

An equally mythical Napoleon has been created by the imagination of his miraculous, unparalleled success—a success which makes him the wonder of history, and on whose shining disc there is scarcely any shadow of disaster. Betwixt Toulon and Waterloo, no doubt, are many triumphs, and the world still gazes in wonder at this artillery officer who conquered so many kings, and so nearly made himself the master of the world. Yet Napoleon's disasters, though, somehow, half the world contrives to forget them, were even more dramatic and amazing than his triumphs. No other historic character, perhaps, achieved success so soon or on so great a scale, and no one was ever more completely and swiftly overwhelmed with disaster. He failed in Egypt; he failed in Spain; he failed in Russia. His Boulogne flotilla was a failure; so was his Continental system. "The most unfortunate general that ever lived, a Xerxes,

a Darius, or Napoleon's own nephew, never," says
Seeley, "underwent such a succession of crushing
disasters as Napoleon in the years 1812–13–14 and
15." If through the scenes of Napoleon's life there
does run the thread of a single plan, it was the plan
for the overthrow of England. All else in his career
as a soldier was but tributary to this. The conquest of the Continent was only a prelude to a final
and gigantic attack on England. "The special and
peculiar work of Napoleon," says Seeley, "is that
colossal attempt to conquer England by conquering
the Continent." Napoleon himself frankly admitted
this. Yet that long campaign against England ended
in Waterloo and St. Helena! All he gained of soil
owned by England was a prison and a grave!

Thiers recites, with the laborious detail of an auc-
tioneer's catalogue, the "six great faults" which, he
says, Napoleon committed betwixt the Consulate and
St. Helena, and which explain why the dazzling noon
of the Consulate faded into the mere nightfall of
St. Helena. (1.) He needlessly broke the Peace of
Amiens and shocked the conscience of Europe by
the legal assassination of the Duc d'Enghien. (2.) He
committed himself to the mad attempt to overrun
the Continent. (3.) He joined with Russia in a conspiracy against the freedom of the world. (4.) He
thrust a Bonaparte on to the Spanish throne. (5.) He
pushed on his Continental system till it involved
him in war with Russia. (6.) He refused the magni-

ficent terms of peace offered him at Prague. This is a succession of blunders compressed into a little more than ten years,—betwixt the assumption of the imperial crown and St. Helena,—sufficient to destroy a dozen great reputations! As a result, just as the Convention, whose aim it was to free mankind, destroyed liberty, "so," says Thiers, "Napoleon, who employed unparalleled intellectual gifts to build up the greatness of France, succeeded in destroying her greatness."

Let it be remembered that Napoleon had not to teach Revolutionary France the secret of conquest. The armies of the Revolution, before Napoleon brought to their aid his marvellous genius for war, had destroyed the first great European coalition; had made Belgium, Savoy, and Nice French departments; had carried the borders of France to the Rhine. Napoleon's own conquests, the phantom republics and kingdoms he set up as tributaries, vanished like mists. And, as a matter of fact, Napoleon lost the early gains of the Revolution, and left a smaller France than he found when he became First Consul. Measured by enduring gains, the Directory was more successful than the Empire. It was under Napoleon, and not under the Directory, that the capital of France was twice occupied by hostile forces. When Napoleon went on board the *Bellerophon*, he left behind him a nation without an army; its capital and its fairest provinces were in foreign occupation; its very existence hung on the generosity of its foes. "What is the trophy of Napoleon?" asks one of his most lenient critics. "Alone of all the modern rulers of France he inflicted upon her a vast and irreparable loss of territory."

Equally in truceless quarrel with facts is the myth of Napoleon's transcendent and unfaltering genius, a genius that never blundered, that never loitered, that had in it a quality of the demonic; and that leaves the tragic failure in which Napoleon's career closes to be explained by the stupidity of his agents, or the treachery of his generals, or the general wickedness of mankind. Of Napoleon's terrible genius for war there can be no doubt. The proofs of it are found written on a hundred battle-fields. Of his genius for administration, again, there are a thousand evidences. His code is still the basis of French law. He did much to reconstruct civilised society after the waste and wreckage of the Revolution. "Nature," says Morris, "gave Napoleon an imagination such as she gave to Dante or Milton; she added a power of calculation and thought such as she bestowed on Newton or Laplace." Of his amazing energy of will, again, there is ample proof.

Mr. Bodley says he has made it "a practice to read the letters of Napoleon day by day, on the dates corresponding to those when they were written a century ago," the letters thus forming a sort of pious breviary for the daily edification of a worshipper of

Napoleon. "The psychology of the reconstruction of France," Mr. Bodley adds, "is revealed in this correspondence." The genius of the Concordat, of the codes, of the administrative system by which France lives, are all there—according to Mr. Bodley—in the letters of this young soldier of twenty-nine!

Taine says the work of Napoleon which has survived him, and is his monument, is modern France! If he imposed despotism upon France he saved it from anarchy. He created that centralised administration which underlies and survives all changes of government in France. "Nothing survives of the Revolution," says Mr. Bodley, "but what was established by Napoleon. Every institution," he adds, "which a law-abiding Frenchman respects, from the Legion of Honour to the Bank of France and the Comédie Française, was either formed or reorganised by Napoleon. If Napoleon had fallen at Wagram in 1809 his fame would have been perfect."

But he did not fall then, and his work must be judged as a whole. It is idle to choose any given point in Napoleon's career and assess him by his performances to that particular date. His career is a unit; it must be judged as a whole. It is true Napoleon created the system of intensely centralised administration, which—happily or unhappily—still is for France its instrument of government. But he gave to France also the bloody disasters of Spain, the tragedy of the retreat from

Moscow, the ignominy of seeing its capital twice occupied by foreign troops. "After Wagram," to use Mr. Bodley's own words, "the lawgiver, the organiser, the statesman disappear, and Napoleon is only the conqueror, conscious of his skill in the terrible game of war, which distorts his imagination and drags him in a furious wanton course to Madrid, to Moscow, and to Leipzig."

But Napoleon's amazing success is not explained by his intellectual gifts. His epoch explains his career. An exhausted Revolution needed a military dictator, and was certain to crystallise into one. If Napoleon had not played that part, Moreau would, or Hoche, or Bernadotte. And though Napoleon rode on the highest crest of the wave, he did not create the tide which impelled the wave. He was fortunate, too, not only in the moment when he stepped on the European stage, and the opportunities which lay before him, but in the weapon which he was able to grasp. The Revolution had temporarily shut all civil careers, and turned the whole energy of France into a military channel. The vast armies of the Revolution, ill-armed, unpaid, half-clad, rich in nothing but enthusiasm and daring, had hardened into a military body such as Cæsar or Hannibal never led to battle. These armies carried, by the strangest moral inversion on record, the generous enthusiasms in which they were generated into mere wars of conquest. They linked, that is, patriotic ardours to the unscrupulous valour of mercenaries.   Napoleon was able to use this, the most terrible military weapon a soldier's hand ever grasped, with the free, unchecked, un-criticised authority of a general who was also an absolute monarch : a monarch who controlled the resources, not of one kingdom, but of half-a-dozen. Seeley sums up admirably the conditions which made the career of Napoleon possible : " An unparalleled army was created, and was then handed over, along with the government of a great European State, into the hands of a consummate military specialist. He wielded this weapon with absolute control, and the result was a series of gigantic military enter-prises, conducted always ably, but for the most part also recklessly, and resulting in some prodigious triumphs, and then in a series of still more prodigious disasters."

Napoleon's intellectual failure is written in dark characters over his whole career.   A wise ruler would never have suppressed the free life of a nation, as Napoleon did that of France.   A great adminis-trator would never have exasperated a whole people, as Napoleon exasperated Spain or Prussia, and so aroused an unquenchable popular revolt against his authority.   Napoleon blundered fatally in strategy when he plunged into the great war with Russia, while his armies were being overthrown by Wel-lington in the Peninsula.   Napoleon, indeed, suffered in his later years from a sort of megalomania, a

ferment of over-stimulated imagination, unchilled
by any regard for sober facts.   A cooler and more
balanced brain would have saved him from the madness of the Continental system, the Oriental extra-
vagance of the Moscow campaign, the gambler-like
recklessness of 1814 and 1815.

What better proof that Napoleon blundered, that
his ends were evil and his methods vicious, that he
miscalculated the forces with which he was dealing,
that he put himself in quarrel with human nature
and with the facts of the world, can be so much as
imagined than the fact that he kindled at last a sort
of general anti-Napoleonic rising ; a revolt of all the
nations and rulers of Europe, and which may be
described as the anti-climax of, and the recoil from
the French Revolution itself ?   Napoleon was overthrown by a rising of whole populations against the
intolerable military despotism into which the French
Revolution itself had crystallised.

But the secret of Napoleon's blunders is moral
rather than intellectual.   He is the supreme example
of great intellectual genius absolutely divorced from
conscience.   He scorned truth.   He worshipped force.
He was absolutely pitiless.   He erected selfishness
into a law.   He counted himself apart from
morality, or above it.   Religion to him was a tool,
and capable of being used for very irreligious ends.
He poured out human blood like water.   He was responsible for more slaughter than perhaps any other

single character known to history. He covered
Europe with battle-smoke. He taught that worst of
creeds, the worship of war. He substituted "glory"
for "duty" in human ethics. He slew his own conscience, and did much to slay the conscience of the
world. Yet all this when seen in retrospect failed to
stir him with a thrill of pity or prick him with a
pang of self-blame.

Napoleon, in a word, had no more moral sense
than a stone. He could not even understand
morality in other people. At St. Helena he declared that Wellington "would seize the throne of
England!" Napoleon, of course, understood neither
Wellington nor England; that opinion, indeed,
measures the whole intellectual and moral interval
betwixt the two great soldiers. Duty was Wellington's law. Napoleon could not so much as understand "duty" as a motive; he knew only selfishness.
It is Thiers, who writes with a Frenchman's bias in
favour of the greatest soldier who ever fought for
France, who traces the failure of Napoleon to a
moral root. He was destroyed, Thiers says in effect,
by his quarrel with morality. His overthrow is explained by the fact that "during a reign of fifteen
years he had made an ill use of everything, of
France, of his own genius, of all that God had
placed under his control." The evil tone of the
French army—the decay of initiative in the generals
and the loss of faith in the ranks—was, like all the

rest, says Thiers, the work of Napoleon, the natural result of his system.

Napoleon thus represents one of the most evil and corrupting forces to be found in history. "No man," says Madame de Remusat, "was ever less lofty of soul. I have never known him to admire, I have never known him to comprehend, a fine action." He probably did not know what truth was. Certainly no other human being known to history lied so systematically, or more coolly employed the terms which belonged to virtue to cover acts which are in the category of vice, than did Napoleon. The Duke of Wellington said long afterwards, "Bonaparte's whole life, civil, political, and military, was a fraud. There was not a transaction, great or small, in which lying and fraud were not introduced." "Scarcely once," said Wellington again, "has he tripped into truth." "Truth-teller was our English Duke;" and it was this strain of falsity in Napoleon which made the great soldier who overthrew him at Waterloo declare of Napoleon that "he never was a gentleman!" Lying ran like a black thread through Napoleon's whole career. There is a lie on his baptismal register, a lie in his marriage certificate; and having lied all through the Consulate and the Empire, he spent his six years of exile in St. Helena in the invention of ever new and ever more improbable lies.

Napoleon's will is perhaps the most characteristic

of all his falsehoods. In it he bequeathed money he did not possess, exhorted his son to practise virtues which he himself scorned, professed a piety which was a sham, scorched his enemies with a "forgiveness" which was as bitter as gall with all hatred, and asked France to pardon the traitors who had "betrayed" her, and whom he catalogued with patient malice. The one gleam of quite Corsican sincerity in the will is found in the legacy he bequeathed to the man who had tried to murder the Duke of Wellington! Said Wellington: "For the payment of all the high-sounding legacies in his will there was not the shadow of a fund. He might as well have drawn bills for ten millions on the pump at Aldgate. While he was writing all these magnificent donations, he knew that they were all in the air, all a falsehood. For my part, I can see no magnanimity in a lie; and I confess that I think one who could play such tricks but a shabby fellow."

Now truth is the very salt of character, the root and sign of a thousand other virtues. Where it is non-existent, any baseness is possible. Gladstone once said of a great political rival that it was doubtful whether he ever possessed any sense of the difference betwixt truth and falsehood; but, if he had, he had certainly lost it, and "for years his mind had been in a state of baptismal innocence with regard to the difference." Napoleon, however, was in a condition of very unbaptized ignorance—a

worse than heathenish insensibility—as to the ethical
difference betwixt a lie and the truth.   It is probable
that, on the whole, he intellectually preferred the
lie, as being the creation of his own brain.   He seriously regarded lying as a sign of superior intelligence!   "Metternich," he said, "approaches being a
statesman; he lies very well."   Nor was this a sneer
on Napoleon's lips, a mere cynical epigram.   He was
accustomed to relate, with entire complacency, how,
when he was a child, an uncle had predicted he
would rule the world, because he was such an
unsurpassed liar!   Napoleon's capacity for lying
astonished even Talleyrand himself, a great artist
in falsehood.   "That devil of a man," he said once,
"deceives one at all points!"

An empire built by genius — no matter how
dazzling—on falsehood, on selfishness, on contempt
for human suffering and scorn of moral restraints,
is pre-doomed to wreck.   To doubt that would be
atheism.   It would be the assertion that the skies
are empty of God; that the universe is indifferent
to evil, or is friendly to it.   But if we are sure of
anything, it is that this is a universe administered
on moral principles, and all its forces are arrayed
against moral evil.   And the empire, though framed
by the genius of an archangel, which is built on a
lie, or linked to a lie, is destined to perish, and to
perish unpitied by God or man.

To test the real quality of the part Napoleon

played in human history, we have only to imagine
that, instead of failing, he had succeeded! Suppose
his armies had triumphed in the Peninsula and in
Russia; he had overthrown England on the sea; his
great flotilla had landed his armies on the shores
of Kent, and England had become a French department, and another Bonaparte had reigned in London!
Is it possible to doubt that, as a result of that
success, throughout the whole world everything men
most value—thought, freedom, religion, happiness—
would have suffered mortal injury? The Napoleonic
world would have resembled, morally, the world of
the later Roman empire. But Napoleon failed, and
his failure was the deliverance of civilisation!

"The Empire," says Morris, "founded on inter-
national wrong, and depending for its existence on
the enforced submission of great races conquered,
but spurning the yoke, was a defiance to law divine
and human; it was a contradiction to the nature of
things; and the methods by which its author upheld
it, harsh tyranny, statecraft, and the Continental
system, were assurances of its speedy overthrow."

England emerged from the long struggle with
Revolutionary and Napoleonic France burdened,
indeed, with a great debt, but clad with a great
fame. She was the undisputed mistress of the sea;
while to the struggle on land she had contributed a
warrior equal in fame to Napoleon himself, and the
victory which closed the long twenty years' struggle

was won mainly by the genius of a British general, and the valour of British soldiers.

It is difficult, indeed, to compress into arithmetic the successes Great Britain had achieved. Her total population when the war closed was only 18,000,000, yet she had 1,000,000 men in arms. She had met and defeated the fleets of the civilised world. Her armies had driven the French out of Spain, and overthrown the Napoleonic empire at Waterloo. She had captured every colony belonging to her foes. Not a single colony remained to an enemy of England at the end of the war. The population of Great Britain and Ireland rose, during this long period of strife, from 14,000,000 to 18,000,000; the national revenue from £17,000,000 sterling to £72,000,000. The public debt, it is true, had expanded in a like ratio; but British exports had doubled in the same period, her imports had increased 50 per cent., the commercial fleet of the Empire had increased threefold.

Great Britain, that is, had waged war on a Titanic scale, and for the period of nearly a generation, and she had grown in wealth and trade, and area and population during the process! There came, necessarily, a great reaction when the war closed; a reaction which itself in turn passed away, and the British Empire entered on a new cycle of amazing expansion, until its flag now flies over one-sixth of the earth's surface and over one-fifth of its population.

And the energy, the long-enduring valour, the exhaustless resource, the magnificent success with which England waged the Great War with Napoleon, are even less matter for pride than the aims which governed its policy throughout the struggle, and the spirit in which the struggle was closed. Napoleon called the British people "a nation of shopkeepers;" and it is the fashion with a certain school of critics to describe British policy as ruled by what may be called "shopkeeping" motives—a wolfish hunger for gain; an unscrupulous passion, not for principle, but for profit.

But it is amusing to read how Napoleon himself rebuked England for not turning her great victory to sufficiently selfish uses. "If," said Napoleon at St. Helena, "your Ministers had paid attention to the interests of your country, instead of intriguing, they would have rendered you the most happy and flourishing nation in the world. At the conclusion of the war, they should have said to the Spanish and Portuguese governments, 'We have saved your country; we alone have supported you, and prevented your falling a prey to France; we have made many campaigns, and our best blood has been shed in your defence; we have expended many millions of money, and, consequently, the nation is overburdened with debt on your account, which we must pay. You have the means of repaying us. We demand, therefore, that we shall be the only nation allowed to trade with South America during twenty years, and that our ships shall have the same privileges with Spanish vessels.' Who could say 'No' to this? It would only have been a just demand, and none of the allied Powers could deny your right to exact it; for it was through you alone, and the energy you displayed, that both Spain and Portugal did not fall. You might have asked, 'Who saved Portugal? Who alone assisted you with men and money, besides having saved your existence as a nation?' . . . England has played for everything or nothing; she has gained all, effected impossibilities, yet has nothing!"

But it constitutes the very honour of England that she exacted no spoils from the conquered. Nearly all the colonies which her fleets had captured were given back when peace was declared. Napoleon, in his will, declared Wellington deserved to be assassinated because he had "sanctioned the crime of having pillaged French museums." This virtuous anger over the "crime" of pillaging museums has a flavour of delightful humour, coming from the soldier who had rifled almost every museum in Europe. But Wellington brought no trophies from Paris to London. England asked for no foot of French soil. Her share in the war indemnity paid by France she gave to the Netherlands. It may be fairly claimed that she came not only with laurelled brow, but with clean hands, from the great struggle.

And she had saved Europe! She had maintained for the great commonwealth of States which constitutes modern Europe, the right to freedom and to national existence. Imagine all that England contributed to the struggle against Napoleonic despotism withdrawn—its fleets and armies and treasures, the statesmanship of Pitt, the warlike genius of Nelson and of Wellington, the proud and long-enduring valour of the English people, that sustained this long strife of twenty years—and would a free Europe have existed to-day?

War is almost, though not quite, the last and worst of evils. It is worth while to endure even the well-nigh immeasurable mischiefs of war to escape the yet worse disaster of lost freedom, of stained honour, of betrayed duty. But what an assurance of the triumph of moral forces, and the final authority of reason in human affairs, it would be to know that the age of war had passed; that never again would the soil of Europe shake to the tread of marching armies, and never again would Christian nations hold discourse with each other from the iron lips of cannon!

That "Golden Age" has not yet come: though the forerunning light of its dawn seems sometimes to gleam in the eastern skies! But if, driven by hard necessity, or summoned by some imperious challenge of duty,—some debt to her own honour, or to the world's freedom and happiness,—England has to set her armies and fleets in array once more against those of some sister nation, happy will it be for her if her cause is as just, and is maintained with an energy as splendid, and a courage as high, as in the great Twenty Years' War for the freedom of Europe with Revolutionary and Napoleonic France !

APPENDIX

Letter from the DUKE OF WELLINGTON to LORD BERESFORD

"PARIS, *August 9th*, 1815.

" MY DEAR BERESFORD,—I received only last night your letter of the 8th for which I am very much obliged to you. The Battle of Waterloo was certainly the hardest fought that has been for many years I believe, and has placed in the Power of the Allies the most important results. We are throwing them away however by the Infamous conduct of some of us; and I am sorry to add our own Government also are taking up a little too much the love of their rascally newspapers, they are shifting their objects; and having got their Cake they want both to eat it and keep it.

As for your Portuguese Concerns, I recommend to you to resign and come away immediately. It is impossible for the British Government to maintain British Officers for the Portuguese Army at our expense even so trifling as it is, if the Portuguese Government are to refuse to give the Service of the Army in the Cause of Europe in any manner. Pitch them to the Devil then in the mode which will be most dignified for yourself, and that which will have the best effect in opening the Prince's eyes to the conduct of his Servants in Portugal; and let the matter work its own way. Depend upon it the British Government must and will recall the British Officers.

I shall hold a language here that will correspond with your actions in Portugal. Ever Your's most sincerely,

" WELLINGTON.

"F.-M. the LORD BERESFORD, G.C.B."

[The above letter formed part of the collection of documents in the muniment chests of Bedgebury, derived from the late Right Hon. A. J. B. Beresford Hope. See Facsimile facing page 376.]

INDEX

NAPOLEON

a portion of Spain, 173 ; reprints in France the adverse criticisms on Wellington in English newspapers, 191 ; gives fresh instructions to the army in Spain after Massena's retreat from Torres Vedras, 214 ; the climax of his power (1812), 269 ; extent of his conquests, 269, 270 ; the beginning of his downfall, 270 *sqq.* ; King of Italy, 270 ; his ambition to make Paris the capital of the world, 271 ; march to Moscow, 270, 271, 272 ; ridicules the idea of Wellington attacking Badajos, 290 ; his reception of the news of the defeat at Salamanca, 330, 331 ; instructions to Joseph Bonaparte in 1813, 357 ; his wrath at the disaster of Vittoria, 383, 384 ; his official account of the battle of Vittoria, 384, 385 ; supersedes his brother Joseph in Spain by appointing Soult to the command of the troops, 394, 395 ; wins the battle of Dresden, **iv.** 6, 88 ; addresses his Council of State at Paris (1813), 40 ; his treaty with Ferdinand, 40, 41 ; abdicates, and departs for Elba, 44, 73, 74, 79, 105, 106, 110 ; destruction of his statue at Toulouse, 74 ; the story of his retreat from Moscow, 79-84 ; issues his twenty-ninth bulletin, 83 ; creates a new army (1813), 84 ; at Bautzen, 86 ; terms offered him by the treaty of Prague, 87 ; refuses the terms of the treaty of Prague, 88 ; three of his marshals defeated, 89 ; falls back to Leipsic, 90 ; desertion of Saxon troops from his army, 90 ; his retreat from Leipsic, 90, 91 : accepts, too late, the terms of peace offered at Frankfort, 94 ; driven towards Paris by the Allies, 98 ; marches eastward, 98 ; letter

NAPOLEON

to his wife, 99 ; on the road to Paris, 102, 103 ; hears of the fall of Paris and goes to Fontainebleau, 103 ; dethroned by the Provisional Government, and denounced, 104, 105 ; deserted by his generals, 107 ; attempts suicide at Elba, 109 ; wishes to reside in England, 110 ; addresses his Guards at Fontainebleau, 110, 111 ; his journey to the coast, 111-113 ; his occupations at Elba, 115, 116 ; his unpaid pension, 116 ; escapes from Elba and arrives in Paris, 120-125 ; meets the troops from Grenoble, 121, 122 ; his meeting with Ney, 123 ; issues a proclamation, 128, 129 ; creates a new army, 130 ; crosses the Sambre, 132, 151 ; his plans for meeting the troops of the Allies, 133 *sqq.* ; his appearance in the Waterloo campaign, 139, 140 ; character of his army, 140-143 ; his accounts at St. Helena of Waterloo, 149, 150 ; confronted by Blücher's army, 152 ; blunders of his staff, 156 ; joined by Ney at Charleroi, 162, 163 ; his delusions as to the plans of the Allies, 163 ; at Ligny, 178, 183 *sqq.* ; fails to pursue Blücher's army, 193 *sqq.* ; his dilatory conduct after the battle of Ligny, 195 *sqq.* ; orders Ney to attack Wellington, 202 ; pursues Wellington, 203 *sqq.* ; failure of his strategy to divide Wellington's army from Blücher's, 207, 208 ; his restlessness on the night before the battle of Waterloo, 209, 210 ; confident of victory, 211 ; disposition of his forces, 223, 224 ; reviews his army, 224, 225 ; his description of the battle-formation of his army, 226 ; plan of attack at Waterloo, 229 ; at the great fight, 231 *sqq.* ; on Ney at Waterloo, 249 ; forms

THE END

Printed by BALLANTYNE, HANSON & CO.
Edinburgh & London

SIR ALGERNON WEST'S REMINISCENCES.

SECOND EDITION. In Two Volumes. With Portraits and Sketches, including Portraits of Sir Algernon West and of the Hon. Mrs. Alfred Lyttelton, by the Marchioness of Granby. Demy 8vo, 21s.

RECOLLECTIONS, 1832–1886. By the Right Hon. Sir ALGERNON WEST, K.C.B. For many years Private Secretary to the Right Hon. W. E. Gladstone, and subsequently Chairman of the Inland Revenue Board.

"In laying down the book our first thought is what an enviable life, our second will be what a delightful character that life reveals. . . . Whether by effort or grace, the writer of this book reveals a genius for making friends even of his readers."—*Spectator.*

"Written with freedom from egotism, with simplicity, discrimination, and faultless taste. . . . Both volumes can be read with unflagging interest, and the certainty that as each page is turned there will be something on the next to keep the attention on the alert, if not to excite a laugh."—*Standard.*

MEMOIRS OF A REVOLUTIONIST. By PRINCE KROPOTKIN. With an Introduction by GEORG BRANDES. In Two Volumes. With Two Portraits of the Author. Large crown 8vo, 21s.

"A very remarkable book."—*Daily News.*

"It is impossible to say too much in praise of these two volumes. Kropotkin has written a fascinating book, and one of the most remarkable autobiographies of the age."—*Bookman.*

"'The Memoirs of a Revolutionist' do not contain an uninteresting page. Prince Kropotkin writes with extreme moderation, without any tinge of hysteria, and he throws light upon a page of Russian history of which too little is definitely known in England."—*Literature.*

THE LOG OF A SEA WAIF: Being Recollections of the First Four Years of My Sea Life. By FRANK T. BULLEN, F.R.G.S., Author of "The Cruise of the *Cachalot*," "Idylls of the Sea," &c. SECOND IMPRESSION. With 8 Full-page Illustrations specially drawn by ARTHUR TWIDLE. Large post 8vo, 8s. 6d.

"In 'The Log of a Sea Waif' Mr. Frank T. Bullen has surpassed all his previous efforts. We have read many stories of sea life, but do not remember to have been so fascinated and enthralled by any of them as by this masterly presentation of the humours, hardships, and minor tragedies of life in the forecastle."—*World.*

"Full of thrilling adventure, admirably told. . . . We must leave Mr. Bullen's touching story of his early struggles and adventures to speak for itself. His descriptive powers are great, his literary imagination is vivid, and he finds abundant opportunities for the display of both."—*Times.*

MORE POT-POURRI FROM A SURREY GARDEN. By Mrs. C. W. EARLE, Author of "Pot-Pourri from a Surrey Garden." THIRD IMPRESSION. Large crown 8vo, 7s. 6d.

"On every topic on which Mrs. Earle writes she has something new to say, for she not only possesses the faculty of thinking out her opinions, but also that of writing down her thought. Mrs. Earle, with rare insight, gives the world a full view of the motive springs of life as 'dreamt of in her philosophy.'"—*Spectator.*

"This second volume has all the charm of the first. It is just the friendly chat of a lady who has not only read books, but knows all about her kitchen, and, if possible, more about the garden she loves. On each, sound, useful information is pleasantly conveyed."—*Punch.*

LONDON : SMITH, ELDER, & CO., 15 WATERLOO PLACE, S.W.

In 7 Volumes. Large crown 8vo, cloth, gilt top, 6s. each.

THE HAWORTH EDITION

OF THE

LIFE AND WORKS

OF

CHARLOTTE BRONTË

(CURRER BELL)

AND HER SISTERS

EMILY AND ANNE BRONTË

(ELLIS AND ACTON BELL)

WITH PORTRAITS AND ILLUSTRATIONS.

Including Views of places described in the Works, reproduced from Photographs specially taken for the purpose by Mr. W. R. BLAND, of Duffield, Derby, in conjunction with Mr. C. BARROW KEENE, of Derby.

Introductions to the Works are supplied by Mrs. HUMPHRY WARD,

AND

An Introduction and Notes to Mrs. Gaskell's "Life of Charlotte Brontë" by Mr. CLEMENT K. SHORTER, the eminent Brontë authority.

CONTENTS OF THE VOLUMES:

1. **JANE EYRE.** By CHARLOTTE BRONTË With a Photogravure Portrait of Charlotte Brontë, from a Drawing by G. RICHMOND, a Photogravure of Rochester and Jane Eyre, from a Water-colour Drawing by FREDERICK WALKER, A.R.A.; a Facsimile of the Title-page of the first edition, and 8 Full-page Illustrations.

2. **SHIRLEY.** By CHARLOTTE BRONTË. With a Facsimile of the Title-page of the first edition, and 10 Full-page Illustrations.

3. **VILLETTE.** By CHARLOTTE BRONTË. With a Photogravure Portrait of M. Heger, Facsimiles of Title-page of the original edition and of a page of the original MS., and 8 Full-page Illustrations.

4. **THE PROFESSOR,** by CHARLOTTE BRONTË, and **POEMS,** by CHARLOTTE, EMILY, and ANNE BRONTË, and the Rev. PATRICK BRONTË, &c. With Facsimiles of the Title-pages of the first editions, and 8 Full-page Illustrations.

5. **WUTHERING HEIGHTS.** By EMILY BRONTË. **AGNES GREY.** By ANNE BRONTË. With a Preface and Biographical Notice of both Authors by CHARLOTTE BRONTË. With a Portrait of Emily Brontë, Facsimiles of the Title-pages of the first editions, and 8 Full-page Illustrations.

6. **THE TENANT OF WILDFELL HALL.** By ANNE BRONTË. With a Portrait of Anne Brontë, a Facsimile of the Title-page of the first edition, and 6 Full-page Illustrations.

7. **LIFE OF CHARLOTTE BRONTË.** By Mrs. GASKELL. With an Introduction and Notes by CLEMENT K. SHORTER. With Photogravure Portraits of Mrs. Gaskell and of the Rev. A. B. Nicholls, a Portrait of the Rev. Patrick Brontë, 11 New Illustrations, Facsimiles of a Letter by Charlotte Brontë, and of a page from Charlotte Brontë's MS. of "The Secret," &c. &c.

** **THE LIFE AND WORKS OF THE SISTERS BRONTË** are also to be had in 7 Vols., Large crown 8vo, handsomely bound in cloth, price 5s. each; in small post 8vo, limp green cloth, or, cloth boards, gilt top, price 2s. 6d. each; and in small fcap. 8vo, bound in cloth, with gilt top, with Frontispiece to each volume, price 1s. 6d. each; or the Set, in gold-lettered cloth case, 12s. 6d.

LONDON : SMITH, ELDER & CO., 15 WATERLOO PLACE, S.W.